Gabriel Alomar Esteve,
1910-1997

Urbanismo

Gabriel Alomar Esteve: Mallorcan Town Planner

Richard Buswell

Published by Paragon Publishing
© Richard Buswell 2022

The rights of Richard Buswell to be identified as the author of this work have been asserted by him in accordance with sections 77 and 78 of the Copyright, Designs and Patents Act 1988.
All rights reserved. No part of this book may be reprinted or reproduced or utilised in any form or by any electronic, mechanical, or other means, now known or hereafter invented, including photocopying and recording, or in any information storage or retrieval system, without the prior written consent of the author, the author's representatives or a licence permitting copying in the UK issued by the Copyright Licensing Agency Ltd.
www. cla. co. uk

ISBN 978-1-78222-910-0

Book design, layout and production management by Into Print
www. intoprint. net, +44 (0)1604 832140

GABRIEL ALOMAR ESTEVE: MALLORCAN TOWN PLANNER

For Hawys

By far the greatest and most admirable form of wisdom is that needed to plan and beautify cities and human communities.

Socrates

All we can ask a man to show is that he has made his world, if only for a little time. If that world lose the life of human purpose, it may even so leave evidences of it.

Paul Horgan: Lingering Walls, 1936

A city is not its streets, nor its squares, but the community of the people who live and live there together, with their groups, their institutions, their ways of living, their traditions, their customs.

Gabriel Alomar Esteve, 1961.

Contents

	List of Illustrations	viii
	Acknowledgements	x
	Preface: Scene one – Palma then and now	xii
1	Introduction	1
2	Palma: a brief history of the city Alomar inherited	6
3	Alomar and the Spanish tradition in town planning: population, public health and movement	10
4	Gabriel Alomar Esteve and his plans for reform	28
5	Reflections on Alomar's plan for the reform of Palma: a critique	41
6	Influences on Alomar's planning ideas	59
7	After the reform of Palma: an American interlude	64
8	Alomar in Madrid	71
9	Alomar and Urban Conservation	81
10	Alomar and *Espaces Verdes*	96
11	Alomar's legacies	105
	References/Endnotes	119

List of Illustrations

1	Medieval Palma in 14C showing succession of walls.	7
2	Map of Palma in 1644 by Antonio Garau.	8
3	Idelfonso Cerdá's plan for Barcelona, 1856.	16
4	'Down with the walls': an 1841 poster from Barcelona adapted locally in Mallorca.	17
5	Bernat Calvet's plan for Palma 1901.	21
6	Alomar's father with his son Gabriel (right) in Barcelona 1924.	29
7	Gabriel Alomar Esteve, in his 20s.	29
8	Cover of Falangist journal *Reconstrucción*, June/July 1945.	32
9	Alomar's general plan showing the twelve areas for reform.	37
10	Palma, lower part of Avenida Jaume III in 2019.	40
11	Palma, lower part of Avenida Jaume III designed by Alomar and Ferragut.	42
12	Reform area no. 1 for the new Avenida Jaume III.	46
13	Avenida Jaume III being built in 1952.	47
14	Site being cleared for the construction of new Mercat de l'Olivar.	48
15	Mercat de l'Olivar in late 1950s.	48
16	Alomar's plan the central area of Palma, reforms 4, 5 and 7.	49
17	Proposal for stairway from Via Roma (La Rambla) to Plaza Major.	50
17a	Stairway to rear of Plaza Major today.	50
18	Reform no. 2, Puig de Sant Pere.	53
19	Reform no. 9, Sa Calatrava.	53
20	Alomar's plan for the eixample/ensanche.	57
21	Population change in Palma, 1900-1960.	63
22	The family home of Alomar's wife located in Mayagüez in Puerto Rico.	65
23	Alomar's plan for a manufacturing community drawn when a student at MIT, 1945.	68
24	José Luis Arrese Marga, a hard-line fascist supporter of the Nazis.	72
	Minister of Housing in 1957.	81
25	Sketch of the title and cover of a book proposed by Alomar.	87
26	The controversial monument by Francesc Roca (1940) at Plaça de Sa Feixina, Palma.	89
27	Alomar's 'Monument to the Fallen' at Sóller.	89
28	Alomar's initial design for Lloseta gardens.	93
29	Gardens of Ayamans at Lloseta designed by Alomar.	95
30	Alomar's gardens at Lloseta in close proximity to the town.	95

31	Aloma's original plan for the garden suburb of Son Veri.	97
32	Alomar's design for the garden suburb of Son Veri.	97
33	A detached house from 1960s on a large plot in Son Veri.	98
34	Street name plaque, Son Moll.	99
35	Alomar's plan for Cala Guya in North East Mallorca for Dr Otto Schlandt.	100
36	Proposed layout of housing at Can Guya.	100
37	Demolition of important buildings, including the Lírico Theatre, to make way for S'Hort del Rei.	101
38	S'Hort del Rei nearing completion c. 1971.	102
39	Alomar's 'palacio' in Sa Calatrava built in the 1950s in the Italianate style.	103
40	Part of the garden of Alomar's home.	104

Acknowledgements

Gabriel Alomar Esteve published a short memoir in 1986. While this has guided my research, it has several shortcomings with, at times, the appearance of a diary; it has little about his early life and education. Part of the second edition of his *Teoria de la Ciudad* (1980) contains valuable reflections of parts of his professional life. He has left a useful archive in the public domain but much of it consists of material that he used to write his memoirs.

This is located in the General Archive of the Consell de Mallorca in a rather desolate part of the western suburbs of Palma, which despite its setting is an excellent place to work. My thanks are to the staff there - and in particular to Sra Isabel Munar who made diligent searches and photocopies to aid my research. As in my previous work on Mallorca, the Biblioteca March in Palma proved invaluable: my thanks to the Librarian and his staff. Secondary sources for this work are readily available in most architectural and planning libraries in Spain including papers in journals and books many of which are available on line. I am particularly indebted to the libraries of Cardiff University in the UK and Universitat de les Isles Balears (UIB) in Mallorca. The internet is, of course, an invaluable source of much information; who today can work without Google and other search engines? A source of many relevant publications is Academia. edu

Newspapers of the period both national and local have proved useful sources including ABC and La Vanguardia at the national level and Diario de Mallorca, Ultima Hora and La Almundaina in Mallorca.

I have been most fortunate in being able to speak at length with my subject's daughters Mari Carmen and Nani, his son Antonio (who also trained as an architect). Dr Biel Alomar Garau, a lecturer in geography and landscape at the University of the Balearic Islands, found time from a busy academic schedule to talk to me about his grandfather and to give me access to elements of his family's archive of which he is curator. All gave up valuable time and much hospitality to answering my many queries, often in their magnificent homes in Sa Calatrava in Palma, at Vin Roma near Muro and at Son Moll.

Without the friendship of my very good friend Dr Gonçal López Nadal, formerly of the economics department of UIB, none of my work on Mallorca would have been possible. His warm hospitality, conversation and memories of Gabriel Alomar Esteve, usually over extended lunches at Son Comparet, will always remain with me. Thanks, too, to Profesora Isabel Moll y Blanes profesora emerita in Contemporary History of UIB whose hospitality enabled important introductions to the Alomar family.

The late Dr Volker Stalmann, a companion in Mallorca for nearly twenty years, with his wife Gretl, acted as a sounding board for many of my ideas on Mallorca and its varied urban and rural landscapes. Near the end of my work on Alomar he sadly passed on: *Requiescat in pace*.

Photographs and illustrations have been drawn from several sources with their permission but especially from Dr Biel Alomar Esteve. Being able to quote from Alomar's oeuvre and reproduce many of his maps from the 1950 published edition of his plan for the reform of Palma is thanks to his kindness. He also kindly provided the image for the book's cover which shows part of Alomar's map of 1943 and an aerial view of Palma today. John Sherwood and Frank Hartles kindly produced digital images of many of the maps and illustrations making this a more attractive book. Many of the photos are from my collection.

While all effort has been made to quote accurately from the numerous sources used in this monograph, and whose origins can be found in the extensive notes and references, the usual academic protocols relating to 'fair dealing' have been observed. Should anyone feel their rights have been breached I would be pleased to hear from them.

Mark and Anne Webb of Paragon Publishing helped me with the early stages of publication, prepared my text and illustrations and arranged for the book's production and its publicity. Their professionalism is much appreciated.

This book has taken much longer than planned largely thanks to the Covid 19 epidemic. Finally, my special thanks are to my partner, Hawys Pritchard, who has helped with translation and corrected many of my infelicitous comments in English and Spanish. She has bravely borne my absences in the field in Mallorca, in the Bookshed at the bottom of our garden and in numerous libraries, over many years while I tried to repay my debt to Mallorca and its people by bringing some aspects of its geography and history to a wider audience.

Cowbridge, Wales and Palmasol, Mallorca.
March 1st 2022
Dydd Gŵyl Dewi and Dia de les Illes Balears

Preface: Scene one – Palma, then and now

This is not a biography but rather an account of one man's working life in town planning. It is aimed primarily at readers of English but his work is little known in the Spanish speaking world. Its story begins with our protagonist – Gabriel Alomar Esteve – and his native city – Palma – and its island setting – Mallorca – whose economy and social organization was transformed in his lifetime by tourism, a set of processes that continue today despite the effects of the Covid 19 pandemic of the 2020s. Its beginning lies in the early 20thC and continues to the 1990s so that the object of his first large-scale venture into town planning has itself been transformed and today the city's citizens are trying to accommodate these new forces into a framework that Alomar only partly created. It may be possible to judge his legacy by examining the challenges contemporary Palma's social and physical structures face, forces that he could scarcely have foreseen. Later in his career, he became involved in Spain's attempts to develop something approaching a rule-based national planning system. He was from the beginning a man with an international perspective which he felt could offer valuable insights for the development of Spanish planning. But it is my view that he became disillusioned with the prospects for *urbanismo* just at the time when tourism was, in part, altering the urban structure of Spain. At that point, he sought refuge in the world of history, perhaps always his first love.

We begin in the early 1940s. Spain was just beginning to recover from the ravages of a Civil War, the ravages that only a civil war can bring. The young architect and hopeful town planner Gabriel Alomar Esteve had served in that war but had seen little or no action having been posted to the northern frontier in the Spanish Pyrenees away from any concentrated fighting. He had returned to his beloved Mallorca in 1938 to see out the war's end at Sollér, a small port on the north-west coast. His training in architecture had been of little value to the Nationalist's effort but towards the end, he was asked to make some alterations to the island's airport and airforce base at Son Bonet.

The war had inflicted much damage on the fabric of many Spanish cities such as Madrid, Teruel and Tarragona, including the infamous bombing of Guernica. Alomar's city had suffered very little, a few bombs from the Republican airforce in 1937. But war damage was not to be the stimulus alone that led Alomar to consider the reform of his city. It suffered much more from the more traditional problems of Spanish cities: poor housing and sanitary conditions, overcrowding, narrow and ill-kempt roads and few open public spaces. Suburban expansion beyond the line of the Renaissance walls had started in the late 19C but it was largely uncoordinated and poorly planned. When he came to examine the needs of the mid 20thC city he had to identify what were the pressing priorities. Palma in the preceding decades was still largely a medieval city in terms of its plan and form upon which new demands were being made: to improve intramural transport, to increase and improve housing provision and its associated hygienic condition, to accommodate the growing native population caused by urbanisation outside the line of the city walls and to recognise the impact of the growing numbers of tourists, that *indústria de los forasteros* – as outlined by Amengual in 1903[1]. In summary, questions of congestion, pollution and population numbers, permanent and seasonal – all this without destroying the unique historical character of the city.

For some, there is an irony in the danger of history repeating itself in the 21stC. Nearly 70 years later similar issues face Palma today. From about 2012 many cities of the world began to suffer increasingly from the modern form of three of these forces: congestion, air pollution and growing population including visitor numbers, all of which are interrelated. Unlike in the late 1930s when Alomar began to approach his task it has been popular protest that has spurred politicians into action, older ones fearful of their majorities and younger more radical ones elected to the city's council.

Planners and architects have struggled to find solutions to the first of these problems by emphasising public transport at the expense of private vehicles despite the car's stubborn presence on urban roads by, for example, investing in underground, metro and tram systems. Traffic management has been used to restrict the movement of certain kinds of traffic into cities, either altogether or at certain times. Vehicles of a certain size may be prevented from entering the central areas or some kind of tax is imposed – a congestion charge.

The quality of the air breathed in cities might have been thought to have improved with the decline of manufacturing and raw material processing in cities but by the 1990s it was becoming poor once more. The smoke and smog of the 1950s may have gone for a while but soon it was replaced by 'petrol fumes', a whole alphabet of noxious gases: CO, CO_2, NOx and particulate matter. It is no longer the outpourings of factory and domestic chimneys but the exhaust gases from vehicle tailpipes that are reducing air quality. In particular, the guilty party has proved to be the diesel engine. The petrol engine may have added mightily to global warming but it is the diesel that is slowly affecting respiratory and other issues and amongst our children, especially in European cities where it has become so prevalent, ironically often thanks to government encouragement. However, the sheer number of vehicles of all kinds means that pollution by smaller units of particulate matter also comes from tyre wear and brake linings.

As the secondary economy of cities has given way to tertiary and then quaternary forms of production so private wealth has taken on a new distribution curve. At the top end, fewer and fewer people command a greater proportion of wealth. At the bottom end, relatively extreme forms of poverty and deprivation can be found, though the quantity remains small. In the middle, the numbers have grown and their share of wealth and resources – especially in its disposable forms – has got larger. And more and more of this middle band, no longer definable by class – upper working, middle, lower-middle – has more money to spend on non-work activities including leisure. The increase in the demand for these activities has come in the form of travel and tourism as prices have fallen. The jet plane from the late 1950s onwards meant that more of this was directed away from a home country's economy. By the 21stC the whole world was available for tourists' consumption.

For port cities such as Palma, a phenomenon of the last twenty years has been a parallel rise in ship-borne tourism on cruise liners. Its origins may lie in 1930s American cruising south among the Caribbean islands but today many parts of the globe are as accessible to such vessels. As demand rose so inevitably vessel size increased: it was easier for ports to accommodate a small number of very large ships (70, 000 tons and up to

6000 passengers and crew) rather than a larger number of smaller vessels. If ports could not accept their size they were left off itineraries. Such vessels are also a relatively new source of atmospheric pollution – and one barely known to Alomar – in that from ships, notably cruise liners, not only emit many noxious gases while in motion but more significantly for a city like Palma do so while tied up in port, often for twenty-four hours at a time.

Add together the decanting or dumping of thousands of temporary visitors from cruise liners to the often millions who arrive by air to the same destination and soon certain places, mostly cities, began to feel the strain. Why cities? Historically they had always acted as magnets for visitors because of their cultural attractions – Florence, New Orleans, Venice etc – they now offered more accessible, more democratic attractions to art and architecture, music, galleries and museums, to now include 'nightlife', fast food, clubbing and commercial sex – attractive to new markets within this newly defined middle class.

But of course, three indicators to which reference has been made are in many ways exogenous: to them must be added that variable that is so often overlooked as a source of environmental stress that town planning has to try to address, namely the rise and rise of the urban population. In Mallorca's case, and in Palma in particular, this is the result of inward immigration both from within the island, from the mainland and significantly from overseas.

Where are the cities in the developed world where the three rising indicators of congestion, air pollution and population growth/tourism often coincide? Mostly they are port or seaboard cities: the West Coast of USA and in Florida, Europe's ancient ports especially those in a post-industrial or never seriously industrialised state, and among the islands and peninsulas of South East Asia. In sharper focus are the cities with the kind of seasonal climates that tourists seek – the Mediterranean regions in particular. Tourists are still driven by a search for dependable warmer climes when their own simply cannot provide these for reasons of geography. And this temporal flow occurs in the north and south hemispheres and across the equator that divides them.

What is the relevance of all this to the reform of Palma's urban structure by Gabriel Alomar Esteve in the 1940s and '50s and his development as a town planner? First, Palma is a good example of the processes described above: car ownership is among the highest in Spain, in pre- Covid19 pandemic years over 200, 000 planes fly in and out of Son Sant Joan airport each year depositing nearly 15 million visitors and the city's port was visited by 886 cruise liners in 2017 bringing thousands of visitors into the middle of the city. For example, in one week in August 2019, 60, 000 cruise tourists disembarked into the historic centre of Palma, more than 900, 000 in the first half of the year[2].

In the last five years, movements have grown up within the city to try to reduce this inexorable increase in visitor numbers. This is not a new phenomenon. Many years ago, local geographers and economists warned of the environmental, economic and social consequences of a small island dominated by a primate city becoming too dependent upon tourism. These pressures first began to be seen in the 1930s in Mallorca when early cruise liners and ferries from the Peninsula began to bring more people. Car ownership rose from the 1930s; the railways were largely closed by the 1960s. The very earliest 'pre-mass' tourists of the late 19C came not so much for the 'sea and sand' but primarily for the cultural attractions of Palma itself – and where were these interests concentrated? – in its historic heart, the Arabic-medieval-renaissance port city of walls, narrow lanes, churches and convents and the townhouses of the aristocracy – mostly characteristic of the 'other' for north European, American and Asian visitors. As we shall see this was the city that the young Alomar grew up in before his translation to Barcelona for his higher education. His ideas for the reform of Palma drawn up in the late 1930s and early '40s, and partly implemented in the 1950s and '60s, were aimed at addressing many of the same quartet of negatives that confront the city today: congestion of traffic and people within the tight corset of a once walled city, pollution from many sources including traffic, lack of hygiene from overstretched housing and social segregation based on wealth and ethnicity, if not in detail at least in broad principle. But at the heart of his plans was the central idea to conserve the historic core of the city. Alomar and the plan reformers who preceded him sought a solution in physical planning – new suburbs, new roads, new urban infrastructure, new architectural forms and functions – whereas today's political processes are seeking to direct the island's monocultural economy (tourism) away from this source of immense wealth and prosperity that has shaped the city since at least the 1960s. The current island and city governments want to reduce Airb&b, uber, cruise liners and the less well off '4S' tourists.

The historic core of Palma on which Alomar's plan was focused has recently been the subject of intensive study by the city authorities and pressure groups (such as Palma XXI), primarily because tourism and well-heeled more permanent immigration have together been exerting considerable pressure on the inner city's structure, appearance and social composition[3]. This revealed that in the 143 hectares of the historic centre the tourist impact is concentrated on the area between the Parc de Mar, the Cathedral and the Plaça d'Espagna including the Plaça Major, Calle St Miguel, Born, Oms and Jaume III, all spaces that will become familiar as this story unfolds. Here the number of 3* to 5* hotels has increased from 38 in 2014 to 144 in 2020, many in converted historically important buildings. Car ownership and use by residents and visitors have increased, assisted by the proliferation of car parks, many underground. Bus data shows the city-region nature of Palma as Alomar predicted with over 16000 passengers per day arriving in the city from all parts of the island. Pedestrian concentration can be found in key areas such as the Plaça Major; footfall can average 2500 to 3000 per hour in Calle St Miguel for example in August. Seven per cent of Palma municipality's population is located in the historic core; accommodation for locals has become a political issue with house prices and rents rising markedly by as much as 30% in the six years since 2012. Rentals have been exacerbated by the rise of Airb&b and by sales of apartments to foreign investors – over 30% of the historic core's population is foreign-born. Finally, the retail and commercial property market has been transformed to satisfy the demands of tourists with the ground floor buildings of many streets converted to seasonal retailing of goods few locals require.

As Palma in the first quarter of the 21st-century experiences a new era of rapid urban change, it is perhaps an appropriate moment to examine the work of a man who foresaw many of the changes required in urban form and function to accommodate them but in his era at a much smaller and less intensive scale. While Gabriel Alomar Esteve's plans may have been visionary, his visions were only partially realised. Maybe his successors have had and will have more success than he did in accommodating modern forces into historical forms. But his plans came after at least two generations of the work of his predecessors in Palma, especially the work and foresight of Bernat Calvet, Gaspar Bennàzar and Guillem Forteza. At least, Alomar was partially successful with his plans whereas those of his predecessors largely remained paper exercises. The plans of his immediate successors in the second half of the 20thC appear to have lost control of planning as originally conceived, leading to more neoliberal interpretations of what cities are for and for whom.

But this was not a man whose vision was confined to his own locality. Alomar emerged as a national and international figure in certain aspects of town planning. An attempt will be made to examine his contribution to the wider field of town planning, beyond the limits of his native island, when he worked for Spain's government in the Institute of Local Government Administration in Madrid. Following a short stay in the United States, he realised that town planning in Spain would be improved if more modern and often foreign ideas could be broadcast and he used his position in the Institute to write a series of texts to aid this process. Eventually, it would appear that his frustration with Francoist bureaucracy and political infighting in the 1960s turned his attention towards a concern for the relations between planning and the historic environment of Spanish cities and the questions about conservation this raised within a European context. He became something of an ambassador for his country in this field. Equally, his love of gardens and the importance of open spaces within cities coloured much of his planning philosophy.

In summary, then, Gabriel Alomar Esteve is someone whose intellectual and professional development led him into wider spheres, perhaps a classic case of learning from the local and specific and broadening out to the theoretical and international.

1
Introduction

In the medieval barrio of Sa Calatrava tucked within the south-east corner of Palma's renaissance walls lies an area once dominated by the tanning yards of the medieval guilds. By the 17C, it was overlooked by the church of Santa Clara, for long a closed convent of the order of Poor Clares. Its forecourt is faced by houses of the surrounding little streets, many medieval in origin. In one of these streets is the narrow Carrer de Sant Alonso roughly parallel to the Bay of Palma. It is a road that goes nowhere, not leading directly to any of the city's walls. About halfway down this street going eastwards, to the right is an archway between a row of these houses. It is blocked by an iron-barred gate. Looking through the bars one is surprised to see the layout of a formal garden very much in the style of 18th century Italy, gravelled paths, pavings, statuary and, of course, a fountain. Beyond is the façade of a grand town mansion, clearly the home of a family of some importance.

But all is not as it seems. The house is a creation of 1950s Mallorca, the fantasy of the architect Gabriel Alomar Esteve who designed it along late Italian renaissance lines to house his wife and three children – Antonio, Mari Carmen and Nani. It was built by acquiring blocks of land that were possibly part of the curtilage of the Santa Clara monastery but which once housed the homes of medieval workers and their masters in a place that faced directly onto the sea but which had become slowly gentrified in the earlier part of the 20th C. It is now protected on the seaward side by the Parc de la Mar built on reclaimed land that allowed the construction of the *paseo maritimo*, a four-lane highway that takes east-west traffic in front of the Cathedral and the remaining walls of the city.

It was to this quiet corner of Palma that Gabriel Alomar Esteve retired after many years of service to town planning and architecture to his native island and his country. Sadly he remains something of an obscure figure to many non-Iberian town planners and architects, perhaps even to some Spanish ones. Among his contemporaries can be found planners of national significance: César Cort, Pedro Bidagor, Pedro Muguruza and Gaspar Blein. He was in correspondence with all of them and worked alongside many of them in Madrid, and yet there is no detailed account of his life's work as there is for some of them save for his brief memoir.[4] But in Mallorca he is a revered figure; his work has left an indelible mark on his native city and helped lay some of the foundations for modern town planning in Spain. This monograph, then, is an attempt to rectify this omission and to try to place our protagonist on the national pedestal where he rightly belongs.

My interest in Alomar springs from something I wrote in a previous work:

> *The city of Palma – Ciutat – presents a particular challenge to anyone writing about Mallorca's landscape. In the medieval and early modern period and again in today's more metropolitan era, and at a time of counterurbanisation, this city has loomed large in the island's history. In landscape*

> *terms, it really demands a lengthy chapter to itself but in fact, so rich and divers is its townscape that only a book would suffice. Readers with a bent for urban history will have to forgive the author if they find his treatment of the city's form and function over two thousand years or more somewhat superficial; it is not for want of interest or competence but for lack of space*[5].

My original intention was probably for a book of essays by different authors on Palma's urban history; this did not materialise. Instead, I became fascinated with the works of Alomar and the times he lived in and through and how the two helped shape each other. I began with the 'local' but soon realised that a proper understanding of the man and his work could only be achieved via deeper contextual studies.

When assessing his work, it is important to recognise three things: first, that he saw himself initially as an architect but that may have been because 'planning' was subservient to 'architecture' and taught together during his era. Secondly, most of his practical town planning was in effect limited to his proposed reforms to his native city – Palma – but which themselves largely built on the basic ideas of a previous generation of engineers/architect/planners, and even then, many of his proposals were not translated into the built form. His other practical plans were limited to small scale developments, many associated with the suburban expansion of Palma and the burgeoning seaside resorts of Mallorca's tourism boom in the '60s and '70s. Thirdly, his influence on town planning in general in Spain came *after* his Palma plan was drawn up and was primarily derived from his time at the Institute for Local Administration in Madrid and as the author of three or four significant books which were used by many as textbooks. His planning ideas were the product of his time – the 1930s to the 1970s – and of his increasingly international connections – but were soon overtaken by the changing culture and economy of Mallorca. After that date, he devoted more of his time to his parallel interests in history and art[6]. The concentration here, then, will primarily be on his contributions to town planning and will only concern itself with his architecture and his art history where they collide.

In the sense that towns planned are cultural artefacts – amongst the largest in the world – Palma has to be seen in the historical and spatial context of the island of Mallorca which in turn should be seen as part of a wider Spain less than fifty years after its Empire failed in the late 19C and in a European context of urban development from its beginnings to the present day. It used to be thought that islands were isolated entities – desert (deserted) islands – cut off from the mainstreams of cultural life: islands are another country; they do things differently there. Today, however, we now know and appreciate that this is far from the truth. From the very earliest times once settled – and their very settlement is indicative of their connectedness – islands were wired into a wider world, constrained only by their technological abilities in crossing water. If this is the case then such islands were nearly always part of cultural movements into and out of their realms.

To be more specific to the subject of this monograph, Mallorca and its city were, historically, more the product of extraneous forces rather than local ones. As we shall show Palma was founded by the Romans, expanded by the Arabs, Berbers and Christians, surrounded by walls – designed incidentally by Italians – because the Spanish State saw it as being at the frontier between European and African worlds. It developed trading links with most of the known world and was industrialised under European economic influences. Each of these cultures brought a planned city into focus. If some of the 'planning' was not of the 'drawn on paper' kind it was, nonetheless, intentional, the product of socio-economic and cultural processes, clearly not solely local in origin.

So too, then, when we examine the planning of Palma as we know it today, we shall see that the progenitors of those drawing-board plans of Alomar's generation although maybe born on the island they were influenced by ideas from elsewhere.

When we come to look at the life in planning of our protagonist we shall see that he was in contact with a wide range of planning cultures and ideas, largely Western but conscious of ideas from Africa and North and Latin America. Alomar's planning education may have begun locally within the Spanish (some would say Catalan) orbit but soon expanded into the Caribbean, the USA and western Europe.

We shall discuss the extent to which his planning notions for modern Palma were influenced by largely Spanish ideas of the 1920s and '30s. He was trained under the Second Republic in the 'radical' city of Barcelona where he was exposed to modernist philosophies but his early ideas were also fashioned following the Nationalist's success in the Spanish Civil War. Were his thoughts shaped by the two regimes' contrasting urban theories? The fact that after 1939 so many theories of town planning in such a tumultuous era existed side by side is a clue to the failure of any kind of Falangist or fascist hegemony. Palma may have been under the sway of a Nationalist mayoralty and gubernatorial control in the late 1930s and '40s but any such overarching, centralist theories do not seem to have fashioned his designs. His plan appears rather to draw on wider and older more liberal ideas. It cannot be described as iconic because of its relations to its predecessors. He was certainly concerned to improve the living conditions of certain inner-city areas. Any economic imperative is clearly discernable in, for example, the construction of Carrer Jaume III where the influence was more likely to have been pragmatic, requiring the support of the financier Juan March. His reforms for Palma seem distant from those of his near contemporaries, Modernists such as Sert and Le Corbusier. If there is one theme that dominates his first foray into town planning it is a historicist one, and perhaps a romantic one, a concern for the historic city in which he grew up.

Importantly, Alomar's plan came at a time when Mallorca – and indeed Spain – was recovering from the Civil War, searching for a new economy based more on small-scale industrial and tertiary activities and the pressing need to find solutions to the older problems of poor housing, sanitation and high unemployment. Above all was the optimism abroad in the city, especially among its intellectual élites, for a new identity, a search that had to embrace extraneous influences brought partly by tourism. It would be some time before the impact of consumerism and increased political autonomy would be felt in the Balearic Islands. Perhaps Alomar's plan, though strongly rooted in an appreciation of the city's past, was, in fact, looking forward to future needs but in 1958, in a letter to Dominico Rodella, the head of urban renewal in Milan, Alomar, reflecting on his experience, described his reforms as '...*un trabajo realizado en un época cuyas ideas estéticas y urbanísticas resultan muy distante de las actuales... Es un eventamento pero realizado con todo respeto a los edificos y a los ambientes de valor*'. (...it was work realised in an era whose aesthetic and planning ideas were very distant from today's... but a project made with complete respect to valued buildings and settings). His historicism is matched by the planner's concern for the city in the future but recognising, perhaps, that his ideas were already being overtaken.

How far did the culture of the Franco regime at the end of the Civil War in 1939 influence his thoughts? It was a frightening and literally murderous regime that sought revenge on all who had opposed the Nationalist cause. To many of the fascist ideologues Spain had to be purged of such elements, contrition had to be sought from those towns and cities who had held out against the Nationalists. One of the most anti-democratic systems of prosecution and the enforcement of a corrupt law saw thousands murdered, imprisoned or sent to labour camps. Mallorca had given strong support to the Nationalists, acting as an aircraft carrier for the Italian airforce based there that harried shipping in the Mediterranean and bombed the mainland cities under loyalist control such as Barcelona, Alicante and Tarragona. The abortive Republican landing in Porto Cristo had been quickly defeated. Most of its forces and supporters were soon rounded up and many executed. After the war at least 500 were shot, including the progressive mayor of Palma, Emile Darder. Military control of the island was imposed and a new civil service put in place; local government was purged of all those who had opposed the Nationalists. Thus, it was, that the city council to whom Alomar's plans had won the competition for the reform of Palma was of a very different colour from the pre-war one. Was this idea for a 'new' Palma part of an ideological shift, seeking a new city to represent a new regime as much as a technological response to the challenges facing the built form by the 1940s?

Following his labours designing the reform of Palma Alomar first took himself and his family abroad to Puerto Rico – an American 'colony' – and from thence to the United States – where relatively short stays were to fashion his ideas on *urbanismo*. On his return, he was soon recruited into the Spanish civil service, to the recently expanded Institute for Local Administration, where he was responsible for developing national ideas in town planning, part of a new coterie of technocrats seeking to direct the country on a new path. His philosophies found expression in a series of books and articles; it was as much an academic role as one of practical 'hands-on' planning. One valuable aspect of this period in Madrid was his establishment of international contacts and visits. These included important links with the British planning fraternity of the 1940s and '50s who were so active in post-war Britain with its new and expanded towns and its regional planning. British planning law was partly the inspiration for the writing and passing of national planning legislation in Spain which, for the first time, helped codify the role of the State against the historically powerful *ayuntamientos* (town councils). A national land-use law (the Ley del Suelo) of the mid-1950s, although subject to much criticism and reform, was a vital stage in Spain's move towards modern town planning. Later Alomar was to examine the broader spatial and regional patterns of economic and urban growth, helping to confront one of the age-old controversies in Spain's history, that of regional development, and of struggles between centre and periphery. It was also a period that allowed him to expand on his earlier ideas for urban conservation, a subject that was to dominate more of his later life in Palma and in Europe.

This monograph's structure reflects these patterns of his progress. If we believe that Alomar was greatly influenced by the urban milieu in which he grew up and that he was deeply conscious of Palma's history, then it seems logical to begin our study with an account of the city's development; this was the physical structure he inherited and in need of reform. The following chapters seek to outline the planning ideas with which he would have been familiar both from his training in Barcelona and from those that had been broadcast in the generations before him in Palma. Chapters 3, 4 and 5 will examine the political context for Alomar's own plan, his execution of it in order to win a competition and a critical analysis of it. It is clear that after this initial success that little actual building was likely to begin immediately. At the same time, his frustration with lack of action spurred him on to expand his planning education further – he was still only 30 years of age when his plan was approved and any training he had had was limited. He felt the need to learn more about Western planning ideas and the only place to do this in the middle of Europe's Second World War was in America. It is this sojourn in the USA that forms the core of Chapter 7. His return to Mallorca saw the publication of his book on the theory of planning in 1947, his Palma plan in book form in 1950 and, at last, work beginning on its implementation. In Chapter 8 we see Alomar becoming involved in the reforms of town planning policy at the national level as part of a new and younger cadre of technological specialists determined to bring post-Civil War Spain more into the European mainstream. He was an important contributor to a key piece of legislation, the Ley del Suelo of 1956. This was a contribution to a national process of modernisation in Spain that helped point the way to the structural economic reforms of 1959. During this decade Alomar spent more and more time in Madrid away from his beloved island and in writing and publishing his most important books about planning. He had now become more of a national figure rather than a purely local one, mixing with powerful figures in the Spanish administration. In the next two chapters (8 and 9) we witness his role in a wider European sphere as Spain's representative on important committees of the Council of Europe. By the 1960s, his interest in town planning was waning and it is an appropriate moment in this narrative to look at two fields very close to his heart that he had always regarded as important within town planning, the conservation of the urban environment and the role of gardens and public open spaces in cities and towns.

We are fortunate that Gabriel Alomar published a short memoir in 1986. While this has been of great value in guiding our research, it has several shortcomings notably the omission of details of his early life. Essentially, it is a memoir rather than a biography, chronological in content, written rather like a diary. He has left a useful archive in the public domain but much of it consists of material that he used to write his memoirs. My task has been to widen Alomar's own story, to provide a more detailed context of the times and to add a critique to his work.

2
Palma: a brief history of the city Alomar inherited

Alomar's ideas in planning and architecture were firmly rooted in the character of the city in which he was born in 1910 and where he lived until he went to the School of Architecture in Barcelona seventeen years later. As a boy, he would have played in the narrow streets around the family home, taken rides on the local trams and later as a young man sampled the numerous cafes and bars in the Casc Antic. Being of a religious bent at a time when Catholicism dominated the social life of the city, he would have had first-hand knowledge of its many churches, especially of Montesion. It is this familiarity with the morphology and the form and function of Palma in the late 1920s and early '30s, including first-hand experience of its urban failings in housing, in traffic and in health and sanitation, that fuelled his growing realisation that the nature of his birthplace was beginning to change that would slowly infiltrate into his perception of what was needed to be done to modernise the city. We know, too, that by the late 1930s he was also familiar with the numerous plans of previous generations of local architects and engineers. . Historically, his had been a city at the crossroads of the western Mediterranean basin forming an important link between Europe and Africa and between Christianity and Muslimism. Its morphology may have given the appearance of a tightly corseted city but by the time of his birth, much of the renaissance city wall had been demolished. It was on the cusp of a phase of suburban expansion that had begun in the last two decades of the 19C but with a deteriorating 'inner city'. For a curious and inquisitive youth, Palma must have appeared to Alomar as a city beginning to change architecturally, structurally and socially.

Palma – 'Ciutat' – the capital of the island of Mallorca and of the Balearic Islands – has a history that marks it out as one of the more noteworthy port- cities of the Western Mediterranean. Founded by the Romans after 123BC it thrived as a Muslim trading centre from the 10thC and after the conquest by the Aragonese/Catalan Christians in 1229 as an important entrepôt, trading, manufacturing and business city in Medieval Europe. It lay on an important hinge between North Africa and Europe. It was for centuries one of a network of such cities that included Genoa, Livorno, Palermo, Naples, Marseilles and the Spanish cities of Barcelona, Màlaga and Alicante and many North African cities. Until Spain's conquest of much of Central and South America with the consequent reorientation towards the west and the Atlantic Ocean Palma was a significant city on the map of the Mediterranean.

From the early days, it was a walled city with encirclements successively including Roman, Arab/Berber, Medieval and Renaissance walls. As with many cities in the Mediterranean, it was the sequence of walls that was to determine much of what went on within them. The intramural space may not have constrained development initially but as the city grew so successive walls with their new technologies were built to enclose extramural growth. Its morphology owed much to Muslim city builders whose *almudaina* (fort) had its own walls with another of the city's encirclement beyond. The narrow streets of what was in effect a Middle Eastern city survived the later Christianising of the townscape in a way that the mosques, bazaars and baths did not.

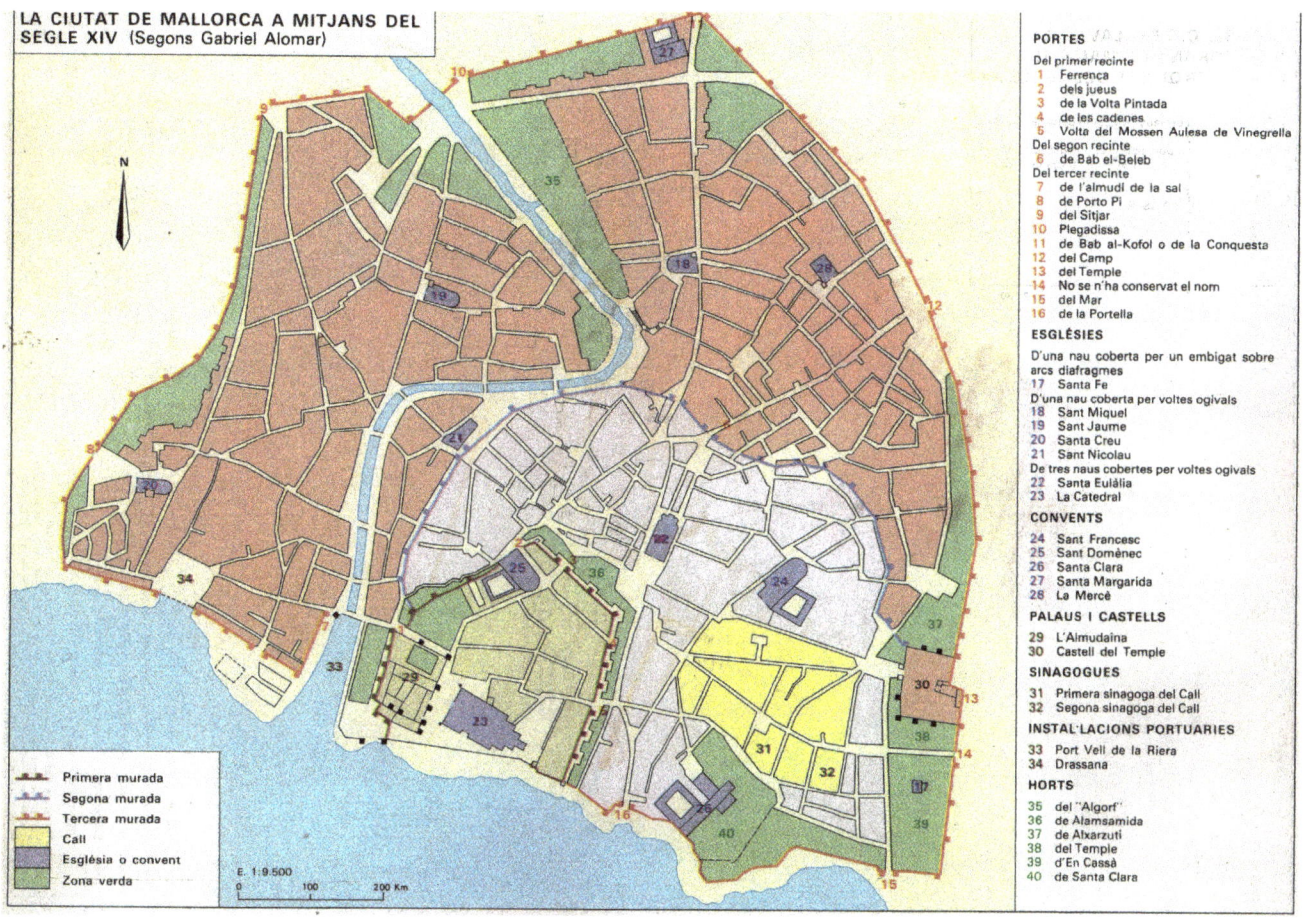

Fig 1   Medieval Palma in 14C showing succession of walls.
Source: Atles de les Illes Balears (1974) (after Alomar, 1950).

Under the 'conquistador' Jaume I the street plan was largely conserved and adapted to new uses. His successor Jaume II built a new circle of walls with ten gates to control ingress and egress for taxation purposes and to protect the city against the corsair and pirate raids that were to persist for many centuries. The final set of walls was designed by the Italian brothers Palearo for Philip II in the 16C to reflect the major technological innovation of the time in the military sphere – artillery – capable of destroying previously impermeable city walls and, from the reverse perspective, of defending them. They planned for a set of straight curtain walls punctuated by a series of ten diamond-shaped bulwarks so that raking fire could be directed parallel to the walls. This eventually gave the zig-zag pattern so common to such Renaissance defence systems in many European countries. These walls were never seriously attacked and proved a major constraint on further urban growth for 250 years, though the gates continued to act for the control of goods into the city. The sea wall limited the development of Palma as a port city as ships grew in size and needed more expansive areas in which to discharge and load merchandise.

A second morphological feature that helped define the city's social and economic geography was the River

Riera whose channel divided the city into upper and lower parts. It had a regime typical of most Mediterranean rivers, that is, in the summer months, it was primarily a dry bed with large quantities of water flowing only in the winter. However, flooding on a drastic scale took place from time to time (1404, 1443 and even in 1618 before the diversion was complete), again typical, the consequences of which were often disastrous for the medieval morphology of the 'low town'. When flowing the river had its uses as a waste disposal system and as a polluted water source. When dry the riverbed acted as the typical Spanish *rambla,* a scene for the *paseo*, part of the 'city as theatre', common in the eighteen and nineteen hundreds. On balance it was judged to be a nuisance at best, a danger at worst. A decision was taken to divert it in 1613, down the west side of the new walls. This entailed building new bridges across it to take new roads leading from the new gates. Its former channel led to the emergence of two new elements in the townscape, Es Born and the Via Roma – the Rambla.

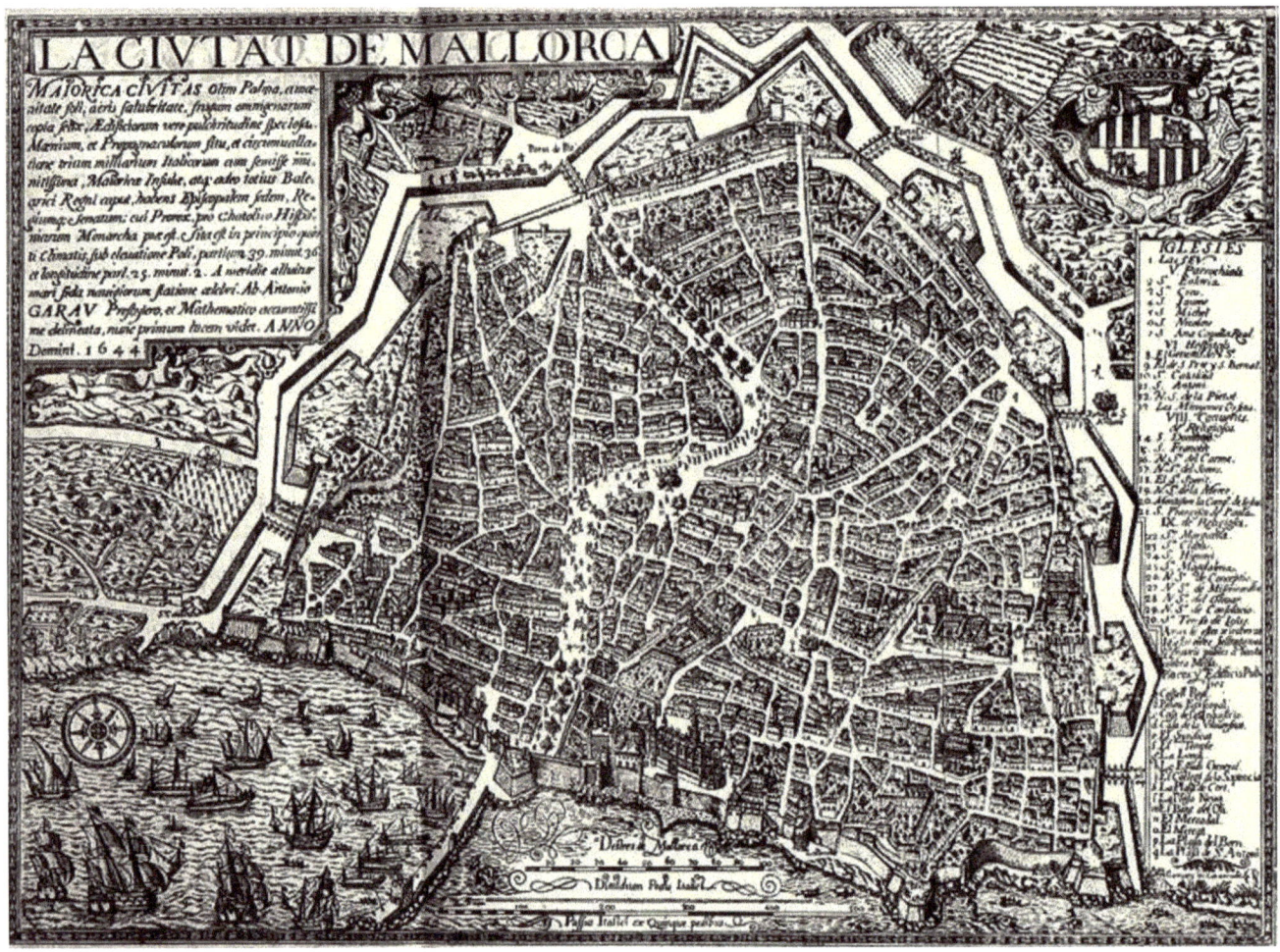

Fig 2   Map of Palma by Antonio Garau, 1644.

A third element, though not strictly morphological, was the city's water supply system. The geology and rainfall characteristics of Mallorca, as in many Mediterranean areas, was not supportive of much surface water, despite the Riera mentioned above. Clean water had to be brought into the city via a series of aqueducts, a process begun by the Romans (though not in the spectacular form as in many other Roman cities) but perfected by the Muslims. Water was brought in via small channels from distant springs, stored in vast underground reservoirs and distributed via a series of *pants,* communal distribution points serving several houses and streets. It was a system that was to survive until the mid 19C.

Upon this physical structure – walls, river, water supply – grew a population sharply divided between a controlling aristocracy and nobility who occupied large town mansions whose opulence reflected their island landholdings, a powerful merchant class located in the central parishes of St Eulalia and Sant Creu and in close proximity to the port, and a mass of labourers, industrial workers and servants. Population numbers grew from 30, 263 in 1784 to 40, 405 in 1840 and to 53, 019 in 1860, all contained within the encircling walls. From an early date, Palma had become an overcrowded and unhygienic city and by the early 19C, it was this characteristic that was to drive the demand for urban reform. Population initially expanded through rural to urban migration as agriculture shifted from fairly intensive grain production to tree crops such as vines, olives, figs and carobs. Industrialisation had always been important in the city including metalworking, textiles, leather goods and furniture mostly for the domestic and Spanish markets. The later 19C saw the introduction of the railway network and the beginnings of a factory based industrial system. Until then, and indeed still today, much industrial output was achieved in small workshops with fewer than five employees. The tertiary industries grew to service the growing urban population, especially in the retailing and banking sectors together with those engaged in the import/export business. Between 1840 and 1877 the population increased by 40%, to 58, 224. By the census of 1901 Palma's population had reached 65, 421 with a density of nearly 330 per ha. Numerous reports – pioneering for Spain – were made on the unhealthiness of the city, the problems of water supply and sewage disposal. Urban diseases were endemic, some harking back to the great medieval plagues such as the Black Death of the 14C, typhus and typhoid and, because of the city's role as an international port, shipborne scourges such as yellow fever. By the late 19C, much of Palma was a congested, dirty, unhealthy and overcrowded city, not unlike so many similar places in the Mediterranean at this time. And, politically there lurked always the danger of social unrest and revolution in such a stressed built environment.

3
Alomar and the Spanish tradition in town planning: population, public health and movement

Besides the physical and historical setting of Palma itself, it is equally important to appreciate the intellectual context of town planning and architecture that Alomar worked within. To what extent was his plan influenced by planning ideas current in the 1920 and '30s?

It is a familiar picture in the genesis of the history of town planning in Western Europe: planning eventually being perceived as a possible solution to many environmental and social problems. It was not until the advent of the Garden City movement of the late 19C that an alternative solution to the ills of cities was to be found in the development of distant but connected secondary settlements – ideas set out in Ebenezer Howard's 'Ideal City' and Peter Kropotkin's 'Fields, Factories and Workshops'[7]. However, there is in Spanish and Catalan culture a marked separation of ideas about the term 'town planning'. As Gordon Cherry pointed out many years ago what might be called 'Anglo Saxon planning' emerged as a discipline from the studies of urban development by such founding fathers as Ebenezer Howard, Patrick Geddes and the Garden City movement typified by Unwin and Parker. In Spain, on the other hand, town planning has its roots in engineering (roads, railways, ports etc) following Napoleonic precepts, in a concern for *higiene publica* and later, in architecture as though the city was solely a physical construct and not a socio-economic one. In Spain, *urbanismo* is not synonymous with town planning. In fact, Alomar himself wrote an essay on this topic which will be referred to below:

> *Esta evolución conceptual del urbanismo ha obligado imperativamente al arquitecto-ingeniero-urbanista – llamémosle planitecto.*

He referred to himself as *planitecto* – a planner[8].

It was against this background of the structure of Palma and the evolving ideas about *urbanismo* in the second half of the 19C that schemes for the reform of *Ciutat* began to emerge. First, it is necessary to remind ourselves of the legal context of 'planning' however it is defined. It is an activity that affects individuals and their property rights. To destroy houses, workshops, factories, churches etc to make way for 'improvements' requires the 'state' to have legal sway over individually owned property if the owners refuse to co-operate. In medieval cities such as Palma, there is a long history of ordinances that gave the local state the right to manage space and buildings according to some sense of the common good when individual rights threatened it. In some cases this was the right of the Spanish State to defend the city against the threat of outside attack especially from the Turkish and Ottoman Empires and their North African regencies; this kind of national ordinance gave rise to the construction of the renaissance walls. For the same reason, Palma housed a considerable share of the national armed forces – infantry, artillery and naval forces -so that swathes of the city were given over to barracks, parade grounds and stores as well as outlying forts such as San Carlos.

At the local level the ayuntamiento – the city council-controlled land and buildings for municipal purposes. Until the *desmortización* (disentailment) of the first half of the 19C, the Church was a very powerful vested interest in the city with more than a dozen churches and monasteries. Mostly founded in the 400 years after the conquest of 1229 such property occupied large areas of the inner city in, no doubt, a spiritually productive way but whose economic value was limited. In many medieval cities, the guilds similarly held buildings and land. The use of this corporate private property was often severely constrained for anything other than institutional activities. In Palma, as in many other Spanish cities located close to national frontiers whether maritime or land-based, the army controlled large areas of the city for military purposes – and the army was under national jurisdiction, not local. Thus what the 'state', whether national or local, could do was often strictly limited until legislation gave the state rights over private property or acquired such sites through purchase. One area where this conflict was much less clear was over the ownership of streets and highways. In an essentially medieval city, the network of roads had emerged over many centuries but it did seem inviolate despite this lack of clarity as to ownership. Roads survived in a way that buildings and the plots they stood on often did not.

Any future planning, then, would have to accommodate public and private needs and rights, reconcile the military and ecclesiastical authorities with those of local government, at the same time devising schemes that could lead to new highways, public open spaces, better housing conditions and improvements in public health. As the power of the Spanish state evolved in the second half of the 19C so national legislation began to demand changes in the structure of its cities and towns regardless of their provincial location. However, in Spain, this centralising force was much less prevalent than in France or Great Britain.

The reforms to urban structure that began to emerge in the second half of the 19C would need the right kind of political structural context for them to succeed. Palma, unlike many other Spanish cities, had historically, and indeed from the time of the Christian conquest in the 13C, been in the hands of a small, but elected elite – *els jurats* – created by Jaume I and based on a model used in Valencia. Until the mid-15C *Ciutat* also ruled the whole island out of which evolved the island *Consell* giving rise to a tension between town and country that resulted in the *germanies* (brotherhoods), conflicts between the wealth of the governing and merchant classes and guilds of the city and the relative poverty of the *part forana*, the inland areas. Although these conflicts were largely resolved in 1523 it was not until the establishment of the Bourbon monarchy (the Nova Planta of 1715) that a new form of municipal government developed. Twenty *regidors* or councillors were appointed directly by the king, Philip V consisting of sixteen knights and four 'citizens', centralizing power in the monarchy. By the 1780s Palma had a population of more than 30, 000 and had become an important manufacturing city as well as a trading port. In the early 19C, the war against France, the alternating liberal and repressive regimes all affected the way Palma was governed.

The city faced numerous economic and medical challenges including the depression of the 1850s and the cholera epidemic of 1865. The success of the democratic period after 1868 and the associated disturbances in the city led to institutional reform and new, more progressive forms of governance but liberals and conservatives continually vied for political control of a city with rising debts, a discontented working class and a pressing need for reform of its physical structure including the demolition of its walls and the building of suburbs, to be known as the *eixample*[9]. The first national legislation for the building of an *eixample* (Catalan. - trans. lit: *widening;* Castillian- *ensanche*) came in 1864 but was limited to Chamberí to the north of Madrid under the Castro Plan. Barcelona, of course, began its *ensanche* in the same year and Bilbao's in 1876. It was not until 1892 that the enabling law was extended to provincial cities including Palma. The first plan for expanding Palma via suburbs was proposed as early as 1877 and drawn up by Pedro Alcantára Peña in 1879, to be succeeded by that of Eusebio Estada in 1885. The introduction of wider suffrage in 1890 would create a more modern city council that might tackle some of these issues of hygiene and overcrowding via a series of committees that dealt with such topics as street cleaning, the regulation of markets, housing and construction. In Palma, the ayuntamiento established a special committee to deal with the demolition of the walls and suburban development beyond them. The road engineer Pedro Garau designed yet another plan for an eixample in 1894 but a competition for other plans saw the success of that of Calvet, to whom detailed reference will be made.

While many observers before the modernisation of the Spanish state that begins in the 1820s had analysed and commented on the parlous condition of life in Mallorca's capital, it was not until the work of a new technocracy of engineers – a product of the national schools of *Ingenieros de Caminos, Canales y Puertos* refounded in Madrid in 1834 – came to the fore that serious solutions began to be proposed. As Hall points out, however, in a social sense the fact that the deleterious living conditions in many cities – contaminated water, lack of sewage disposal, fetid air, noise etc – also affected the middle and upper classes as much as the proletariat, it meant that there was a political impetus for reform led from above[10]. Also, there was a slowly growing philanthropy for the condition of the poor so that space also had to be found for a locus for their care; in an earlier generation in Spain and Italy, these were manifest in the *misericordia* (poor house, especially for orphans). Funding such large scale reforms as town planning and public buildings had to come from local energies at a time when local government in the modern sense as we know it in Britain had hardly begun in Spain, and in any case, had limited tax-raising powers. The notion of progressive taxation to pay for reforms was a long way off.

In many Spanish cities, the question of who was to inhabit these new *ensanches* was widely debated. Initially, the middle and professional classes were to be the clients of the house and apartment builders but the demographic urban expansion in the last quarter of the 19C was largely fuelled by rural to urban migrants who had little experience of urban living and brought many of their less sophisticated practices with them notably all those disadvantages associated with outright poverty: unemployment, overcrowding, poor hygiene and begging.

One of the key areas of concern was for the health of the urban population of Palma. High death rates, high rates of infant mortality and shortness of life led to a concern for the rate of demographic growth: cities were supposed to demonstrate a population dynamic – a relationship between population growth and economic development was believed to exist. Historically there had always been the fear of diseases entering the city via its major port so that elaborate rules, both local and national, for quarantine and the isolation of disease represented themselves in the form of dedicated areas and buildings[11]. As in many other cities in the 19C, one of the greatest fears was an epidemic of cholera of which the island suffered four outbreaks in the 19C. In Mallorca, the authorities' principal weapon was containment using *cordons sanitaires* which were supported by contemporary medical evidence but seen almost as 'declarations of war' by the local population[12].

The 1880s saw the rise in the importance of a medical profession in Mallorca with an epidemiological emphasis; measurement and quantification were as popular socially in Mallorca as they were amongst the British intelligentsia at that time. A leading figure was Enric Fajarnés Tur whose published work on death and disease was to have a profound effect on attitudes towards public health in the city[13]. His work followed a national movement begun in the 1870s for the improvement of the collection of medical statistical data:

De su lectura y/o interpretación se producía la visibilización del problema sanitario y se desprendía su posible solución en forma de actuación normalmente pública legitimada por los propósitos del programa higienista. Este programa en su versión urbana se fijó en el derribo de las murallas, la canalización del agua y del alcantarillado, la higiene de las viviendas para evitar el hacinamiento y la mala ventilación, la construcción de ensanches, etc. (Whether the hygiene reform programme was effective depended on how the nature of the sanitary problem was perceived. The urban version of this programme paid attention to the demolition of the walls, the channelling of the water supply and the sewage system, the hygiene of the houses to avoid overcrowding and bad ventilation, the construction of suburbs, etc.)[14].

The availability of these new statistics enabled provincial cities such as Palma to provide a snapshot of the healthiness of the city particularly in terms of causes of death. Higher death rates amongst men coupled with the drafting of men into the armed services in the late 19C plus a rising rate of overseas migration thanks to the lack of economic opportunities, all led to a belief that a declining or stagnant urban population would lead to further economic decline. Palma, it was thought, suffered less from many of these urban malaises than other contemporary European cities thanks to its beneficial climate. Higher than average natural increases also meant that it did not rely so extensively on rural-to-urban migration to sustain its population. In other words, Palma may have been an increasingly unhealthy city in an objective sense but was better placed than many comparable cities, probably because by the last two decades of the 19C it did not yet display the really poor environmental qualities associated with large scale industrialisation. However, an increasing population in a situation of limited housing supply meant a continuing subdivision of properties leading to deleterious overcrowding that in turn led to poor health, especially in areas such as Puig de Sant Pere and Sa Calatrava. Despite this early concern for health very little progress in this field was made. Even in the Franco era architects and planners still saw sanitation as a major issue in Spain's cities; the Falangist Serrano Suñer remarked that "the key to town planning policy was sanitation. Given that the existence, strength and health of the nation come first, aspirations to national greatness should be based on achieving a strong, healthy Spanish citizen, in a salubrious and comfortable home, in a hygienic city or village"[15].

In addition to concerns for the public health of the city, another topic that attracted the attention of those concerned about the city's development was intraurban movement. The medieval street patterns derived from their Muslim predecessors made the movement of goods and people from one part of the city to another very difficult especially in the historic centre, the *casc antich*. This was exacerbated by the physical geography of Palma which divided it into upper and lower sections so that stairways were used to link the lower part of the city to the upper town. The street pattern presented two problems: the intramural movement of goods and people especially from the port area to locations across the city and secondly extramural movements in and out through the city's gateways. The coming of the railway in 1875 resulted in a shift of the centre of gravity northwards. This was complemented by the establishment of new large factories at or beyond the city's periphery as defined by its walls. Clearly, there was little or no room for steam-powered factories in the dense network of medieval streets. As we shall see, the military controlled the walls and laid down strict criteria for the location of industrial plant with respect to them. New extramural suburbs such as Santa Catalina and La Soledad had already emerged by the 1880s.

The port of Palma developed its first seaward quay and mole early in the 14C; before that ships had beached on the sands in front of the seawall. A new quarter – the *raval de mar* – had grown up in the 13th to 15thCs in response to the latter but it was characterised by the same restricted street topography[16]. With the arrival of steamships after 1850 seaborne trade increased rapidly in association with the island's growing population and an import/export trade to support the new or expanded industries. This was especially true after the opening of the Suez Canal which increased access to the East Indies and Asia via the Mediterranean rather than the Cape of Good Hope[17]. Once the railway system was linked to the port in 1931 then a considerable expansion of space for warehousing and shore portering was required.

This does not mean to say that land-use changes *within* the city walls were not forthcoming. New streets, new *plaças*, new public open spaces were added to the inner city's topography in the 19C. Doubtless, they might contain elements of town planning but in essence, they are better seen as 'property development' that, in some cases, had some public benefit. In the 1820s both the Born and the Rambla were built or improved as 'theatrical spaces'. In the 1830s the *desamortació* of Mendizábal involved the acquisition and demolition of as many as twenty-five church properties over the next forty years, including the huge gothic Sant Domingo convent and church whose site was redeveloped by Sureda and Abrines. This created an opportunity for new wide streets such as Conquistador (1845) that improved links between the high and low parts of the city and, on the site of the convent of Sant Filip Neri, the Plaça Major. But these spaces did little to relieve the conditions of the poorer sections of society. There remained sharp segregation between the rapidly increasing working classes and the *bottifares*. The holistic or more comprehensive kind of town planning was to come in the next century.

The last quarter of the 19C saw a noticeable increase in the city's population from 60, 000 in 1877 to 65, 500 in1900 – by then more than a quarter of the island's population – bringing further pressure on the *casc antich* that led to unplanned expansion beyond the city walls to accommodate new workshops and factories. Hostalets (1883), Capes (1892) and La Soledad (1891) – suburbs all to the east of the city centre – were typical extramural accretions. To the west, Santa Catalina had grown up initially as the suburb associated with the port, the home of sailors, fishermen and a whole variety of sea-related trades focussed on the ancient hamlet of Sant Magi. It was given formal planning recognition by the 1896 plans of Pere d'Alacántara Peña and the city's architect, Antoni Sureda[18]. As we shall see, the principal constraining factor linking these new western suburbs was the valley of the Riera which had to be bridged and all around Palma were the restrictions imposed by the walls.

The emergence of planning ideas in Spain

It was against this background that solutions to the sort of urban problems described above began to emerge. Some were concerned with public health, some with economic development and circulation and some with housing. As a way forward, our concentration will be on those ideas that took a more holistic view from the relatively new science of town planning. It is necessary then to say something by way of introduction to the origins of town planning as a discipline in Spain.

There were many cities in early 19C Spain that suffered the familiar pressures within their walled confines: Madrid, Barcelona, Seville, Cadiz, Gijon and many others demonstrated the need for relief of this pressure[19]. Naturally one first turns to the work of the pioneer in Spanish town planning Idelfonso Cerdá Suñer, an urbanist whose work was shamefully neglected for almost 70 years[20].

Idelfonso Cerdá[21]

Born at the end of the Napoleonic Wars, Cerdá trained initially at the Llotja School in Barcelona but received his professional training as an engineer at the School of *Ingenieros de Caminos, Canales y Puertos* in Madrid, graduating in 1841. This school, only re-founded in the 1830s, was clearly modelled on the similar establishment in France, part of the liberal and modernizing movement in Spain at that time. A progressive, he was elected as a member of parliament for Barcelona in 1850 but more importantly became a Barcelona city councillor in 1854. This was at a time when that city was undergoing serious political unrest and was suffering from many of the environmental problems identified above; to many, the two were not unrelated. After studying the social conditions associated with working-class housing he developed his *General Theory of Urbanization,* published in two volumes, the first in 1859, that contained a social analysis of Barcelona in its appendix which sowed the seeds for his plan for reform – the Plan Cerdá – in volume two in 1861. His work contained most of the factors requiring urban analysis that were described above: air pollution, water supply, congested working-class housing, difficulties in intraurban movement, lack of space for industrial expansion, the introduction of railways into the townscape and expansion of the port – all within the constraining six-kilometre corset of Barcelona's city walls[22]. The parallel with Palma's location and urban structure will become obvious. His detailed socio-economic analysis of the city – it runs to nearly 700 pages of text and tables – showed that of a working-class population of about 54, 000, 88% were 'mere' labourers living a marginal existence and whose average life span was only 23 years. In the two cholera epidemics of 1854 and 1865 over 10, 000 people died. One of his most telling correlations was between mortality and density of population[23]. Given the density of population in Barcelona at that time of 856 inhabitants per hectare – the highest in Spain – this is hardly surprising. His other principal contribution was to recognize the importance of market forces in any redevelopment of the city. New roads would be a defining feature of his plan; before reform in the 1860s the old city contained 200 streets less than 3m wide, and 400 less than 6m[24]. He re-established the economic principle that the construction of new highways could be funded by developers if they were granted building rights on land on either side of the road, a funding mechanism that benefited public and private interests alike. He also recognized that for there to be any demolition and reconstruction of the built environment for public benefit then land and property owners would have to be compensated[25]. Later we shall ask the question of Palma's historic planners if Cerdá and his ideas were to serve as a model.

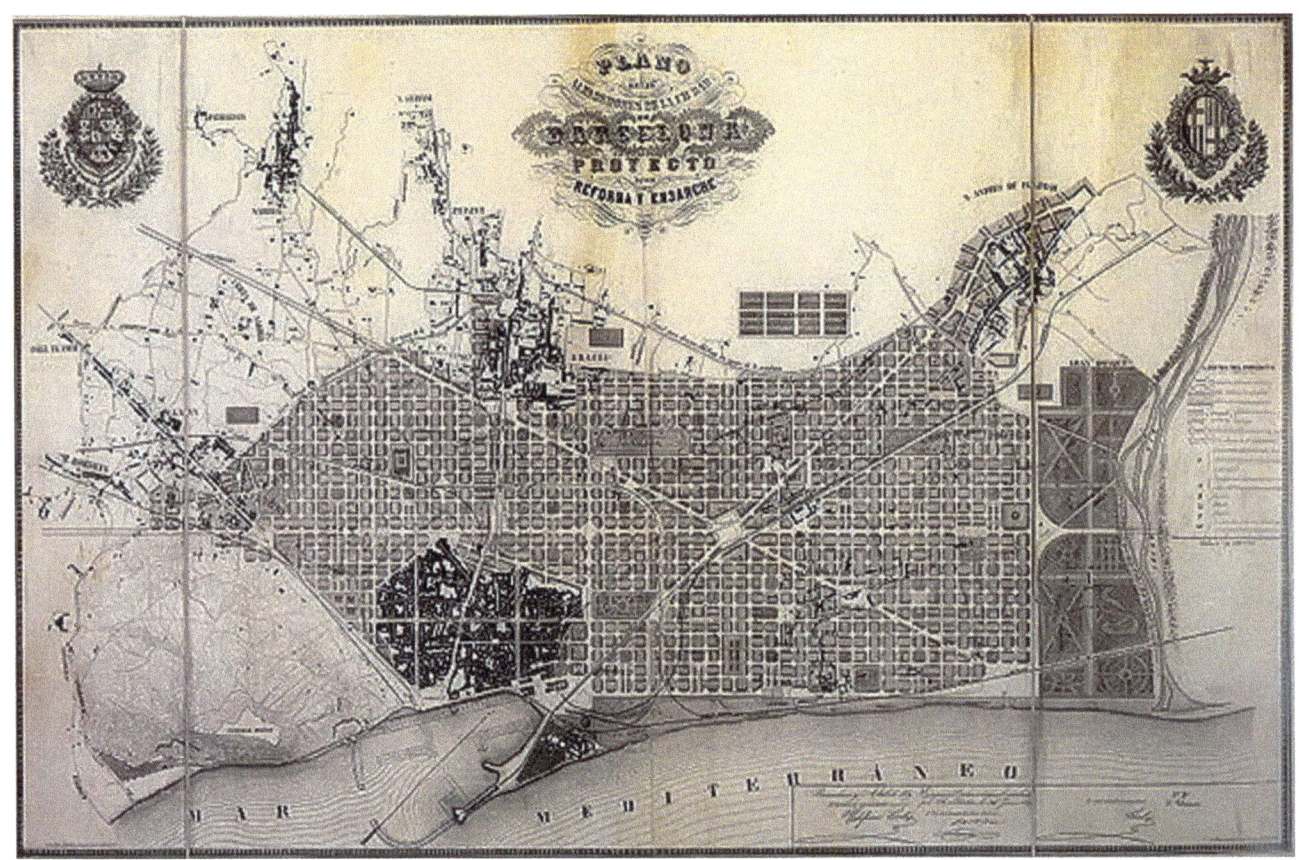

Fig 3   Idelfonso Cerdá's plan for Barcelona, 1856. Source: Wikipedia Commons.

Steven V. Ward reminds us of the innovatory, even revolutionary, ideas of Cerdá in a wider European context with the story that the great Haussmann offered to buy Cerdá's plans for Barcelona with a view to their application to the French capital[26].

Cerdá's ideas were not the first reforms to surface in Barcelona but they were perhaps the first to be based on detailed spatial and social analysis. The benefits from demolishing the walls had already been identified by, amongst others, Pedro Felipe Monlau (1808-71) – a Barcelona doctor, whose monograph *Abajo las murallas!!! Memoria sobre las ventajas que reportaría Barcelona y especialmente su industria de la demolición de las murallas que circuyen la ciudad*, was published in 1841.

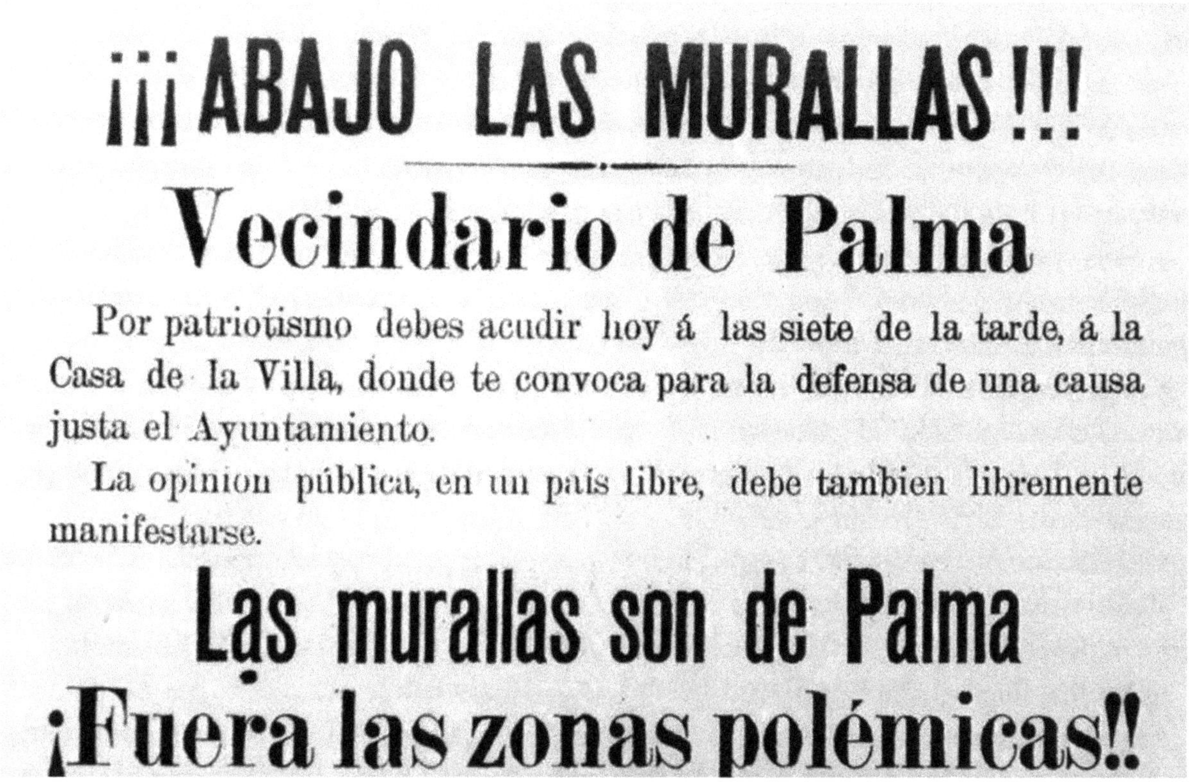

¡¡¡ABAJO LAS MURALLAS!!!
Vecindario de Palma

Por patriotismo debes acudir hoy á las siete de la tarde, á la Casa de la Villa, donde te convoca para la defensa de una causa justa el Ayuntamiento.

La opinion pública, en un país libre, debe tambien libremente manifestarse.

Las murallas son de Palma
¡Fuera las zonas polémicas!!

Fig 4 'Down with the walls': a poster adapted locally in Mallorca from Pere Filip Monlau's campaign in Barcelona of 1841.

Indeed, the Bourbon walls of Barcelona were already being partially demolished by the 1840s but it was at the time of a textile workers' strike in 1854 that a wider attack was made on them:

> '... every citizen of Barcelona who could wield a tool... was out on the ramparts'. The strike was brutally suppressed but '.. the muralles, those implacable stone compressors of misery, kept coming down', a task not completed until 1865 when the seething discontent of the city began to be addressed by 'planning not by grapeshot'. It was no coincidence that a demand for revolutionary social change was linked to the physicality of the city's walls[27].

This was the context for Cerdá's main contribution to ideas about town planning, that the expansion of cities beyond their ancient walls – the addition of suburbs to relieve the intramural pressure, in effect the creation of a new city – might be a solution to the social problems of the overcrowded and oppressed working classes. His notion of the *eixample* was for a geometrically planned network of streets, avenues, *plaças* and land blocks for building, especially low-cost housing, to be developed outside the walled city, as though the removal of the corset with the breaching and demolition of the walls could give rise to a great exhalation – a loosening of stays. In essence, his plan was for a new city on previously unoccupied farmland, an extension, not an internal reform of the old city. We now know, of course, that his planned city was not built as he drew it. An ineffectual city council, political corruption and developers' greed from the outset began to undermine the detail of his scheme. The socialistic principles of social intermixing were soon corrupted and a familiar pattern of economic segregation appeared. As with many medieval New Towns, including those designed under the ordinances of Jaume II in Mallorca, whose street plans were laid out early, the infill of Barcelona's building blocks took a long time. Cerdá's meticulously drawn and very regular plan made it from drawing board to the ground in only the barest of outlines.

If Cerdá's theories formed the basis of 'modern' town planning in Spain then two physical constructs dominated thinking from the last quarter of the 19C to at least the Civil War, some might argue until the Ley de Suelo of 1956 to which Alomar was to be a significant contributor. These were: the eixample or extension (i. e the expansion of the city at its edges) and the reform of the historic cores of cities. There is a tendency in the history of town planning in Spain to concentrate on a series of case studies of cities as though each one was a unique example (exceptionalism) whereas in fact there were attempts to establish a national framework for planning, that recognised urban development problems as symptomatic of an industrialising and slowly urbanising society. Even by the last third of the 19C Spain remained largely an under-industrialised and under-urbanised society relative to much of Europe. The proportion of its population classified as urban in 1877 was 14. 28%; even by 1900, this had risen to only 16. 84%[28]. However, these data conceal some important changes going on in Spanish cities at that time. Politically, it may be characterised by its fluctuating stability – the Carlist Wars, shortage of resources, unrest in the remains of the Spanish Empire, regional inequalities, the formation of new working-class political structures etc – but certain cities were growing and industrialising especially in the north of Spain. Urban infrastructures for water, gas and later electricity were slowly being introduced. Horse trams gave way to electric versions. As national railway systems grew they inserted stations and bridges into the urban fabric as did port and harbour structures. Suburban expansion became increasingly necessary as densities rose: the ensanche became a way of expanding cities at their edges – *extensible por simple prolongación de la retícula básica, con adición de nuevas manzanas modulares (*extendible by the simple expansion of the basic grid with the addition of modular plots)[29]. A series of the larger Spanish cities developed plans for expansion via ensanches before those of Calvet and Bennàzar for Palma and finally, by Alomar. But these could hardly be described as part of a *national* plan or planning system. They continued to reflect the dominance of the ayuntamiento, a measure of Spain's continuing, less centralised, more devolved political structure. It was not until the passing of *el Reglamento de Obras, Servicios y Bienes Municipales* in 1924 that national standards for the municipalities were laid down. This gave guidance on planning matters for towns with over 10, 000 population ranging from road widths, green zones, identifying areas that could or could not be built on, establishing the differences between urban cores and 'extensions'. Continued under the Dictatura of Primo de Rivera, it was not until the municipal congress held in Gijon under the auspices of the Second Republic that ideas for a national land-use planning law began to emerge. This was not to materialise until the groundbreaking Ley de Suelo of 1956 in which Alomar played an important part[30]. Under the Second Republic, the only major additions to this legislation were associated with housing development by the *municipios* but all-in-all the improvements were minimal and did not address the increasing problems posed by the growth of Spanish cities in the pre-Civil War period although it did permit the extension of certain cities such as Badajoz and Bilbao. It also highlighted not for the first time, the acute problem of housing supply, particularly for the growing urban working classes. This tension between planning per se and housing was later to lead to problems of reconciliation for Alomar, a topic to be addressed in a later chapter. At this time, the question put simply was: should building plots and the licences that went with them be given priority over having a land-use plan which would allocate their distribution via zonification? Merely taking in lands immediately adjacent to such cities to permit expansion was inadequate. What was needed was a national, or at least a regional planning framework, a plea voiced at the Congress for Municipalities held at Gijon in 1934. Once the war was over the new government established the Instituto Nacional de Vivienda, a body nearly always dominated by the ideology of the Sindicatos de la F. E. T y de la J. O. N. S (the Falange). It was estimated that there was a national housing shortfall of nearly 1. 4million units against a background of increasing rural to urban migration in many Spanish cities in the '40s and '50s, made more difficult by the political control of levels of rent and the categorisation of housing as *viviendas protegidas* and *bonificables*. This national housing development policy continued for many years with little reference to the municipalities.

The question arises as to the extent to which the city of Palma was affected by these tensions, the extent to which its ayuntamiento was obliged to follow these national policies, an atmosphere into which Alomar hard to project his plans for reform.

Palma, its early planning and its eixample (ensanche)

The importance of the ideas of Cerdá for Barcelona, if not their actual practical application, were to resonate through the Catalan territories. The second half of the 19C saw links between Barcelona and Palma consolidated by steamships, industrial development, imports and exports and investment. Barcelona became a centre to which many Mallorcans turned for cultural inspiration, often associated with the revival of the Catalan language, and for their higher education. The tremendous development of manufacturing industry, especially in textiles, showed Mallorcan entrepreneurs what might be achieved in an environment that lacked the traditional north European resources of coal and iron. Barcelona also acted as a mirror for the constraints on the urban growth associated with demographic transformation – the dramatic increases in urban numbers, the problems of high death rates, overcrowded housing conditions, worryingly poor levels of urban healthiness. Mallorca too had a growing problem of these internal pressures contained within a circuit of walls, walls that had rarely if ever been attacked and served little defensive purpose. Of course, the parallel should not be taken too far: Palma's history is not the history of Barcelona, nor in detail, is its urban morphology.

Palma's early planners: Alcántara Peña, Estada, Calvet, Bennàzar, Forteza

Historically, Palma, like Barcelona, had been subject to requests for the demolition of its walls before the emergence of Cerdá's ideas. In the reign of Isabella II (1830-1904, queen of Spain from 1833 to 1868) a local town councillor (*regidor*) had called for the demolition of the walls on the grounds of improving public health and, with regard to the seawall, for improving the port facilities. In any case, the ayuntamiento had already considered the building of the first extension, Santa Catalina, and later to the east, La Soledat in the 1880s. Similarly, a series of articles in the *Revista Balear de Ciencias Medicas* in the 1880s, on the healthiness of the city, identified the need to expand beyond the city walls; Mallorcan doctors were well aware of the progress that had been made through the 19C on communicable and other diseases that were related to such factors as housing conditions and water supply[31].

At this stage, it is important to remember that Alomar's eventual plan was one for *reform* and by no means one that could begin *tabula rasa*. Not only did he inherit a city with a considerable history he also had before him a considerable number of plans that had not been fully or even partially executed. As we have already hinted Alomar saw his reforms as a series of *proyectos* (projects), each one dealing with a specific part of the city or a particular issue. Together his plan may be said to have had a certain unity of purpose – 'a better, more efficient city' – but that would only have been achieved if all his projects had been completed, which they were not.

Having covered the basic morphological history of Palma and the early emergence of planning in Spain, it is now necessary to consider the work of his predecessors in the planning of Palma.

Pedro de Alcántara Peña

Alcántara Peña began his education and early life as an artist but turned to the law graduating from Barcelona in 1849 partly paying for his tuition in paintings. Later he became interested in the layout and function of Palma when he became master of fortifications. In 1859, as part of a study of the history of Palma's successive fortifications, he presented a report to Palma City Council in which he considered for the first time the need to extend the city beyond the walls in an ordered way as previous works had been uncontrolled, without the necessary facilities and infrastructure. In a time of relative peace, the growth of the population and its increasing industrialisation Peña raised the question of the role and purpose of the walls in a series of newspaper articles. He suggested the walls should be demolished to create space for the growing city. Unfortunately, the control of the walls and the adjacent areas were in the hands of the Army and without its agreement little could be achieved. Despite its interest in his proposals, no progress could be made without Madrid's support.

Eusebio Estada

In 1885 a most influential work was published that was to set in train most of the reforms being called for. This was *La Ciudad de Palma, su indústria, sus fortificaciones, sus condiciones sanitarias y su ensanche* by Eusebio Estada who had been influential in the construction of the first railway in Mallorca. The book's very title reveals its comprehensive nature, embracing all of the factors said to affect the future welfare of Palma. In the second edition of 1892 Estada set out a description of the general condition of Palma which may not have had the detailed statistical analysis of Cerdá's work but which followed very much his methodology and reasoning. He saw the reform of Palma's built environment as necessary from a number of points of view. In addition to the need to improve public health, to provide better working-class housing and to lower densities of population, Estada realised that for Palma to become a *modern* city it would need additional space for industrial location. This proved difficult within the city's walls because under a military edict of 1856 the army had established zones where industry was not permitted. After all, it might compromise the defensive role of the walls, even though they no longer had any strategic value[32]. In summary, he argued for the demolition of the walls and to reclaim from the military the *'zonas polemicas'* where industrial development was prohibited. The limit imposed on building heights meant that the density of population in some of the *zonas* was responsible for the unhygienic living conditions and high rates of mortality amongst the overcrowded working classes[33]. It meant that larger-scale steam-powered factories were initially located outside the walls in the new *barrios* of Santa Catalina, La Soledat and El Molinar.

At the same time, there was clearly a popular movement for the demolition of the walls led by the reforming Republicans and Liberals. One of the first areas within the city where these feelings were expressed was that within the sea wall, such as the neighbourhood around La Llotja and in Puig de Sant Pere, areas especially affected by diseases like yellow fever[34]. But the demolition of the walls had to be complemented by the building of new suburbs beyond them; the need for an *eixample* in Palma can be traced back to at least the 1880s. There was also a pressing need to improve the port facilities – a symbol of modernization like industrial progress – was also related to this geographical area but again, was opposed by the military and naval authorities. Much of the seawall was demolished in 1873. Numerous applications followed for the demolition of stretches of the walls including the need to create an opening for Eusebio Estada's railway line and station in the north of the city. To improve access to the industrial suburb of Santa Catalina, plans were put forward for that section of wall between the *baluade* of Sant Pere and the Santa Catalina gate.

Bernat Calvet

In response to these demands, the ayuntamiento established a competition for the design of an *eixample* in the area beyond the demolished walls. This was won by Bernat Calvet, another engineer, with his plan *Proyecto de Ensanche de la Ciudad de Palma de Mallorca,* finally approved in 1902. Of all the plans before Alomar's, this was the one that influenced him most. Indeed, many have argued that Alomar's reforms followed Calvet's rather too closely.

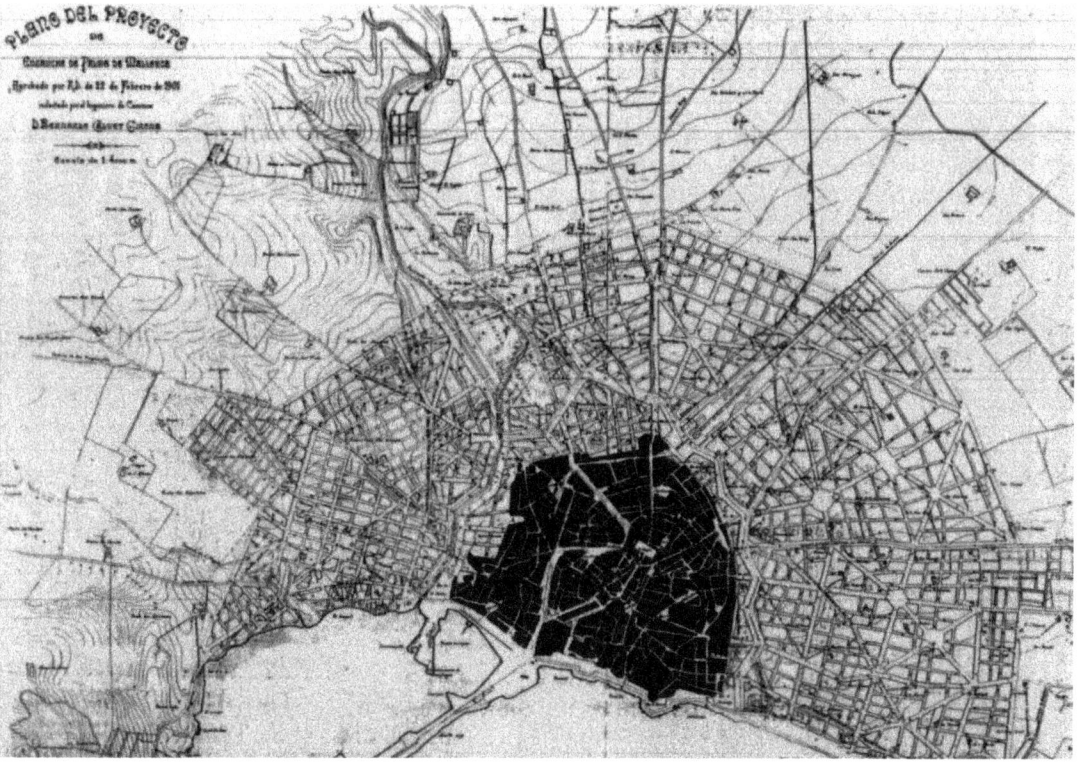

Fig 5   Bernat Calvet's plan for Palma 1901. Source: Wikipedia Commons.

Calvet faced several problems in extending the city via an *eixample*. The first was: how large should the expanded city be? Should it be large enough to contain the existing population but at a lower density, thereby improving living conditions? Should it be large enough to contain population growth into the 20th century? If so, what new densities of population should be targeted in the eixample? The second area of concern was the acquisition of rural land and its conversion to urban form. The land outside the walls was a mixture of large estates in the hands of the remnants of the nobility and smallholdings the result of 19C land reforms aimed at providing *quarterades* for the landless peasants. Having identified the need to improve intraurban movements and external access from the city to provincial towns, a third concern was for the size and capacity of any new roads. The latter was influenced by the paradigm that had emerged from the School of Engineers since its foundation, namely for what Seguí Aznar called *un conjunto de grandes vias, las radiales y las de ronda* – a set of orthogonal and diagonal routes radiating from a series of centres (*plaças*), enabling the eixample to be divided into a number of regular geometric forms. In this sense, Calvet was not following the precepts of Cerdá in Barcelona and Castro in Madrid, the result of their training as engineers[35]. He devised a hierarchy of roads – 40 metres wide, 20 metres and 10 metres, performing a hierarchy of functions: the latter purely internal, the middle size to link various *barrios* together and the widest size for links to external settlements and for ceremonial purposes (*grandes paseos*). The larger roads which radiated out from the centre were to link the 'capital' with the principal provincial towns – Inca, Llucmajor, Manacor – as a stimulus to their development especially in terms of manufacturing and to improve access to new markets. He saw this as a form of rational, efficient planning descended from the Haussmannian ideas used in Paris. Whereas Cerdá had tried to insist on his plan providing a uniformity of combining social classes, occupations and economic activities across Barcelona, Calvet proposed a much greater element of broad zoning. The western part of the city was to have fewer principal roads and would contain the accommodation for the better off professional and military classes – *un barrio residencial* – but the east and north would become the commercial and industrial centres of the city[36]. Along the *gran paseo de ronda* (ring road), to be constructed where the walls once stood would be public buildings such as theatres, museums and libraries. For the housing blocks (*manzanas*) Calvet again did not follow Cerdá's socialistic principles of uniformity of provision that included gardens and patios but instead suggested a variety of housing types both in terms of height and volume, maintaining his own idea of *la ciudad horizontalmente*. As an engineer Calvet had little concern for the architecture of housing; *manzanas* were simply land-uses. The geometrical regularity of the plan also presented an opportunity to introduce on a wider scale such amenities as gas (not widely available in the city until 1927), water supplies and a sewage system, all part of the modernizing movement. It was Calvet's plan that was to dominate the planning of Palma for the next half-century. It had, however, a number of weaknesses, the first of which was that it did not specify land uses in the *eixample*. The second was that he underestimated the growth of the city's population by about one hundred per cent. Thirdly, the brief he was given by the mayor of Palma largely ignored the planning requirements of the *casc antich*: the restoration of old buildings in the medieval streets, the effects of lowering densities, the creation of new throughways and more open spaces and questions of social segregation[37]. It was as though all of Palma's problems would be solved by building the *eixample*. Calvet's plan was very much that of an engineer and a highway engineer at that. These omissions would present many opportunities and challenges for the next generation of planners including Alomar.

Gaspar Bennàzar

In the next half-century, a series of municipal architects and planners was to offer schemes for the reform of Palma's built environment. The first significant one of these was Gaspar Bennàzar, the first of Palma's planners with training in architecture. Although he originally enrolled in the School of Engineers like his predecessors, in 1899 he graduated from the School of Architecture in Madrid. Appointed as the Palma city architect he had a special interest in the major public buildings and in ecclesiastical architecture. In 1902 he joined a team of engineers and architects given responsibility for the demolition of Palma's walls and the implementation of Calvet's plan. Bennàzar himself brought forward a series of proposals for the reform of the city's built environment in his *Plan General de Reforma de Palma*, published in 1916. In particular, he was one of the first to recognise the city's potential as a tourist destination, tourism being an economic activity that was then beginning to be promoted[38]. Bennàzar realised that for this to come about the city would need to improve its infrastructure considerably including reforming its public health, its water supply and its hotels. At this time the 'beach' was not seen as the principal resource for tourism; the city itself was a major attraction and he recognized the potential of the historic core of Palma but it too would need 'reforming'. Calvet's plan, on the other hand, had been primarily concerned with the expansion of the city beyond its walls once they were demolished. There was a tension between these two objectives: the reform of the old city and planning its extension or *eixample*. Most of the proposals for reform of the interior were focused on improving the internal movements within the city, largely by proposing a series of either new or widened existing streets *à la* Haussmann to improve industrial development, retailing and tertiary functions[39]. The introduction of mule-drawn trams in1891- the network was largely electrified after 1914 – meant the system was limited to the wider streets. The first private automobile seen on Palma's street appeared in the early years of the century although numbers were slow to increase. Bennàzar quickly saw the importance of improving circulation overall especially between the upper and lower parts of the city and between the port and its immediate hinterland via a sort of 'cross' of routes. At their junction would be *el centro neurálgico de toda la ciudad*[40]. A second contribution was to 'oxygenate' the city by widening existing roads and plaças and by planting trees. Many reformers had recognized the need for a new central market for Palma. Bennàzar proposed a location on the site of the old Plaça de l'Olivar, served by a series of new roads whose construction would involve the demolition of a number of religious houses, many of them of considerable architectural importance.

Bennàzar had also to consider the *eixample* proposals of Calvet; they were, after all, the principal raison d'etre for the reforms as originally set out by Eusebio Estada and approved by the ayuntamiento in 1897(See Fig 5). He followed the criteria that had been established, that is, that the line of the demolished walls should contain a new circular road around the old core of the city with numerous sections of *eixample* beyond. In addition, Bennàzar proposed not only changes to improve access to the recently modernized port area begun by Pou in the 1870s[41] but also a *'grand parque'* to the west that would embrace the area around the historic Castell Bellver and the recently expanding El Terreno suburb bringing it into the city's ambit[42] and provide a *paseo maritimo*; to the east would be a *ciudad jardin*. These would act as suburbs for the city's middle classes – areas of low density in a green environment; naturally, some have seen the influence of the British garden suburb movement here. On reflection, however, it appears as a somewhat romantic construction.

Perhaps the strongest criticism of Bennàzar's plan was that it lacked sympathy in its treatment of the historic core of Palma with too much demolition necessary for the construction of the major roads he proposed. Many of his schemes for the expansion of the city and of the port area seem to have more in common with the fantastic than the objective needs of a growing city.

Guillem Forteza Penya

By the mid-1920s architects and planners working in the Catalunyan regions would probably have graduated from the School of Architecture in Barcelona and not from the School of Engineering in Madrid. An architect-planner, Guillem Forteza Penya from this School, was critical of the Bennàzar plan for two main reasons: first, in his *L'art de construir les ciutats i la reforma de Palma (1921)*[43] Forteza supported the late 19C ideas of the Austrian urbanist Camillo Sitte. He decried the early emphasis of much Spanish planning on the technical solutions of engineering, public health and housing improvements to the neglect of the city as an expression of artistic culture. Instead, he advocated the application of a historicist approach to the study of ancient cities as a means of promoting the aesthetics of city planning, conserving the traditional routeways and open places of the city with an architecture dominated by gothic ideals. He was especially critical of the geometric approach to eixamples as advocated by Cerdá and others: *'cosa sols compatible amb el* genius loci *de les ciutats Nord i Sud-americanes, inadaptable per tots conceptes en el nostres països'* (which is only compatible with the genius loci of North and South American cities, unattainable for all examples in our country) preferring the sinuosity of medieval layouts advocated by Sitte[44]. He went further saying that these geometric plans were an affront to 'our' Mediterranean.[45] Secondly, by 1930 Forteza had to accept that the planning of any city was beginning to be confronted by the demands of the motor car; previous plans had said too little about traffic congestion. Mayol Amengual points out that although his training would have made Forteza more familiar with modernist ideas, in general, they found little favour with him but those associated with circulation had to be addressed[46]. Despite the introduction of an urban tram system, horse-drawn traffic dominated Palma well into the early 1930s and by then motor vehicles were beginning to have an impact on the patterns of movement in the city. The *avingudas* (new avenues) would eventually provide a new ring road for the core of medieval Palma but movement across the city, both east-west and north-south, soon emerged as a major issue restricting economic activity, especially in the growing tertiary sector of offices and shops. He noted that the main pinch points were at three places. First, where the roads from the north and north-west met at Raconada de Santa Margalida and clashed with traffic generated by the railway station. Secondly, where roads from the east and north-east met at St Antoni Gate and thirdly, where port traffic had to fight its way through the city centre[47]. Like his predecessors, Forteza focused on the construction of new throughways – a circular road from Conquistador to Oms that would improve links between the high town and the low town and two Gran Vias, one connecting the city centre to Raconada de Sta. Margalida and another 15m wide joining the second congested area, Porta St. Antoni, to the centre. His plan also called for the then quite radical idea of zoning, derived from early American planning theory, with separated areas for residence, business, industry and leisure pursuits. Perhaps, surprisingly, he also advocated segregated housing on a class basis[48]. But all-in-all, Forteza will be remembered as an architect not as a town planner.

Palma by the late 1920s and 1930s

These decades were, of course, a turbulent period for Spain in many senses. It had fortunately avoided the direct consequences of the First World War but the economic impact had been considerable, making imports of materials and goods difficult and expensive but at the same time permitting Palma to market its goods to combatant countries. The wars in Morocco had sapped the strength of Spanish manhood through the cruel system of conscription. Emigration to Latin America similarly had a deleterious effect. Politically the failure of the weaknesses of the monarchy under Alfonso XIII led to the dictatorship of Primo de Rivera. Still not recovered from the loss of the American and eastern colonies, Spain was a poor and backward country in many respects by the late 1920s. Later affected by the world depression, nonetheless, the cities began to see a modernising of their functions. The first half of the thirties although wracked by political strife, especially in the north, is now seen as a period of rapid economic growth. The second half saw the outbreak and pursuit of the Civil War (1936-39). Whereas the first might have seen further progress in urban reform and development under the influence of industrialisation and migration into the cities, the latter was characterised by destruction and stagnation. However, for a relatively remote city like Palma, the decade was somewhat different. In the first half, many new industries were expanded and tourism began its take-off towards the mass end of the spectrum. The late 1920s saw a number of large hotels constructed on the island and a distinct improvement in the promotion of the island as a tourism destination; in addition, the number of cruise ships entering Palma's harbour increased dramatically[49]. The expanding suburb of El Terreno to the west of the city began to emerge as a major centre for tourists, especially Americans[50]. However, the need for further suburban expansion continued to be seen – as it always had since the late 19C – as the solution to the city's ills.

The years immediately following the Civil War were catastrophic for Spain and Mallorca and its capital, Palma. To ensure that Spain did not enter the Second World War on the side of the Axis powers, the Allies isolated Spain economically including cutting off its fuel imports from aboard via a blockade. At the same time, Franco and his government pursued a policy of what became known as autarky or self-sufficiency, theoretically cutting itself from international trade. The result of this, for example, was to deny large parts of the country adequate food supplies and building materials. In Mallorca and Palma, there was a determination nonetheless to proceed with the modernization of the city that earlier plans had failed to complete. Although the city was bombed by the Republican airforce during the Civil War, the damage was very small compared to that inflicted by Nationalist forces and their German and Italian allies on Peninsula cities.

Much of the technical infrastructure may have been in place by the 1940s, especially the supply of electricity and gas, the development of the tram network and some health and education facilities but certain land uses such as retailing and modern office space were in short supply while large areas of the city were given over to the military (*els quarters*), seen as a necessary element in the urban form by the national government. To improve communications along the seafront, schemes in the 1920s and '30s had begun to demolish what was left of the sea wall and its *baluades* (bastions) which conservationists wanted to preserve as historical monuments[51]. It was becoming clear that what Palma needed was a new and comprehensive plan to bring it into the second half of the 20C. As we shall see, however, Alomar's proposal succeeded where others had failed, not because they had fundamental weaknesses but it was more of a case of timing in relation to the prevailing political and economic climate.

However, the key to any such planning had always lain with the success or failure of the eixample that had been advocated by all of the 'modern' planners of the city: Estada, Calvet, Bennàzar and Forteza. By the late 1930s what progress had been made with this suburban development? María Dolores Ladaria Beñares identifies many reasons for the slowness of its development including the failure to implement improvements in the city's sewage system the need for which had been emphasised for more than 100 years. This would involve public investment which was not forthcoming; only houses of a certain standard (and price) were equipped with bathrooms. The fear of the great plagues of the 19C still haunted the city; tuberculosis was a particularly virulent disease in Palma. Secondly, the walls and their related infrastructure had simply taken too long to demolish completely. The failure of the army and the city council to come to a deal over the *zonas polemicas* hindered the release of land and its development for housing. The decision to demolish the walls may have been taken relatively early in the 1870s but serious demolition did not begin until the turn of the century. Questions of land ownership and sale in the area to be suburbanised were unresolved for too long. Thirdly, the bureaucracy involved in these complex processes was too inflexible and slow, not simply at the local level but especially so nationally in what had become an increasingly centralised state under Franco. There was much debate, too, on what might appear to be less significant matters in the eixample such as street width, plaças, parks and public open spaces – that is, the allocation of land uses which might be seen as public goods and non-profit making. Who was to pay for this land that was lost for building; how were landowners to be compensated? This was an issue that had confronted Cerdá and his Barcelona eixample many years before. Other arguments revolved around who was the eixample to be for? In Barcelona it was the middle classes who had benefited most; in Palma, it was important that the working classes from the overcrowded centre should be offered affordable housing in order to lower the pressure on the core. But progress was slow: of the 88, 000 inhabitants of the city in 1930, only about 12, 000 were living in the eixample. In the century's first decade, only 223 building permits were issued, of which only 159 were for actual construction. By 1927 only 569 building permits were for housing, 368 for building apartments and 232 for building plots. This slow uptake can be attributed to the low growth in the economy before the 1930s, the continuing impact of emigration and the effect of diseases such as the Spanish flu of 1918[52]. As far as layout was concerned the plan for the eixample remained that designed by Calvet. It added a new set of spaces to the urbanised area of the city – the edge growth of suburbs – but it did not seriously address the problems of the congested *casc antich*. The reforms planned by Bennàzar in 1918, as we have seen, were a mixture of the pragmatic and the fanciful. While municipal architect he had overseen the demolition of some of the walls and gates – much of whose fabric was of immense historical significance – and had concentrated his efforts on the spine of the city from the port, the Born and the Rambla towards the Plaça d'Espagna. While road improvements were made by him to improve the flow of people and goods across the city, Bennàzar might best be seen as an architect more than a town planner. His main output was in creating many new contemporary buildings in the city such as s'Escorxador (the municipal slaughterhouse) and the apartments above the bars Cristal and Triquet, after all, his career was characterised by work in the public and private spheres. May there not have been what today we would call a 'conflict of interest'? His more imaginative work on the proposals for garden suburb type expansion in Palma's western fringes was confined to paper plans and never built. The task of the comprehensive reform of Palma – city centre and suburbs together – was to be Alomar's inherited task.

4
Gabriel Alomar Esteve and his plans for reform

The objectives were to solve the problem of adapting the old town to the new circulatory, hygienic and social needs of the time, to reform certain degraded internal areas, as well as to link, in order, a series of peripheral urbanizations arisen in lands outside the official ensanche. Of the urban plans that were conceived at that time, almost none were brought to reality. Therefore, one of my goals was for the project to be realizable. With this idea, I divided the Internal Reform Plan into twelve "partial reforms" thinking that more than half would remain on paper.

Interview of Gabriel Alomar Esteve in the series 'History of contemporary urbanism', COAM (1989): Biografia de arquitectos urbanistas, *Revista urbanismo,* 105, 8, 91-97

In addition to the plans of his predecessors outlined in the previous chapter, it can be argued that Alomar's prizewinning plan for reform was also the product of three other forces: his own first-hand experience of growing up and living in Palma, his education and training in architecture and town planning and the pre-Civil War ideas and theories prevalent in Spain in the 1920s and '30s.

Family and educational background

Alomar was born in 1910 in the family house in Palma in the Carrer de Sol located in what had once been near the Jewish quarter of the city in medieval times. His family originated in Muro municipality in the north of Mallorca where they were owners of an estate that was probably granted to the monastery of Sant Feliu de Guixols by Jaume I after the conquest of 1229. This was broken up into a series of *possession*s (smaller estates) in the 16C, today all near Km4 of the Sineu-Muro road. Each of the branches of the family had a substantial house in the town of Muro. This was a family that clearly thought of itself as a member of the upper-middle classes to be addressed as '*don…*' or '*o honor…*'[53]. By the first half of the 19C, they had established themselves in Palma as conservative gentlemen attended by their womenfolk, children and servants[54].

Gabriel Alomar Esteve wrote a memoir published in 1986 but unfortunately, it only covers the forty years of his life from 1939; essentially it is chronological[55]. Given the relative prominence of the man and his family, it is puzzling as to why he omitted from it his childhood, education and early life. Where possible these earlier features are expanded here. As a boy, he spent his summers on the family's Muro estate. He was a voracious reader, especially of Romantic novels, and enamoured of the countryside. It was here that he first developed his interest in local history especially of the town of Muro and its buildings; it is likely that these juvenile experiences helped direct him towards architecture[56].

Fig 6   Alomar's father with his son Gabriel (right) in Barcelona 1924 Source: Courtesy of Gabriel Alomar Garau. ©

Fig 7   Gabriel Alomar Esteve, in his 20s, seated near the building that later became the current headquarters of the Colegio Oficial de Arquitectos (Official College/Association of Architects) Source: Courtesy of Gabriel Alomar Garau©

Of his early education and training and what really attracted him to the subject, we know little other than that his father asked a distant but famous cousin Gabriel Alomar i Villalonga to act as his tutor[57]. The latter was an intellectual and man of letters who had become radicalised by his time in Barcelona in the 1880s. He was particularly influenced by the regional movements in support of the Catalan language. A polemical writer he eventually became the Republican ambassador to Italy and Egypt at the time of the outbreak of the Civil War and as a result, spent the remainder of his life in exile. Another influence may have been an uncle, a priest who served in the Cathedral. Whether these men were instrumental in young Gabriel becoming an architect is difficult to judge.

Alomar's education and training

His high school education was under the auspices of the Spanish Christian Brothers, a fairly tough religious order. Like most young men of that era, he took a broad range of courses in the classics but with enough maths and science to permit his entry into the Institute in Palma as preparation for his acceptance by the University of Barcelona. Here he had to spend his first two years (1927-29) taking maths, physics, chemistry and geology as preparation for entry into the Superior School of Architecture[58]. This seven-year course emphasised maths, drawing, mechanics and materials, including *estereotomia* (building in stone). It was not until 1931-2 that he was able to take the first of four planning courses available. And planning at the School was undergoing new forces of change[59]. In 1931 a new director of the Architecture School was appointed – Alexandre Soler i March – who managed things without appreciable change in the teaching of architecture in this revolutionary period but he did succeed in introducing town planning into the School's curriculum, a subject known at that time as *urbanologia* with Amadeu Llopart as its first professor[60]. He had held a chair in the school since 1918 but in *topografia* and *geodesia*. Interestingly in 1942, he was to act as an assessor for Alomar's plans for the eixample in Palma.

We know that Alomar's training in architecture in Barcelona emphasised the classical traditional styles of Spain. No doubt, like most would-be architects of that era, he would have had to make numerous measured drawings probably of gothic and renaissance buildings but later it was with a planning project that he won the first-class diploma for architecture with a display of *'cuadros relatives al proyecto de reforma interior de la cuidad de Palma de Mallorca'* (illustrations relating to the internal reform of Palma) at the National Exhibition of Fine Arts in Barcelona in 1942[61]. La Vanguardia's correspondent reported that:

> '... *Mr. Gabriel Alomar Esteve ...By means of a large map of the city, one can see how careful the author was, first and foremost, to ensure that the most outstanding monuments appear unscathed, in a way that fully stands out for their best display and contemplation. Accompanying this plan are drawings demonstrating reforms to be carried out, such as the unilateral expansion of Calle de San Miguel; a staircase down to the Rambla, from the Plaza Mayor; the modification of the Calatrava neighbourhood, etc; Ideal evocations, of sober guidelines, inspired by Roman influences in details that we recognize as interesting, but that we are unsure if their character fits in the environment for which they were conceived'* (Author's translation)[62].

It led to him being appointed as honorary municipal architect of Palma, with a responsibility for town planning, remarkable considering he had only taken four courses in that subject as an undergraduate in Barcelona and had no practical experience.

He had entered higher education at an almost revolutionary period and in a city that was at the heart of change. By 1934, the year he graduated, Barcelona was in turmoil and had been for months, as 'feudal' Spain sought to smash Catalonian identity[63]. Would this place and its social and political movements mould his perceptions, in particular, of the way he saw cities and their plans and architecture?

Architecture and Planning in Spain in the 1930s and early 1940s

At this time – the era of the Second Republic (1931-36) – architecture and design were experiencing modernizing, even revolutionary, feelings. The Modern movement in the rest of Europe was beginning to affect the education and training of practitioners in Spain. Influenced by CIAM ('International Congresses of Modern Architecture'), perhaps the most progressive group to advocate change was GATEPAC (Grupo de Artistas y Técnicos Españoles para el Progreso de la Arquitectura Contemporánea)[64]. It was founded in Zaragoza in October 1930 in order to publish a magazine with which to disseminate ideas that pushed the boundaries of the current state of architecture in Spain. There were three groups – in Barcelona, Madrid and San Sebastian – with the publication of the magazine acting as a common link; 25 issues were published between 1931 and 1937. Of these groups, the most effective was that located in Catalunya, where 'modernizing' was almost an art form beginning with the 'moderne' movement of the late 19C. But this Republican period was one in which more liberal, modernist and rationalist ideas in architecture and planning were to the fore. Alomar must have been exposed to these contrasting and conflicting ideas. Soon after his studies were concluded the Spanish Civil War broke out, forcing him to return to Mallorca where eventually he was drafted into the Nationalist Army before he could begin his practice. By the end of the war, he was part of the *Inspeccción de fronteras* stationed in Pamplona, later transferring back to Mallorca first in the anti-aircraft unit at Port de Sóller and then in the administrative service of the airport, a post which called upon some of his architectural skills[65].

Even before the war broke out – indeed earlier in the 1930s – the philosophers and supporters of the anti-Republican movement were beginning to set out new theories in the field of architecture and planning. With their success in the Civil War, such theorists were able to promote their schemes with more confidence – and more importantly – with the initial support of the Franco regime. A series of important organizations and national conferences were to help shape post-war thinking in planning and housing[66]. To begin with, these were led by the Falange, the fascist ideological organisation that had some influence over Franco and his ministers. Three principal elements dominated thinking in the Falange: the symbiotic relationship between the Catholic Church and the State, the importance of the family in Spanish life and social organisation, and autarky – essentially an economic idea but one which fostered the separateness and uniqueness of Spain that had to be safeguarded and protected from 'foreign' influences.

In architecture and planning these three factors were also brought to the fore. The Falange concentrated on four areas in its attempts to shape national policy after the Civil War: the damage to the physical urban fabric of Spain caused by the war had to undergo a period of reconstruction as a matter of priority but any rebuilding, particularly of housing, had to be designed along Falangist principles. So, secondly, the family as the core of the Catholic Church in practice was to be the important social unit – not the individual, not the community. Thirdly, was the principle that housing, especially in apartment blocks, should contain a variety of social classes. Finally, the country needed a symbol of its new position in the form of a capital city that reflected its new values. This was to be the Imperial City of Madrid, raising the prospect of reliving the glories of the former Spanish Empire. In terms of focus Madrid fulfilled at least three of these objectives[67].

Fig 8   Falangist journal *Reconstrucción*, June/July 1945.

López Diaz quotes the Falangist architect Pedro Muguruza[68] as saying the example of the cities of the medieval Reconquest and the American colonies were significant in conceptualising the City for the Movement. Within this, the role of social housing was not only to promote the family but it was to be the means of combating social class: 'As architects, we may note that until now separate and distinct neighbourhoods have been built for various social classes, which naturally encouraged and excited the class struggle. And now we want neighbourhoods for people who are united by a common purpose, and in each of these areas will be found the entire social hierarchy from maximum to minimum'. This would prevent neighbourhoods favoured by radical cadres – the great fear by the Falange of communist and anarchist workers. Zoning by social class was to be avoided. In fact, Falangist ideals were rarely translated into practice despite the work of the National Housing Institute and its plan for housing, 1944-54, which recommended the construction of 1.4million homes. Only half this number was built mostly in war-torn Madrid. Here, and in other Spanish cities, the rapidity of organic, barely planned suburbs and growth resulted in satellite cities and socially segregated communities. In the light of this and the shortage of building materials brought about by economic autarky, most Falangist ideas were not accepted by the Franco regime[69].

Against this political background, the question arises as to the extent to which Alomar was influenced by Falangist ideas, perhaps even to the extent to which such ideas might have become 'rules and regulations', even 'laws'. It might be imagined that, after all, Franco's Spain was a centralist state not tolerant of divergent thinking but as we shall see that was far from reality. We know that in 1938 a group of Mallorcan architects including Alomar attended the Congreso de Arquitectos Falangistas held in the Escorial. This aimed to establish the directions of the new architecture[70]. We also know that by 1946 Alomar was rejecting *el reduccionismo tradicionalista de los años 40* (the reductionist traditionalism of the 40s) in architecture in favour of a more modernist approach[71]. In the event, economic autarky meant the hopes and aspirations of the Falangists were not accepted by the regime as it struggled to manage the beginnings of mass urbanisation that were to dominate Spanish demographics for at least the next 50 years. Gradually, a new technocracy in housing and planning, of which Alomar was to become a part, would win out over the ideologues of the Falangist Movement, and indeed of many other factions. In practice, however, political nepotism and simple corruption would, in the long run, undermine the aspirations of most planners in central government.

Alomar's development of his longer-term ideas on planning began much earlier and was to be greatly influenced by several events including earlier visits to Paris and Frankfurt that he undertook in 1934, the year of his graduation[72]. In 1937 he married his cousin Maria Angela Esteve Bianchi from Puerto Rico[73]. This gave him access to the wealth from this source and it gave him a 'colonial home' for him and his family. A second influence was his sojourn in the United States at MIT in 1945 as we shall see but this, of course, came after he had drawn up his plan for the reform of Palma; it was more influential on his later work. A third factor was his outward-looking attitude towards planning in other countries especially in Great Britain. To this end, he later travelled widely where he met many planners, sometimes at the behest of the Spanish government, but more often at his own expense and motivation. But all this was to come later and it is important at this stage to try to concentrate on explaining the reasoning behind his 1942 plan for Palma.

Like many of the pioneers in town planning such as Ebenezer Howard, Thomas Mawson, and Thomas Adams, Alomar had little formal training in the discipline initially. His qualification in architecture may have exposed him to some of the principal ideas; he could not fail to be aware of the major previous plans for his native city and many of those of the Peninsula. His first sally into town planning was undertaken at the behest of Archbishop Miralles of Palma – who had conducted his marriage service – when he was asked to undertake a preliminary study of the *eixample* of Palma for the diocese[74].

If, by today's standards, Alomar had limited training in town planning and little actual experience, what encouraged him to take on such a prodigious task at the age of only 30? Did he have a reforming zeal for the condition of his native city, some kind of social motivation? He was certainly aware, at least empirically, of the shortcomings of Palma economically, environmentally and socially, particularly in its medieval core. Anyone who lived in the city in the '30s and '40s could not have avoided the serious deficiencies in housing and public health. In his autobiography, he talks of the difficulties of city life under autarky after the Civil War and the need for rebuilding those areas damaged by aerial bombardment[75]. But he underplays these difficulties. Mallorca like so much of post-war Spain was almost starving with shortages of wheat, largely thanks to the inefficiencies of the autarky policy with even the meagre bread ration being reduced. There was a desperate shortage of skilled labour and a massive shortage of raw material and energy supplies. Looking back it seems a most curious decision by Alomar to put so much of his physical and mental energy into the subject of urban reform. Was he, then, motivated by any kind of political ideology, including some of the political bases for town planning that had been circulating nationally to which we have referred earlier? Did he think that Mallorca and the Balearic islands deserved a more worthy capital; were there any grandiose thoughts like those that some were advocating for Madrid? Did he see it as a challenge to his artistic imagination, an aesthetic desire to improve the appearance of Palma? Had he looked at the previous attempts of reform, and simply said, 'I can do better than that'? Or are these questions better directed to the Nationalist government that had taken over Mallorca, the earlier liberal and Republican polity having been swept aside early in the war, with the mayor of Palma Emili Darder and many of his fellow counsellors having been murdered?

This raises the important question of the political context of the times in which Alomar first drew up a plan for the reform of Palma – especially its inner core – which was entered for and won a prestigious prize in Barcelona. By this time the Civil War in Spain had ended but the country was entering a most difficult phase of post-war austerity, in turn, affecting the Balearic Islands including Mallorca and its capital. Earlier Mallorca had declared for the Nationalists and, in order for its support to be recognised nationally, set about the purge of those who opposed its cause. This was led by the *africanista* General Manuel Goded Llopis, despite his initial promise to guarantee the security of the city. The Nationalist coup released the beginnings of terrible repression between July and September 1936 including the open murders of Republicans, trade unionists and communists. The swiftness and the comprehensive nature of the repression suggest it had been planned beforehand. To instil a reign of terror dead bodies were left in the streets of Palma; hundreds were executed, without due legal process, in the city's principal cemetery including many of the city's most important political figures. Eliminating the main figures in the city's bureaucracy was also a key policy: introducing 'correct' managers into the ayuntamiento had earlier been tried under a previous dictator Primo de Rivera. Garcia Ruiz, as the new civil governor, quickly appointed Mateu Zaforteza Mussoles – a military man – as mayor of Palma for three years, between 1936 and 1939. The city council now consisted of ten new councillors with sixty-two heads of department being removed from office. This move had ideological origins; in theory at least, the new state was to be technocratic rather the democratic. The Republic, in opposing the island's Nationalists, sought to restore normalcy to Mallorca by force including the bombing of the city and the disastrous invasion of the island by Bayo's forces in August 1936 which only served to heighten the repression. To strengthen the defences of the island Italian air support was sought largely funded by Juan March Ordinas's wealth, the man who had been Alomar's early patron and later financier of part of his reform of the city when it came to be built in the early '50s. Bishop Miralles, another early patron of Alomar, publically thanked the Nationalist leaders in Mallorca for their defeat of the Republicans. Against this background of terror, repression and assassination, what motivated Alomar to pursue his plans? Surely, there were more pressing needs he could have addressed.

But, of course, Alomar was eventually to respond to a competition established by the new post-war town council so the question is equally directed at the ayuntamiento. What motivated it at this most inauspicious time to decide to reform the structure of Palma? Were there, for them, ideological motives such as those mentioned above? Were they influenced by direction from the centre i. e. Madrid? Or was this simply a local initiative? Were the needs of the city so pressing at this time that reform had to be implemented? In some ways, it was a continuation of schemes begun in the previous era. During the preceding period from 1931 under the Second Republic, Mallorca and its Ciutat were governed by a coalition of the left, dominated by Esquerra Republicana Balear. A key liberal moment was the election in 1931 of Emili Darder, a doctor and scientist, to the town council with responsibility for sewage, water supply and housing which derived from his interest in epidemiology. On becoming mayor in 1933 he was in a strong position to implement new policies including the building of new roads such as Avenida Alexandre Rosselló which was to become part of the inner ring road that followed the line of the former walls. He was anxious to improve the health of the city and internal movement, topics that had concerned earlier town planners. He succeeded in making Bellver Castle part of the city; he promoted the construction of houses for workers and public gardens, promoted measures to solve the problem of unemployment and, interestingly, improved the urban structure of the city and its traffic management including introducing pedestrian crossings. When the Nationalists took control of Mallorca during the Civil War the Republican local government personnel (elected members and officers) were replaced by military and Falangist placemen. Gabriel Riera, the military governor later became mayor; the distinguished Mallorcan architect, Franscesc Casas became a councillor in 1940[76]. Given the earlier moves made under Republican governance and the placing of Casas on the council the eventual decision to advance the cause of Palma's reform is perhaps not so difficult to understand. However, the cultural values of the city – or at least of its Nationalist leaders – were shifting in line with Nationalist and Falangist thought. The State and the local state took on new meanings, the Catholic Church had many of its former policies and its position within the state restored, liberal views in the media were repressed and artistic and architectural values became more nationalist and less regionalist. There was also a sense that the perceived separateness of Palma and the Balearic Islands from the mental maps of Spanish politics at this time may have enabled Ciutat to advance its own cause independently. Spain's central government was too often focused on ridding the country of 'reds' and freemasons in the old regime that its behaviour was not as centralist as many might imagine. Nonetheless, Palma was not immune from the new Spanish ideologies and Alomar's plan had to take cognizance of this fact. As already pointed out the plan and its architect were the product of the times.

But what 'times' were these? The immediate social and economic environment could surely not have been worse. In addition to the repression under successive civil and military governors, the mayoralty was in the hands of centralist powers; there was little or no room for debate, certainly not dissent, especially in such less relevant fields as architecture and town planning, at least not until after 1959. Palma's economy was at a standstill, manufacturing employment in the island fell from 39% in 1936 to only 18% in the late 1940s, imports of finished goods, raw materials and above all food supplies were at a historically low level. Rationing applied in nearly all sectors, as it does so often in immediate post-war years. Mallorca starved. With little economic vigour to stimulate activity social energy was in recession too. Literature and the arts felt repressed, public expression of moral and political needs was limited to dark corners of the city thanks to an atmosphere of terror as throughout the '40s and much of the '50s opposition to political orthodoxy was put down, even eradicated. So-called enemies of the regime – liberals and intellectuals – were imprisoned, some even in Nazi concentration camps in Germany where they perished. Some of the opponents of the regime managed to escape either in the early days of the war or later, only able to make any kind of contribution from abroad.

In this kind of setting, then, was this the most appropriate time for Palma's city fathers to indulge in plans for urban reform? Was a new city to be a symbol as well as a practical expression of *Mallorca va reviure* (Mallorca brought back to life)?

Alomar's plan

On 30th March 1940, at the instigation of Gabriel Riera, the mayor, and Fransesc Casas – a leading councillor and city architect – a meeting was convened to discuss ideas for the reform of the interior of Palma and to establish a planning competition[77]. The original brief was to include the reform of the ensanche and the extension zone (the earlier unplanned suburbs) but the emphasis was on the reform of the inner, historic core. The jury established to judge the various entries was headed by the mayor and two independent architects from Barcelona, Llompart and Vilaseca plus two local representatives, Miguel Forteza (a road engineer and brother of the architect Guillem) and the architect Enric Juncosa. Entries were shortlisted and Alomar's successful proposal was announced on 26 April 1941. The architect Francesc Casas[78] came second collaborating with the engineer Antoni Parietti[79, 80]; other plans submitted included those of Roberto Oms Gràcia[81], Enric Matas Ramis[82] and Berenguera Ramon Carreras. Guillem Forteza had also submitted plans but withdrew them when his brother was appointed to the panel. Sadly, many of the details of these other plans are unavailable, making comparisons impossible. Eventually, Alomar's plan was formally approved by the Council on February 12 1943. Later his plan was widened to include a scheme to improve the links between the various extensions that had grown up in the city's suburbs and the old part of the city, something that became more important with the increase in population and internal traffic in the 1950s. Mallorca had few private cars in the late 1930s; even by the early 1950s only about 800 cars were being registered each year[83]. Nonetheless, the essentially medieval road network of the centre was clogged with horse-drawn traffic (and polluted with mounds of horse manure!) and a dense tram system. In this sense, Alomar's plan had a certain element of foresight, looking forward to the rapid increase in road traffic after the 1960s. Also, the ayuntamiento was looking for schemes that would improve the sanitary condition of the inner city. In particular, the local authority was anxious to solve the problems of health and hygiene in two inner-city districts – Sa Calatrava to the east and Puig de Sant Pere to the west, both within the city walls – through a programme of controlled demolition. To Alomar, an early conservationist, these two districts represented very significant places within the city's history and culture; he was determined that where practical the essential characteristics should be protected and their public health problems solved in another way[84]. Alomar hints also that any approved plan ought to lead to the

Fig 9   Alomar's general plan showing the twelve areas for reform. Source: Alomar, 1950. By kind permission of Gabriel Alomar Garau©.

creation of work for the many soldiers returning from the Civil War[85]. The Plan when finally approved in 1943 showed the principal components leading to a coherent scheme for the whole urban area: a plan for the reform of the interior, a plan *de la zona d'extensió* and the *eixample*, with the *avingudes* providing the geographical dividing line[86]. (See Fig 9).

In analysing Alomar's plan, one inevitably asks: to what extent was this merely an elaboration or extension of the plans of previous workers such as Calvet, Bennàzar and Forteza whose schemes were never fulfilled? He describes the background to his plan in his book published in 1950[87]. However, many of his comments on his plan were to be *post hoc* and appeared in his textbooks as well as his memoir. He reflected on the need for '*ciudades gigantescas, sino ciudades humanas*' (massive cities but human scale cities) for example, in his *Theory of the City* of 1947[88]. It is interesting to speculate on what might have happened to his ideas for Palma between 1943 when his plan was approved and 1950 when it was published in book form; in that time he and his family went to Puerto Rico and to the Massachusetts Institute of Technology (MIT). One also has to ask about the influence in this period of his collaborator the architect José Ferragut Pou, whose name occurs on several of the maps of the projects for Palma's reform. While a great admirer of his work Alomar describes him as *un carácter difícil* but one of the more influential figures in his life[89].

At a purely local scale, Alomar addressed four principal themes: circulation and traffic, hygiene and sanitation, the aesthetic appearance of the city and historic/artistic relationships. The influence of Calvet's earlier plan is plain to see but Alomar sought to integrate his (Calvet's) eixample with the historic core in a series of twelve reforms covering nearly 280, 000m2, together with plans for the area beyond the limits of the eixample – what he called the 'pseudo-urban' area. This is believed by some to have been a late addition to his plan that was inserted after his return from the USA[90]. It is a mark of his perception of the changing nature of the city at its edge with a need to embrace the numerous settlements that together occupied an area greater than the eixample but which were clearly part of Palma's function but beyond its then-current administrative boundaries. In fact, this could have been achieved under the old Municipal Statute of 1924[91]. It eventually enabled the development of the *polígonos* (industrial and trading estates) and extra-suburban housing of the 1970s and '80s. Lastly, Alomar pointed to the need to create new neighbourhoods, communities and barrios, a theme he was to develop in his later books as a central part of his planning philosophy.

In about 1955 in a series of handwritten notes – written incidentally on notepaper of the Ritz Hotel, London – Alomar retrospectively outlined his thoughts for his plan and some reflections on it by that date. After a brief introduction to the city's history, he notes the need to open new ways inside the old city, clearing certain slum zones and preserving certain neighbourhoods interesting for its (sic) character and old movements. Secondly, he suggests listing in order, for economical reasons only, all the streets open at present and the development zones. For the reform of the interior, he notes that most of his proposals have been committed by the city council to a private corporation which is making a good job of it – not exactly a neutral sentiment as the company was founded and partly owned by himself! The new lots created are sold out, he wrote, and being built on by private enterprises mostly separate flats as middle-class residences (this appears to refer to Jaume III and the land to east and west of it). While the new blocks are generally dignified, attempting to preserve the style of the old city, perhaps they are too demodé which could be objected to. He is much less happy with the development zones, constrained by the existing buildings and a lack of green zones – 'not good planning at all'.

Even though he feels the reform of the interior of Palma is a very interesting and successful experiment, his notes then go into a riff about his dissatisfaction with local politicians and planners who are not prepared to make a good job of his plan. 'But I have more important work in Barcelona and Madrid and I have not time to waste in local problems in which are involved questions of local and personal politics that I don't like'[92].

By 1944 Alomar had clearly become frustrated with the lack of progress in converting his plan into 'bricks and mortar', a frustration that stemmed from the economics of the time dominated by Franco's policy of autarky that meant there were insufficient materials available for the sort of construction that Alomar envisaged, frustration that came from the growing infighting between the different elements in the regime, particularly the ideologies of certain architects and planners in the Falange as to what cities in the New Order were to look like, frustration that came from the different priorities being broadcast especially those emphasizing housing development above *urbanismo* and, of course, frustration with the shortage of investment capital that would be required.

Alomar may have submitted his plan successfully to the city council but it was clear that it had no funds for building development, indeed, the protocol at that time demanded that the private sector undertake construction, including all the risks that that entailed. By the time when work on at least some of the projects should have started the city council's political composition had changed once more. In his search for developers, he and Ferragut sought the advice of the new mayor, Juan Coll, who suggested that Alomar use his own company to carry out the works and approach the Catalan company Construcciones y Urbanizaciones S. A. to finance it. By 1947 no progress had been made. Alomar turned to an old friend of his father the banker Félix Escala, a director of the Banesto bank, who suggested he approach his former employer Juan March Ordinas, Spain's richest man and financier of the early days of Franco's insurrection. Alomar has already been involved with the management of the building and landscape works at the enormous estate of Sa Vall for Juan March at the beginning of his career, suggesting that he was familiar with project management. By 1945 he was involved with plans for March's palace at the foot of Carrer Conquistador which suggests both parties were also familiar with the problems of undertaking urban reform in Palma. In the event, March agreed to fund at least three of the projects via a company that Alomar had revived for the purpose, EUSA (Edificaciones y Urbanizaciones S. A.): Jaume III, the new l'Olivar market and the Plaça Major – at three per cent, providing that 50% of EUSA's shares were allocated to him. EUSA was later to become one of the largest construction companies in Spain – an ample return on his original investment. In addition, March insisted on joining the board of Alomar's company. Other members included Emilio Tramullas from March's banking firm, a lawyer Lluis Almany and Alomar's co-worker on Jaume III the architect, José Ferragut.

The financing did not proceed without its difficulties. The tax payable on developments of the kind envisaged in the plan contained a large element of what was in effect capital gains tax (*contribución sobre majores*), including that on properties that increased in value by their being contiguous with any new building. The owners of such properties complained bitterly about this. EUSA was not able to benefit from this 'added value'[93].

We have referred to the need to obtain the land upon which to carry out these large-scale developments, and soon EUSA was faced with claims for compensation. Some of these could be met but others resisted leading to threats of expropriation. Just as Alomar had limited experience of managing a complex business organization which he now had to do, so too, he had little knowledge of valuation for compensation[94]. The powerful Truyols family was one of those claiming compulsory purchase so their estate at the lower end of

Fig 10   Palma. The lower part of Avenida Jaume III in 2019; arcading designed by Alomar, built in 1950s. Source: Author's photo.

the Jaume III development had to be compensated by the building of a new town palace (casa Villalonga), designed by Ferragut, and at the company's expense[95].

At a more personal level he was increasingly aware of his limited appreciation of more modern ideas in town planning, not those of Nazi Germany or Fascist Italy which some of his profession in Spain were drawn towards at that time for ideological reasons, but those more liberal visions that could be found in British and American practice. As a man who felt he was not dependent on governmental approval for his work either financially, politically or morally, this feeling of independence, coupled with his frustrations, drove him to seek succour elsewhere, first to Puerto Rico, the birthplace of his wife, and then to the United States.

5

Reflections on Alomar's plan for the reform of Palma: a critique

The context

It might be profitable to begin by examining the political and ideological context of the time when Alomar was beginning to devise his reforms. It was after all a time of upheaval leading to civil war and the imposition of an almost totalitarian regime. It is too simplistic to ascribe to the Franco regime the same degree of centralism, for example, as was seen in the Soviet Union under Stalin. Spain under *El Caudillo* was hardly a totalitarian state. Franco*ism* barely existed; there was never one dominating ideology that could go by that name. Indeed, some have seen the Civil War as a transitional era in the long history of Spain, between the alternating liberal, conservative, monarchist and republican periods before 1936 and the eventual constitutional monarchy under Juan Carlos and his father and then Felipe VI. The Civil War might be seen as another military intervention to re-establish the historical status quo. This is not to accept, of course, the bloody suppression of Republicans, communists and anarchists, the ruthless murder of opposition to the regime and the indiscriminate use of terror as has been recorded by Paul Preston[96].

What characterises the Franco era is the lack of any overarching central view, and certainly not of policies towards planning and architecture. Too many tensions arose during the war and survived it: geographical ones related to regionalism, political ones related to visions of reviving imperial glory, and tensions between town and country and Church and State. What emerges in urbanism at this time is a series of conflicting and competing visions, including Alomar's own as expressed in his Theory of the City (1947).

Carlos Sambricio has identified five challenges that the Franco regime faced during and immediately after the Civil War:

i. reconstruction policies.
ii. a new model of the city, not the previous social democratic one.
iii. housing for the middle classes who supported the regime to keep them 'on side'.
iv. construction of what today we would call 'affordable housing'.
v. pursuit of autarky in urban development.

Reconstruction was increasingly seen as an economic necessity under autarky and not as an architectural priority despite the privations of post-civil war conditions in Spain[97]. In the field of urban planning soon after the Civil War Spain simply produced a melange (rag-bag?) of ideas for urban development, the only common

Fig 11   Palma. The lower part of Avenida Jaume III - palacio for Solleric family above arcading, shops below, c. 1955 by Ferragut and Alomar. Source: Author's photo.

denominator was to reduce the priority for affordable working-class housing for those who had supported the Republican cause. Some fantastic ideas surfaced about the nature of the city ranging from one Falangist, the Count of Montarco's notion to burn down most of Madrid 'while keeping firefighters in some of the most important buildings' to Ramon Serrano Suñer's idea of abandoning Madrid because it had supported the Republic, with a new capital at Seville. In housing, it was party officials and workers who were members of Falange who benefited immediately after the war. It might be thought that the Falange as a political party with considerable influence would have provided the intellectual or ideological leadership in planning. There were certainly members who expressed clear views on the future of urban development for the post-war period. Many commentators, however, preferred to revert to reliance on previous legislation dominated by the 1924 municipalities act. One vociferous advocate of change was César Cort[98], one of the founding fathers of 20thC planning in Spain, who continued to cite the significance of Cerdá's theoretical work at the meetings of the Federation of Town Planning and Housing first established in 1939 and hosting a series of congresses up to 1954[99]. However, this was largely a talking shop which only served to highlight the considerable diversity of views we have referred to. At the first, in 1940, Serrano Suñer – the leader of the Falange – advised that,

'the existence, strength and health of the nation come first, aspirations to national greatness should be based on achieving a strong, healthy Spanish citizen, in a salubrious and comfortable home, in a hygienic city or village... The State powers have entrusted most of the responsibility for construction-related matters to the municipal powers; and he solemnly declared, *'that all architectural undertakings should inescapably, necessarily and obligatorily be subject to Political approval',*

a statement that was more observed in the breach[100]. At its meeting in Barcelona in 1942, Ortega y Gasset reminded members that town planning was a tool to overcome class divisions to be moderated by a housing policy, a position which was very similar to the longstanding Falangist vision for the city. By the last of these congresses, held in Palma in 1954, the emphasis had shifted to Cort's later concerns for ruralising the city and urbanising the countryside, a theme closer to Alomar's own call for public open spaces in and near the city and accessible to its citizens[101].

It might be the case that some of Alomar's ideas that were to manifest themselves in the Plan of 1943 were the result of the diffusion of ideas from elsewhere. In Spain planning may not have been imposed by a central power, for example, but surely there is evidence that certain theories, Cerdá's for example, were well known at the time. However, one of the problems in analysing Alomar's reforms is the absence in the book-form of his plan of the conventional *'before* and *after'* or *'as is'* and *'proposed'* illustrations or detailed maps; it is sometimes difficult to understand what is being lost in his proposal. Alomar would have been well aware of 'classical' examples of planning such as those of Haussmann and more contemporary grandiose schemes such as Mussolini's Via dell Imperio in Rome as well as those for Spanish cities, especially Madrid.

The Projects (See Fig 9)

In part, his reform was to produce a city for the future. It consisted of twelve projects:

1. The construction a new throughway in the north of the city - Carrer Jaime III and the creation of a new urbanization on the site of the old Hort d' in Moranta, preserving San Felio. This would be linked to a new promenade along the left bank of the Riera – the Paseo de Mallorca.
2. The sanitary improvement of Puig de Sant Pere in the south-west corner of the city and Sa Calatrava in the South-east.
3. A new link from the port to the Plaça d'Espagne and the beginning of the circular (sic) street Oms.
4. To straighten and widen Carrer San Miguel.
5. To connect the west side of the Plaça Mayor to the Rambla (Via Roma) with a series of staircases.
6. To build a new market to be known as Olivar[102].
7. To improve the penetration of the roads from Manacor and Inca towards the centre of the city.
8. To preserve the San Francisco area through a pathway toward the Lluchmajor road.
9. To improve the sanitation of Sa Calatrava in the south-east corner of the walled city.
10. To link the entrances of the Manacor and Inca roads across Carrers Conquistador and Jaime II.
11. To build a new communicating road from San Nicolás through Pas del Quint to Brondo.
12. To link Plaça del Cort with the Born, via a Gran Vía.

Plans exist in the mind of the author or authors in the first place, plans which in Alomar's case he described as being 'his life's ambition'...' so labouriously developed over many years at a stretch '... 'as if it were my child', and then on paper[103]. Drawn plans, however attractive – and Alomar's certainly were – have to convince the political authorities who might give them approval. Finally, success would depend on winning finance for the plans and securing developers and construction companies who can convert the hopes and aspirations into concrete form. Alomar's dreams were to almost founder on these last two points. By 1946 having won approval in principle for his reforms from the Palma council as early as February 1943, Alomar had great difficulty in getting local building firms to submit contracts, nearly all found the schemes too risky with insufficient return on any capital they might invest. At the same time, it would appear that his main rival in the competition for the original plans, Francisco Casas, tried to win support from other construction companies and their political supporters, namely the architects Enrique Juncosa and Antonio García-Ruiz. Juncosa, according to Alomar, 'has become one of our worst enemies, a real devil's advocate for our cause'. Alomar took the opportunity to raise some of the issues surrounding his planned reforms the most pressing of which was the local opposition stemming from arguments about compensation for land and property owners. Partly as a result of this, as will be shown later, it took a long time for his plan to reach the construction phase. A decade after the plan's first submission Alomar had to seek support from Pedro Bidagor Lasarte, the head of planning in the Dirección General de Arquitectura in Madrid. Translating plans into built form proved to be no easy matter.

The most dramatic of these projects was the new avenue of Jaume III which was to be highly commercialised, definitely bourgeois with its high-class shops – including later a department store – the first in Palma – its hotels and, of course, the city mansions of the Villalongas and the Truyols. It has been described rather fancifully as Palma's answer to Fifth Avenue, New York. However, some believe that Alomar's vision for this thoroughfare was more influenced by his experience of Italian towns, often characterised by arcaded pavements sheltering the shopper from the hot sun and the sudden downpours so typical of the Mediterranean climate. As to scale, Jaume III is hardly Hausmannian in width.

Although there is little evidence that the central government's policies for the development of cities were directly involved, *'schemes implemented by dictators almost always involved the modernization of historic centres by means reminiscent of Haussmannization, namely cutting wide avenues through densely built-up quarters, often the districts inhabited by working-class opponents*'[104]. This proved to be much less so in the case of the construction of Jaume III. One observer believed that only 44 houses would have to be destroyed in the process but it was to create space for more than 800 dwellings and a link between the west of the city and *'unos de las puntos vitales de la ciudad, la encrucijada de la llamada Fuente de las Tortugas, al final de Paseo de Borne'*(one of the key points in the city, the junction of the end of the Born and the Tortugas fountain'), the exchange, on balance, being worth it[105]. The creation of Avenida Jaume III did affect the location of some workshops including a cotton factory in Carrer Bonaire, the loss of the La Concepción convent and of some gardens and open spaces and the expropriation of quite large proportions of several hundred square metres of the land and palaces of the Villalonga and Truyols families. Naturally, there was some resistance on behalf of landowners but these were overcome without resort to the courts. In their place arose the main cross axis, Bonaire, and the new *barrio* of Santa Maria del Sepulchre. Local opinion was divided on the possible benefits of the new *carrer*;

some lower-class housing and minor streets were eventually lost to these higher-class apartments, shops, and townhouses[106]. Most of the new apartments would be built in new streets running at right angles to Jaume III. Alomar himself argued that his new thoroughfare ran through largely unoccupied land next to the Riera river in the Huerto d'en Moranta that lay inside the renaissance walls – '... *ha permanecido sin edificar*' (has never been built on) – making way for a modern urbanization on the huerto[107]. In designing Jaume III Alomar was the progenitor of the arcades that line either side of the street. This thoroughfare may have been seen by some as somewhat grandiose and 'Haussmannian', linking Santa Catalina across the Reira with the head of the Born but Alomar was never a great supporter of the French architect. The arcades were seen by Alomar as '*calles porticades. . . traditionales en nuestra cuidad antigua*', a succession of arcs and columns creating a rhythm as in a musical score, one of the basic themes in art, *siempre bella*', a reference to Italian architecture including the modern Via Roma de Turin of 1934-38 and as seen in Bologna, towns which Alomar had visited in his youth. However, a most important figure in the actual architecture of this first project, whose work should not be underestimated, was José Ferragut Pau. It was he who added the detailed architecture *above* the arcades. He was to contribute numerous buildings in the 1960s to Alomar's basic plan including in Carrer Baron de Santa Maria del Sepulcro, in Carre Bonaire and in the Paseo de Mallorca, in addition to those in Jaume III itself. In 1964 Ferragut wrote to his fellow architect when Alomar was working for the Comisaría General del Patrimonio Artistica Nacional regretting the loss of architectural unity, lamenting that rather than acting as a demonstration of what could be achieved '...*lo que se habia ordenando ha quedado perfectamente desordenado*" (...what could have been achieved by control became perfectly messy), nonetheless, it was Alomar who had laid down the plan – indicative lines on the map with only architectural guidelines[108]. In the plan for the Jaume III area in the published version of 1950 (p. 51), both men are listed as authors.

Alomar, *as architect*, had advocated for his historic core of Palma a constrained layout for his street plan, perhaps more influenced by Sitte, a classical style rooted in regionalism and the use of local materials for his architecture but it was Ferragut and his collaborator Juncosa who designed much of what we see today, especially in the streets of apartments at right angles to the principal thoroughfare in the 1950s and later in the Paseo de Mallorca in the 1960s. One detail of the plan that taxed those responsible for traffic flow was the junction of Jaume III and Plaça de Tortugas but a late submission to the city council by EUSA showed a solution that was finally approved. While the reforms were clearly aimed at reducing traffic congestion through the city, and in particular at junctions like this one, it would be wrong to take Alomar to task for not having the foresight to predict the explosive growth of urban transport and population numbers that coincided with the boom in tourism from the 1970s. Had he been able to do so, then he might have had to include at least the kind of wide avenues envisaged by Haussmann in Paris, or worse, some kind of urban motorway system that ruined so many other European cities – the very antithesis of his planning philosophy. The actual building of the apartments and the *carrer* took many years to complete; it was not until the late 1970s that Jaume III took on the aspect that we see today. Notwithstanding, together the planner, the architects and the builders created a unity of expression in Alomar's *proyecto numero uno* that today dominates that quarter of Palma.

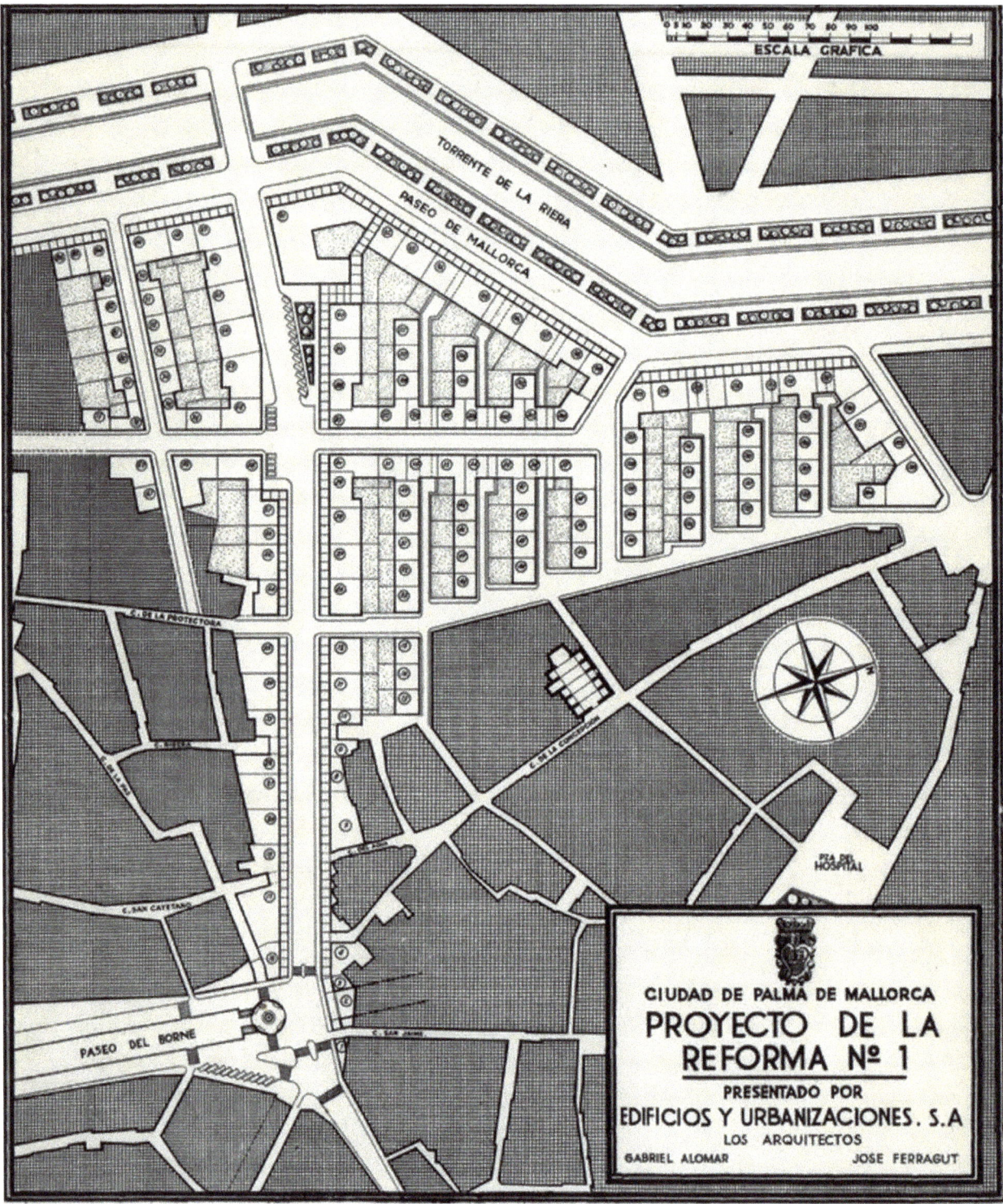

Fig 12   Reform area no. 1 for the new Avenida Jaume III with housing (not built), linking Santa Catalina to Plaza Tortuga (El Borne). Source: Alomar 1950. By kind permission of Gabriel Alomar Garau. ©.

Fig 13   Building Avenida Jaume III, designed by Alomar, about 1952.

A somewhat contradictory characteristic of Alomar's reforms was the decision to build a new market for stallholders selling fruit, vegetables, fish and charcuterie for the benefit of local working-class consumers in the days before supermarkets, to replace the old Plaça Major – Palma's *'zoco indigno'*, its Arab souk[109]. A plaça major, said Alomar, had to be the heart of the reformed city, its civic and geometric centre but the existing site had become run down, overcrowded and unhygienic, unworthy of its real purpose. What was needed was a market that met modern standards in a new location whose relocation would permit the subsequent 'proper' development of the Plaça Major. Many previous planners including Bennàzar and Forteza had eyed this site's potential for redevelopment. The former had included it in his wider reform plan for the city but which was not adopted. In 1931 the Madrid government approved the expenditure for the market and Guillem Forteza was appointed as architect. Being of a more modern outlook he refused to accept Bennàzar's designs and opted for a pre-stressed concrete structure. Before construction could begin – it was finally approved by the city council in 1935 – the Civil War intervened. On its conclusion and the adoption of Alomar's plan in 1943 it was he who actually succeeded in allocating this space for a new public market[110]. This scheme too involved the demolition of buildings of architectural significance including the site of an old convent that was proposed for release onto the market by the abolition of entailments by Mendízabal as early as 1832. In addition, many small alleys were lost that included a variety of industrial activities including an important foundry. The building had a budget of over 12 million pesetas but Alomar complained later that some of the developers exceeded the height of surrounding buildings spoiling the appearance of the area[111]. On balance, the scheme may have created many jobs at a time of high unemployment but it did involve the displacement of some of the local population.

Fig 14   Site being cleared for the construction of new Mercat de l'Olivar.
Source: Courtesy of Mercatolivar.com.

Fig 15   Mercat de l'Olivar in early 1950s. Source: Courtesy of Mercatolivar.com.

Largely designed by the Valencian architect Vicente Valls Gadea, with some modifications by Alomar and Enrique Juncosa, construction began in 1947 but probably because of the shortage of materials at that time especially cement, it was not officially opened until January 1951[112]. It was the second of his twelve projects and, like Jaume III, it was financed by EUSA and Juan March's money[113].

His third project was the Plaça Major and the need to integrate it into the wider townscape.

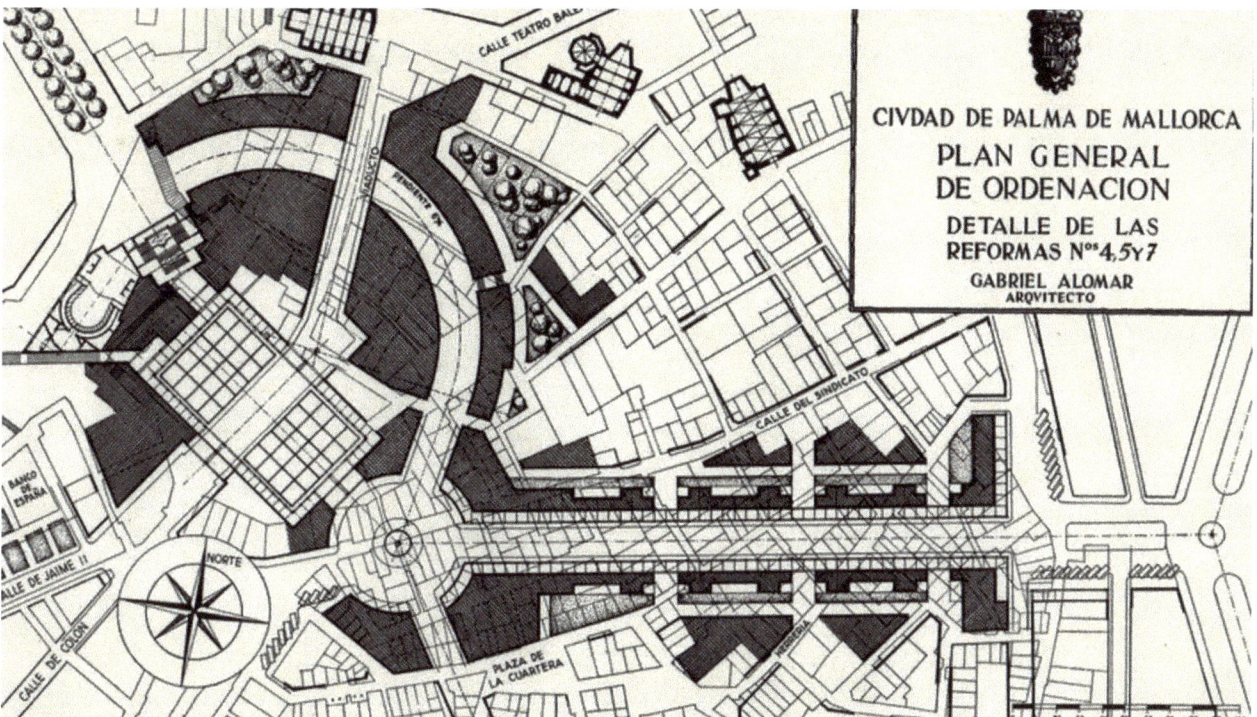

Fig 16   Alomar's plan the central area of Palma, reforms 4, 5 and 7, little of which was built. Plaza Major lies to the left. Source: Alomar, 1950. By kind permission of Gabriel Alomar Garau. ©.

Originally the site of the Inquisition (the convent of Felipe Neri) and before that the site of executions in the Muslim city of Mayurqa. Following the disentailments (*desmortacions*) of the 19C it was built as the sort of structure familiar in so many Spanish cities, nearly all based on the space of the same name that was originally built in Madrid in the 16C in the reign of Felipe III and later much reformed to give its largely present-day appearance in the 18C by Villanueva. Palma's version had become in the 19C the site of many commercial activities including the city's fish market. The Plaza in Madrid stood on a hill and access was by a variety of stairways, including that from Calle de Cuchilleros. In Palma's version, Alomar's main objective was to try to link the plaça on the north side to the Rambla, renamed the Via Roma following wartime fascist Italian influence, by a new and massive stairway. His solution was essentially architectural rather than one of planning perhaps following the Madrid solution.

Fig 17   Proposal for a stairway from Via Roma (La Rambla) to Plaza Major. Source: part of the entry to Barcelona exhibition, 1942. ©

Fig 17a   Stairway to rear of Plaza Major today. Compare with Fig 17. Source: Author's photo.

When the land beneath Palma's main plaça was excavated in the 1960s to create an underground shopping centre and car park, access to the surrounding streets by road was achieved, and eventually, a planning solution was reached although access and exit to the car park remain problematic. The architecture of this planned stairway reveals all of Alomar's classical leanings; sadly, what remains of the original conception is rarely used by pedestrians today and stands as a rather gaunt monument to a previous era.

Although Alomar divided his reforms into twelve projects, he saw them leading to the reform of the inner city as a whole; together, the twelve were a means to an end. Later, we shall discuss whether he was successful in this holistic ambition. Between the initial drafting, the publication in book form in 1950 and the beginning of construction many economic and political changes were to take place in Palma.

As we noted above local opposition stemming from arguments about compensation for land and property owners created delays. 1950 Alomar solicited the support of Bidagor in Madrid for his plan. It would appear that Alomar had asked him to write to the mayor of Palma to find a way forward, particularly in relation to the local opposition to parts of the plan. Bidagor suggested that the green spaces could be reduced in size where owners had sacrificed them to increasing building density in exchange for limiting growth at the city's edge. For the *casc antich* Bidagor noted that of the twelve projects four were already being carried out and of the remaining eight only occupied 9% of the historic area. For these Alomar and Bidagor appeared to agree that expropriation should not proceed. The city council was urged to reapply to the national government with a new scheme in which urgent reforms should be prioritised and proceeded with and others annulled. Those considered most urgent were the road widening schemes in projects 7 and 8 (roads to Inca and Manacor) which would provide the required solution to the traffic problems identified by Alomar. Bidagor also supported a modified scheme for Sa Calatrava (no. 2) in which the access road to the gateway to the port could be carried out gradually and the unsatisfactory sanitary conditions improved.

In conclusion, the influential head of planning in the Madrid civil service, Pedro Bidagor, gave the city council the clearest support for Alomar's plan when he wrote:

> *La Jefatura de Urbanismo considera que la Reforma de Palma, principalmenteé por la forma en que se realiza además de su interés local tiene un interés nacional, ya que problemente serviria de ejemplo y estímulo para otras ciudades que se hallan en condiciones similares.*
>
> *Sería lamentable que la marcha inicinada con tanto empuje se viera detenida a mitad de camino. Los prejuicios que se irrogan(;) en todas los empresas de este tipo sin indudablemente, pero por encima de ellos, debemos considerar la razón superior del bien colectivo de la ciudad.* The planning authorities are of the opinion that the Reform of Palma, mainly because of the way it is being approached, is not only of local but also of national interest in that it is likely to serve as an example and stimulus for other cities in a similar situation.
>
> It would be regrettable if the activity begun with such enthusiasm were to lose impetus half-way through. The negative aspects that crop up during all enterprises of this kind are undeniable but over and above these we must bear in mind the most important aim of the collective benefit to the city (of Palma). [114]

Progress on all fronts proved not to be possible. First, was the need for a supply of capital at an affordable rate. We have shown that while the financier Juan March was prepared to advance monies at 3% interest for the development of Jaume III initially, few other investors from the construction sector seemed willing to risk taking on some of the other projects; the local banks were especially reluctant. By October 1949 Alomar records that EUSA had already spent in excess of twenty million pesetas on three projects: Jaume III, l'Olivar Market and Plaça Major; another company had committed to improving the link between Plaça del Cort and the Born[115]. Secondly, there was the question of compensation for landowners whose buildings would have to be expropriated and demolished to make way for the new schemes; landowners would need to be able to calculate any likely increase in economic rent following redevelopment and this proved unlikely in the immediate post-war circumstances. There were serious attacks on his plan in respect of this issue in the press, especially in a long piece in La Almudaina by Cañellas in June 1949 in which Alomar's plan was described as something of a romantic dream that had persuaded the ayuntamiento to accept it; at its heart was the notion that the benefits of the public good of the reforms would outweigh those of private property. Cañellas drew on municipal laws going back to the 1860s to show that this was not the case here: the *sueño* had become, for him, a *fantasma* [116]. Alomar's daughter even recalls her father telling her he was threatened with murder by some of his opponents[117]. Much of this kind of opposition lay behind the need for Bidagor's letter above. Compulsory purchase without compensation was little known at this time. In any case, Alomar points out that the town council had few funds to offer sufficient indemnity. Clearly, there was a conflict of priorities between the business community and the ayuntamiento and the latter was divided in its support for those projects that required a commercial outcome. In effect, this left the Plaça Major and the new market as the only ones of likely public benefit (Juan March had underwritten the development of Jaume III)[118].

So, what of the remaining nine projects? In reality, very little was achieved apart from the examples quoted below. Mallorca's population and its politics were beginning to change markedly from the mid-1950s onwards. Its economy was shifting towards further industrialisation and to the tertiary and quaternary (service) sectors under the influence of large scale inward migration and the growing tourism industry. The focus of attention shifted to the supply of working-class housing for the new Spanish immigrants in places such as Molinar and Es Rotlet in the east of Palma. Away from the city, it was the new coastal resorts where real estate developers could make considerable sums with little planning control, and investment followed them. The political situation was moving if only slowly towards a more decentralised form so that city governments had rather more autonomy, a reflection in Mallorca's case of a move away from the influence of Falange and Francoist ideas, towards more diverse views that, even here, Alomar had found it difficult to come to terms with; he quickly wanted to absent himself from the local parochialism – and probably – corruption. As we shall see, he was later recruited by Madrid where he sought to find solutions to some of the difficulties he experienced in Palma in new ideas for a national planning policy.

The proposed reforms to Puig de Sant Pere (part of project no. 2) have come under much criticism over the last seventy years. This area in the far south-west of the walled city certainly suffered from poor sanitation, crumbling unsanitary buildings many of them centuries old and providing very poor quality accommodation in multi-occupation for families with low incomes. Alomar's idea was to sweep them away and replace them with modern facilities, at that time an obvious solution to a pressing socio-spatial problem. His detailed plan for the area reveals a series of four blocks of apartments with spectacular views of the harbour. But nothing was done.

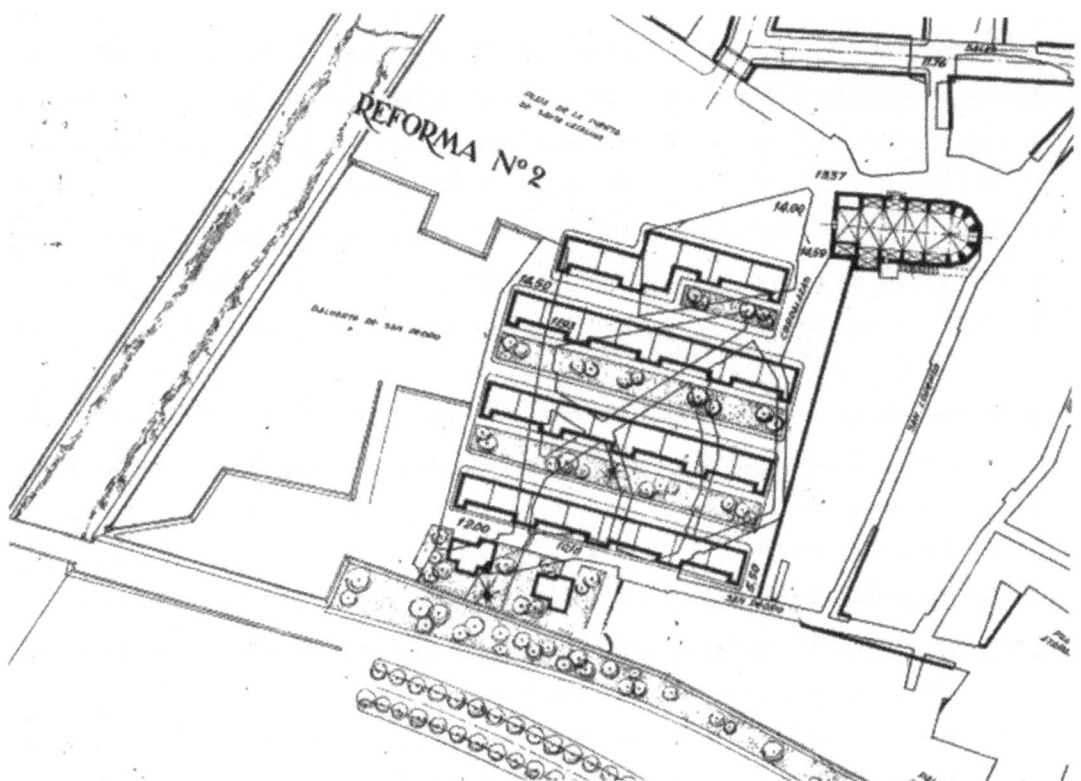

Fig 18 Reform no. 2. Puig de Sant Pere in the South West corner of historic Palma. Source: Arxiu Municipal de Palma.

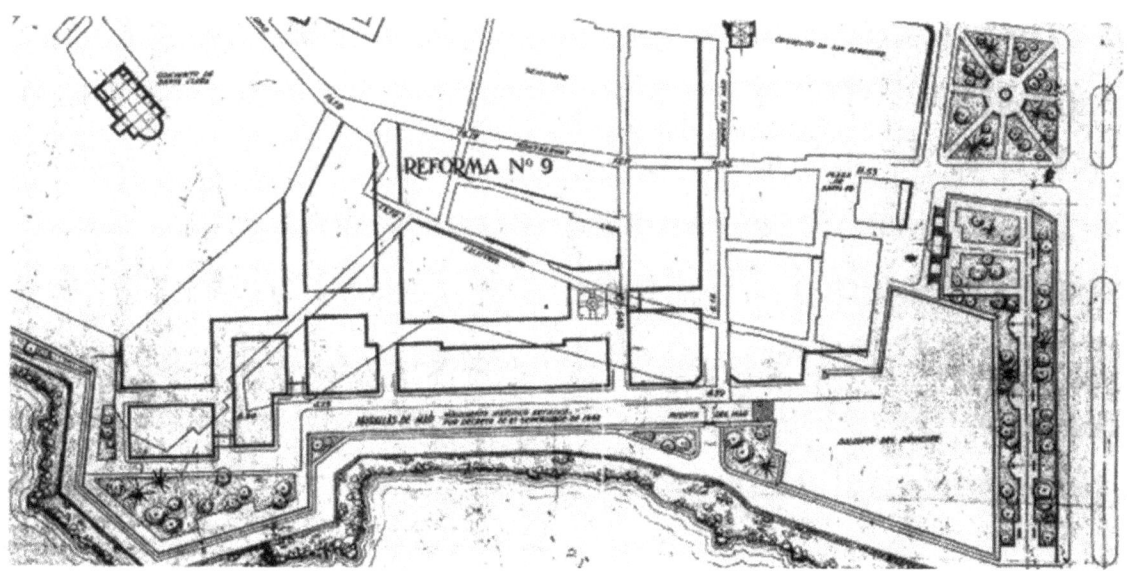

Fig 19 Reform no. 9. Sa Calatrava in South East corner of historic Palma. Source: Arxiu Municipal de Palma.

It was not until many years later by which time the conservation lobby had become much more vocal and the value given to the area changed. In an exhibition mounted in 1975, the year of European Architectural Heritage, which ironically Alomar had helped to establish, the Balearic College of Architects laid out their reasons for the reform of the area. These were solidly rooted in its historical/architectural significance, drawing on the experience of other European cities that had faced similar challenges such as Bologna, Copenhagen and Brussels. The guiding philosophy was to be 'conserve not renovate', encouraging existing economic activities and their growth, retaining the high density of buildings and spaces (*manzanas*) and finally trying to maintain the sense of community by involving the local population. This would mean,

> '*será necesario abandonar el conjunto de normas y reglamentos urbanísticos convencionales para tratar separadamente cada caso, no solamente teniendo en cuenta la tipología del inmueble rehabilitad sino también su composición sociológica, su población, sus relaciones de vecindad, sus relaciones culturales y experiencia de sus habitantes sobre la utilización del espacio*'. (It will be necessary to abandon the set of conventional urban rules and regulations to treat each case separately, not only taking into account the typology of the rehabilitated buildings but also their sociological composition, their population, their neighbourly relations, their cultural relations and experience of the inhabitants about the use of space)[119].

Again, ironically, many of these criteria would have by then (1975) been approved by Alomar. However, a major stumbling block to the future use of the area lay with the Army's ownership of the *baluade* (bastion) in the corner of the walls. It was offered to the city in the 1960s who refused it take it on. Finally, it was sold to a private developer, Gabriel Munar Carbonall and Vich Pous SA, who wanted to convert it to a casino. Joana Roca Cladera recalls '... *the company that owned the Bastion (Baluade de Sant Pere) started to buy the houses in the neighbouring block, took the roofs of them and declared them as derelict with the aim of demolishing them, to isolate their singular building from the poor and deteriorated neighbourhood. The houses were in poor shape. Since the 1940s the owners had made no investments in them, because the General Plan drawn up by Gabriel Alomar in 1940 envisaged new, sunny buildings with sea views*'[120]. Considerable demolition of ancient properties took place without planning permission, including a large section of the western wall which had to be rebuilt to its original structure. In 1964 a scheme for army housing was proposed that was totally inappropriate for this historic location[121]. By 1981 this zone had 259 houses and a population of 729 by which time a team of young local architects that included Alomar's son Antonio and Joana Roca Cladera succeeded in obtaining Madrid's approval for the scheme of rehabilitation referred to earlier, perhaps the first of its kind in Spain[122].

The remaining projects were nearly all associated with improvements to the road network of Palma including radial roads that penetrated the city such as the Manacor, Llucmajor and Inca roads. An examination of these routeways today – and indeed from personal experience – shows that such roads have been widened and extended to accommodate later traffic. Lined with shops, offices and apartment blocs they have acted as linear extensions of the city, a feature of so many west European cities from the 1930s onwards, a response to increases in car ownership and motorised traffic that later generations of planners have tried to deal with but with little success. Instead, the plans of the 1960s, '70s and '80s have focused on trying to take traffic *around* the city via the Cintura, itself now heavily congested so that road widening schemes, new roundabouts and junctions are frequently being introduced to add capacity and speed up flows. In 2019 a second outer ring road appeared.

The major highway that was built later along the coast and port area – the Via Marítima – was an exception to this make-do-and-mend approach. Alomar may have foreseen the need for this road but it had its origins in the west of the city between the old port of Portopi and the first mole where the beginnings of a *paseo marítimo* were built in stages. It was not until the engineer Joan Roca designed the existing highway in the late 1950s that the circuit by the sea was begun. It was opened by the Caudillo in 1960. Many opposed its initial construction claiming that this urban throughway would separate Palma from its historic and aesthetic connection to the sea, flanked by a large area of car parking, of which Alomar did not approve. It was not until the new city plans of the 1970s that the reclamation of large areas from the sea created a large new platform dominated by a lake and fountain below the magnificent Gothic cathedral, affording protection to the historic waterfront below the retained south walls including such iconic buildings as the Llotja and Consuelo del Mar and connecting the city to new suburbs developing westwards such as El Terreno.

Other road improvement schemes were to assist the flow of traffic within the historic centre particularly from the port towards the stations in Plaça d'Espanya. Again, most of these were to be achieved at a time when Alomar had long given up his concern for the planning of Palma and when traffic problems had become even more acute.

The final topic, related to urban conservation, was one Alomar listed among his twelve projects for the core of Palma, the historic zone in the southeast corner of the city, Sa Calatrava (part of project no. 9).

It is difficult to assess why this important area was not subject to more attention by Alomar but it would appear that this was the result of a conflict of interest between the city authorities and the architect. In 1980 he described the former's demand for blocks of apartments for reasons of hygiene as 'truly foolish' rather than instead of his proposal for *chalets* (low-rise housing) overlooking the sea with their own gardens, an aesthetic in tune with the area's historic past[123]. Perhaps he saw its historic architecture and its association with so many significant industrial activities such as tanning (*blanqueries*), the settlement of the Jewish population in *el Call major* in medieval times and its churches such as Montesion, as worthy of conservation once the sanitation problems of the area had been overcome. This can be contrasted with his proposals for Puig de Sant Pere in the opposing southwest corner of the city where he recommended wholesale clearance. After decades of neglect, Sa Calatrava has become a contested space as the process of gentrification advances under neoliberal forces where town planning has been reduced to being dictated to by market forces[124].

As prices of property and land in the 'aristocratic' part of the historic city began to rise so pressure increased on the zones immediately adjacent – Santa Catalina to the west and Sa Calatrava and Sa Gerreria to the east – creating a twofold division of land with areas immediately facing the sea being developed as high-class residences (including Alomar's own home between Sant Alonso and the seafront) and the ancient, overcrowded, industrial working-class zone inhabited for so long by a transitioning community. Today, this tension can be ascribed to the failure of the local authority to confront a problem identified by Alomar more than seventy years ago in his plan and, as we have seen, supported by the influential Bidagor. Until recently, largely unrestrained market forces have now changed the value of this zone to the increasing exclusion of its original inhabitants: the bourgeoisification of the area, a theme to be discussed in the final chapter[125].

As for the remainder of the city, there is the case of the need for suburban espansion. The history of town planning in Spain from the late 19C onwards is dominated by the ensanche, that the only solution to the ills of the country's cramped and often walled cities was to create new extramural suburbs. In addition to Cerdá's scheme for Barcelona which we have discussed, perhaps the most extensive were the ensanches to the north and east of Madrid. Here, Carlos María de Castro (1810-1893) was much influenced by Cerdá where he felt *'...Barcelona's ensanche was so complete and conscientious...so well written and full of precious details that we have not hesitated to choose him as a model and follow him step by step in what is applicable to the locality on which we have to operate'* [126]. Of many enigmas in Alomar's plan for Palma, despite these national examples and despite his early work for the Bishop of Mallorca on this subject, it appears to be focused almost entirely on reforms to the historic core. Was this another of his somewhat romantic ideas about cities, to do with size and human scale and avoiding sprawl? Much of his later planning theory but based on his Palma experience, as we shall see, now seems out of touch with the mainsprings of Spanish planning at that time.

As published in book form in 1950, Alomar's plan was primarily concerned with Palma's centre seeming to give less consideration to the future needs of the city beyond the renaissance walls. Calvet's plan of 1901 had perhaps identified this need and planned for it but, of course, little was done. Suburbs had indeed grown up from the late 19C to the outbreak of the Civil War including, for example, Santa Catalina across the Riera, Son Armadans, Pere Garau, Son Gotleu and Soledad Nord but in general, Alomar saw these early developments as anarchic, often related to new industrial developments as in La Soledad and the developing railway lines as they penetrated the city[127]. María Dolores Ladaria Bañares has made a detailed analysis of these from 1868 to 1927 and shown that very little planning was involved beyond the laying out of a general street network. Developers submitted individual plans and building licences for plots of land that they acquired which, once approved, were developed with little or no control except those relating to the current building regulations. However, they evolved as one of the major urban locations for industrial development, much of it in the form of small-scale workshops, and for the majority of housing.

The ensanche or eixample

> ...there are three basic points on which the municipal policy regarding the Extension Zone should be based. The first is the definite limitation of the developable area to avoid that this area of the city, frankly, which is already out of proportion with our economic capacity and continues to grow. The second is the establishment of a Plan of Alignments drawn up according to a set order, to which all new plots of building land must be subject, without exception. The third is the formation of a Building Ordinances Corps, controlling the use of the land, the heights (maximum, minimum, or fixed) and the volumes of buildings – Ordinances that are based on the corresponding Zonal systems.
>
> Gabriel Alomar Esteve: *The Reform of Palma*. 1950. Author's translation.

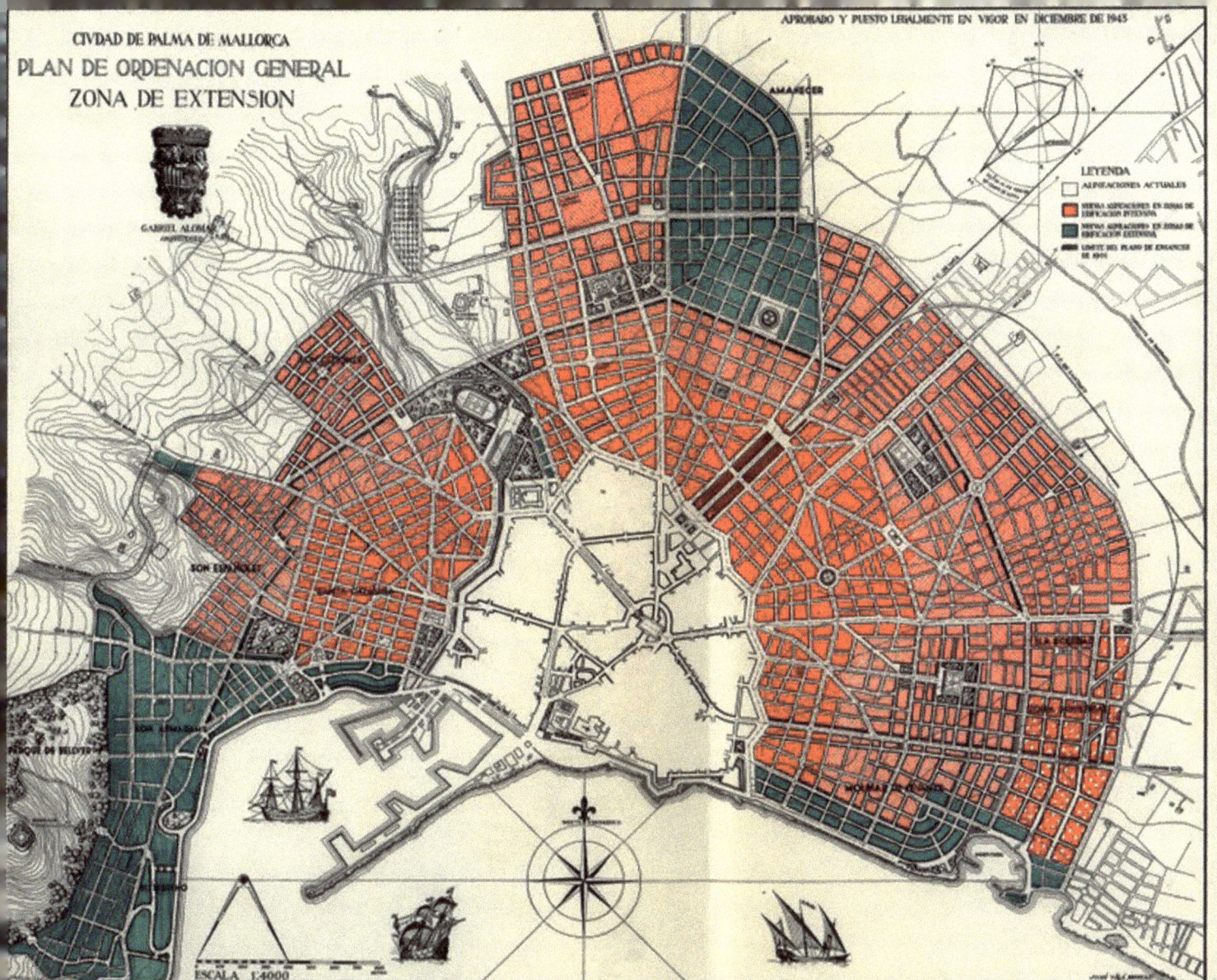

Fig 20   Alomar's plan for the eixample/ensanche. Source: Alomar 1950. By kind permission of Gabriel Alomar Garau. ©

Alomar saw that the increase in the city's population during the 1930s would need accommodating in its extramural suburbs; by 1940 Palma's population had reached114, 405. By the 1950s 70% of the city's population would reside in areas such as these, with the historic centre having only 30%. By 1960 population numbers had risen to 153, 084, nearly all this growth having taken place outside the line of the old walls. This kind of development, as foreseen by Alomar, should only be done within an agreed plan that took into account many of the variables that were also so important in the historic city: housing, sanitation and movement. His plan for the suburbs is not detailed and appears a reluctant addition to his overall scheme for Palma. In the map of what he called the extension zone in the 'new city' Alomar distinguished between areas that could be developed extensively, that is, with lower densities, and intensive zones. This reveals what appears to be a pattern of segregation perhaps best exemplified by the areas to the southeast of the historic city with prestigious sites on the seafront and the industrial area adjacent to the north including La Soledad that was linked to the radial routes to Manacor and Llucmajor. Other extensive zones including El Terreno and Son Armadans in the southwest around some of the public open spaces he hoped to create and in the far north on the edge of the city overlooking rural landscapes in Amenecer. Altogether creating a three-zone city – the historic core, the ensanche of the late 19C and this new *zona de extrarradio* – but one which showed the separation of functions, perhaps the beginnings of an American style zoning policy. More importantly for Alomar was the need to have a plan for Palma's expanding edge that prevented the growth of unregulated pseudo-urbanization where speculators laid out their blocks of building land (*parcelas*, *manzanas* and *solares*) converting rural, or at least fringe-belt land, to urban land and benefiting from the increases in value. This was a topic he was to address later in 1955 in his books on planning theory which coloured his ideas leading towards the national Ley del Suelo of 1956.

In the end, of course, a city is a system, a system of interrelated parts internally and with economic and social relations externally so it is necessary to judge Alomar's Palma as a whole, a topic that will be addressed in the final chapter.

6
Influences on Alomar's planning ideas

The theories of town planning that emerged in Britain in the late 19C were largely influenced by Ebenezer Howard's Ideal City and the Garden City Movement of Thomas Adams, Parker and Unwin, Mawson etc. All were founded on the idea that urban growth would have to be accommodated *outside* the existing, industrial, cities of late-Victorian Britain and at some distance from them. This would permit lowering densities in such cities and act as a stimulus for development in rural areas, acting as intervening opportunities, slowing down the rate of rural to urban migration. This approach to planning was well understood in Franco's Spain but it did not attract the same degree of attention as in Britain notwithstanding the Falange's concern for the relations between town and country. In *practice*, nearly all of Spain's city plans in the early part of the 20C were designed to lower the central densities of their historic cores while expanding the cities at their edges via ensanches. This was especially true of the two great cities of Madrid and Barcelona but repeated in a small provincial city such as Palma, surely under the continuing influence of Idelfonso Cerdá. However, from the 1930s there had been some opposition to the idea of the 'geometric' planning of the modernizers whether in new settlements or in the ensanches of the larger cities. Some Fascist societies certainly had a liking for the massive and the monumental, in Spain's case later exemplified by the Escorial and Franco's personal involvement with Valle de Los Caidos, but Falangist thinking about urban and architectural ideals was against the contemporary European support for 'modernism' exemplified by the work of Sert and Le Corbusier[128]. But this is a contested field: defining "Francoist" or even fascist architecture and planning is fraught with difficulty. As Daniel Domenech has written: *It has thus become impossible to achieve unanimity on such contested issues as the nature of Francoism, and whether it was essentially reactionary, or in a qualified sense could be seen not just as modernizing, but even fascist, and hence revolutionary in a strictly right-wing, nationalist sense"*[129]. For example, the INC (Instituto Nacional de Colonizión, founded in 1939) had shown in its plans for individual (mostly rural) towns a morphology-based on 'a loose grid centred on an enclosed and at times arcaded plaza major' but those attending the 1949 National Assembly of Architects argued for a return to something approaching the Spanish vernacular but in a modernized form with an emphasis on less rigid, more organic forms[130]. We know from his *Theory of the City* (1947) that Alomar was influenced by biological structures and relationships and by the aesthetics of the medieval built form[131]. He saw the urban community as –

> '… *una integración de seres humanos, constituida en determinada área geográfica y con un cierto grado de unidad en relacion a algunos importantes aspectos de la vida. Los hombres que habitan una ciudad integran evidentemente una communidad que se halla establecida en un conjunto especial de estructuras fisica y aún una de las más características,*' which might be transliterated as 'a concern for human ecology with the ecological relationship of peasant households to land being possibly transferred to

the urban dweller and the urban environment.' Failure causes *debilitatión* (weakness)[132].

The morphological notions of Sitte[133] also influenced Alomar as they had of one of his influential contemporaries, Guillem Forteza, who, in his *L'art de construir les ciutats i la reforma de Palma* (1921) wrote of his opposition to the then dominant ideas of engineers and hygienists, reformers whose approach to planning was essentially technical. Alomar considered Sitte's 19C idea of applying the aesthetics of the medieval city to the modern city referring to his artistic principles, including organic unity, to create *ambientes agradables* – the aesthetic relations between the street, the plaza, monuments, the fountains – what Alomar called *una armonía natural*[134]. It is worth noting that Alomar's influential book was published shortly before the National Assembly of Architects 5th meeting in 1949, from which a visit to Palma was organized[135].

At a wider geographical scale, Spain was also beginning to consider what a later generation of geographers would call the system of cities, that dominant major cities were part of a spatial hierarchy arranged according to a rank-size rule, theoretically at least. The relative failure of the Garden City movement in the UK was said to be attributable to a lack of regional planning at the time, that is, being able to integrate new towns like Letchworth into a wider, functional spatial framework. In the United States, the Regional Plan of New York showed an alternative to the theory of the self-contained Garden City. In Spain as early as the first decade of the 20C Núñez Granés had explored the need for links between Madrid and its surrounding settlements as part of a regional system[136] so the by the1920s the notion of regional planning per se was being considered[137]. Although the Municipal Statute of 1924 gave considerably more power to the ayuntamientos, in the field of planning it tended to pitch one municipality in a region against another, supporting *extensións* rather than regional systems[138]. It has been criticised for concentrating almost entirely on improving roads in cities. In social terms, it tended to benefit middle-class urban areas but could do little in the planning of cities beginning to experience increasing rural to urban migration by the 1920s. In other words, planning under its auspices was partial and piecemeal and not at all comprehensive, subject to the whims of individual cities and towns. Nonetheless, it remained the principal piece of national planning legislation until the coming of the Ley de Suelo of 1956[139].

In the case of Alomar's scheme for Palma in the 1940s it meant that any plan had perforce to focus on 'core' (the *casc antich*) and 'periphery' (the *eixample*) as in Eusebio Estada's plan of sixty years before, despite the city's overwhelming dominance in the Mallorcan urban hierarchy and the island's space economy. It has only been since the mid-20C that settlements such as Marratxí, Llucmajor and Calvià's coastal towns have become more integrated into Palma's city region, and even then mostly by organic development rather than via any regional plan. Eventually, the 1973 spatial plan treated the whole island as its 'region', perhaps the result of Alomar's thoughts aired a decade earlier[140].

We have shown earlier that the influence of late 19C and early 20C plans on Alomar's plan but to what extent was his plan a direct descendent of planning ideas expressed in the decade immediately before his own was published? Despite the modernist movements referred to above, under the Second Republic town planning was rarely at the top of the national agenda. In the difficult years of the early 1930s, any developments tended to spring from the analysis of the city that had persisted from earlier historical periods – mostly still focused on overcrowding and sanitation. For example, Emili Darder Canaves, originally President of Palma's Municipal Health Commission, a doctor with socialist leanings, was able to continue his concern for the sanitary condition of the city when elected as Mayor under the Second Republic. This was one of the few occasions when the city was able to advance the nineteenth-century hygienist policies that had their origins in the work of Montlau and Oliver referred to earlier[141]. Alomar would surely have been conscious of this aspect of the need for reform in Palma's infrastructure. Similarly, his ideas were tempered by considerations of the potential influence of motor transport on the functioning of the city, and in Palma's case, the impact of tourism. Nonetheless, any development proposals were largely refinements of old ideas; there was little true innovation.

The Civil War 1936-39 had a devastating effect on many cities not only from the relatively new military strategy of aerial bombardment but from the widespread use of artillery. Cities such as Barcelona, Madrid, Teruel etc suffered considerable damage to their built form so that any post-war planning for many of them was centred for some time on rebuilding. In the case of Palma, the bombing had been carried out by Republican 'planes in May and December 1937: the damage was not extensive[142]. A major priority for the Nationalist government in terms of urban development was obviously the repair and rebuilding of damaged cities in the devastated zones. At the same time, the ideologies of the New State were beginning to be broadcast to the planners and architects of the time many of whom, of course, were long-standing practitioners. Alomar could not have failed to recognise the words of one of the most influential town planners in the immediate post-war period, César Cort (from a book review):

> *La vida municipal es la base de la prosperidad de la nación. No hay nación grande con municipios abandonados, enclenques torpes o venales. Y, no hay posibilidad de organizar las corporaciones locales, sin un ideal que guíe los afanes de sus lectores y unos conocimientos que se an garantía de acierto en gestió. Este libro…persigue el propósito de interesar a las gentes en los problemas municipales, de ofrecer a los ediles un compendio de las principales cuestiones de Urbanología, que diariamente han de someterse a su estudio y decisión y, sobre todo, de preparar el ambiente nacional para quien breve puedan traducirse en realidades los ideales que vamos a exponer con el fin de que nuestras futuras ciudades se amolden a las características de nuestro clima, de nuestros usos y costumbres; ciudades para españoles; ciudades nuevas distintas de las que se ven en países extranjeros; ciudades agradables para los que en ellas viven; ciudades sin privilegios; ciudades cristianas, en fin, donde la vida comunal sea grata a la inmensa mayoría de sus pobladores y no regalo para unos pocos a costa de la pesadumbre de los demás.* (Municipal life is the basis of the nation's prosperity. There is no great nation with neglected municipalities, be they weak, clumsy or venal. And, there is no hope of organizing local government without an ideal to guide the efforts of their leaders and some knowledge that will guarantee success in their management. This book, perhaps presumptuous, is aimed at people with an interest municipal problems, to offer councillors a handbook of the main issues of Urbanology (town planning), which daily they have to confront and make decisions about and, above all, to prepare the national environment for the ideals that we are striving to translate into reality, to demonstrate that our future cities adapt to the characteristics of our climate, our uses and customs. Cities for Spaniards, new cities different

to those seen abroad; pleasant cities for those who reside there, cities without privileges, Christian cities – in short, where communal life is agreeable to the majority of people and not a gift for a few at the expense of the suffering of others)[143].

It was a call to arms, even if one tempered by Falange ideology, but then, is not all town planning as much a product of political ideals as of possible technical solutions? It is true to say that Alomar's prize-winning plan for Palma was drawn up *before* these kinds of ideologies gained currency under the Franco regime but much of the building, of course, took place post-war. Could this be one of the reasons – alongside the economic and political reasons we have already alluded to – why only three of his reforms were completed, the remaining nine failing to meet the new circumstances of city governance?

Alomar's early experience of Palma

Following his concern for the aesthetic of earlier times might it not also be worth considering the influence of the urban environment in which Alomar had been brought up, a notion raised earlier? His love of the small town of Muro, where he spent many holidays, was one of the older towns of Mallorca, characterised by a rather irregular street plan with small houses facing onto the streets, houses mostly having Arabic and medieval origins in terms of their layout and design. Studded through this townscape would have been the townhouses of the local senyors including that of the Alomar family. Alomar's memories of the 1920s – his adolescent years – spent in Muro were of *un vertader museu d'aquitectura vernacula* (a veritable museum of vernacular architecture) which was in many ways unique, a product of its local geography with houses built of the marès blocks – *pedra arenisca fina local llavorada amb una admirable perfecció* (fine local sandstone worked with an admirable finish). It would have been an environment of small spaces and close proximities. However, the social-spatial structure continued to reflect the divisions between the senyors and the small-sized middle class and the poorer classes in terms of housing and the locations of the townhouses of the better off, set in distinct streets, a reflection of the continuity and timelessness seen in the 1920s[144]. Would these patterns perceived by a schoolboy come to influence his future planning theories? Much later in life, he was to write a detailed analysis of the 'planned' towns of the Ordinances of Jaume II where historical and planning themes would coalesce[145].

His second urban experience as a young man was that part of Palma where his parents lived and where he went to school. Sadly, his memoir does not begin until 1939 when he was aged 29 so our assessment of the influence of Palma's streets and buildings is mostly conjecture. We know that he spent much of his time in the *casc antich*, and especially in his barrio to the east of the Cathedral, a truly medieval townscape even to this day. But it was a city on the verge of change in the first three decades of the 20thC:

> *La vieja ciudad de Palma, con unas murallas imperiales, con sus peraltados lienzos, con destacadas puertas y orgullosos escudos, que perfectamente delimitaban una ciudad tranquila, donde la paz se estaba desvaneciendo, asi como el orden sosegado, la vida apacible se estaba rompiendo, y el que su generacion, a pesar de no ver la demolición, en gran parte percibio el desbordamiento de antiguo recinto, sepultados los baluates, con un afran de reforma en momentos de verdadera anarquia...* (The ancient city of Palma, whose undulating stretches of imperial walls with their fine gateways and proud escutcheons had perfectly contained a tranquil town, was gradually losing its tranquillity, its orderly functioning and

its peaceful rhythm of life. His generation, though not witnessing actual demolition, for the most part, recognised that the city was overflowing its ancient limits beyond its fortifications a consequence of an appetite for reform at a genuinely anarchic period...)[146].

No doubt in his teens he would have discussed these changes and the many plans being proposed in the period before the Civil War with his more liberal friends and family, and fellow architects. He could not have failed to have seen the modernisation and growth of the city's economy in the 1920s and more especially in the 1930s. New manufacturing industries such as textiles, footwear and metalworking, in many cases witnessing a shift to larger units of production. New and expanding services activities some of which were related to tourism but which also saw a rise in consumerism and personal services, all of which led to a relative growth in population even before the 'boom' of the late 1950s.

Palma Population	1900	1910	1920	1930	1940	1950	1960
Absolute nos.	63937	67544	77418	88262	114405	136814	159084
Index (1900=100)	100	105.64	121.08	138.04	178.93	213.98	248.81

Fig 21   Population change in Palma, 1900-1960, Source: Barcelo Pons B (1970): Evolución reciente y estructura actual de la poblacion en la Islas Baleares. Madrid, CSIC, Tables 1 and 4.

We have already referred to the numerous plans for the reform of the city brought forward by others between the demolition of the walls and Alomar's time in Palma during the Republic and the Civil War which the local press publicised. Alomar's plan of 1940 was a response to all these forces: personal and professional experience, national and local political pressure, and contemporary planning theories.

7

After the reform of Palma: an American interlude

By the early 1940s, Alomar had become tired of the immediate after-effects of the Spanish Civil War, particularly the confusing political state that included the clashes between various groups within the government. The tensions between the fascist-leaning Nationalists led by the Falange and the other cliques – the monarchists, the Francoists etc, Alomar found difficult but it was the economic policies based on autarky and national self-sufficiency, the emphasis on industrial development and above all, the shortages of essential raw materials and imports that frustrated him most. In the construction sector, for example, licenses for private works carried out by architects in Palma declined from 739 in 1940 to only 128 in 1945, largely the result of the shortage of building materials. Industrial employment fell from 39% of the working population in 1935 to 18% by the end of the 1940s, compensated somewhat by the rises in the tertiary sector. He recounts that life in Spain had become untenable thanks to these post-civil war conditions. The island was particularly affected by these shortages and through much of the 1940s, it was close to starvation. Ration cards became obligatory, queues for food became the norm and the birth rate dropped noticeably[147]. At the same time, political repression continued accompanied by 'legal' appropriations of property and goods from the regime's opponents. These stresses may not have been so evident in Mallorca as in some parts of the Peninsula but a strong resentment for the execution of respected figures such as Emili Darder, the continuing imprisonment of more liberal leaders, the general air of censorship and control, all led to a depressing atmosphere that an energetic professional like Alomar found increasingly difficult to accept. Here was an architect/planner who was to make a significant mark on Palma's townscape and economic future but who found his plans for reform only partially being acted upon. He found the repressive regime made his life '*insoportable*'. The architectural work he had been undertaking for the March family at Lloseta and Sa Vall was well underway or largely complete. He had reached an impasse. As a planner, too, he was more and more aware of his limited education in this growing field for which there was no Spanish source. He was acutely aware of movements in Europe and North America that ought to benefit Spanish practice. It was against this uncongenial background that he began to look abroad for his own personal development. With Europe still at war until 1945, and thereafter likely to be engaged a programme of reconstruction, his gaze turned inevitably to the Americas, and particularly to the USA.

Relations between the USA and Franco's Spain were not exactly cordial even though the Americans were anxious to take advantage of possible new trading relationships. Alomar needed to find an entrée to the American higher education system that he hoped would provide a solution to his aspirations in planning. This was to come via Mallorca's historic links with emigration to another island in the 1920s and '30s and more importantly from his family connections to this island – Puerto Rico – a Spanish speaking territory commanded by the USA since the war of 1898 and hence, a possible doorway to the United States. His route to the USA via Puerto Rico was motivated by this family connection but nonetheless, it seems a curious choice. Puerto Rico was in effect a true colony of the United State. Invaded by American troops and heavily bombarded by the US Navy in 1898, the island was initially run by the military. Like Cuba, it was seen by the Americans as a place for plunder with the rich soils soon taken over by American corporate interest for the production of sugar cane, funded by American capital but worked by the island's peasantry at wages at half the level of the mainland, workers who lived in the most appalling rural conditions. With little political representation and suffering racial intolerance Puerto Rican society was governed by some of the most inept and corrupt governors appointed by US presidents including in the 1930s Franklin Delano Roosevelt.

In 1937 he had married his cousin María Angela Esteve Bianchi from Puerto Rico. Her father had emigrated from Artá in Mallorca in the late 19C and married into an influential local landowning and commercial family, the Bianchi[148].

Fig 22   The family home of Alomar's wife located in Mayagüez in the west of Puerto Rico, a substantial mansion of the 1920s designed by Sabás Honoré, one of Puerto Rico's most famous architects. Source: Pinterest.

Alomar had access to considerable wealth from this source and it gave him a 'colonial home' for him and his family. When his wife's income was added to his growing professional income, this enabled him to follow a career not encumbered by too many concerns for money; this Caribbean source continued for many years after his death (see below)[149]. Because of his wife's Puerto Rican (and therefore American) citizenship – and probably her social standing – she was able to obtain an American passport. His time in Puerto Rico was to prove significant in the development of his planning ideas thanks to the American administrators working there, something that will be examined in some detail later. It was while staying in Puerto Rico with his wife and daughter that he decided to go to the USA in search of exposure to American theories and practices the best source of which was likely to be American universities. Being a man with some understanding of the hierarchy of American colleges at that time, he drew up a list of places in which he might study; they were all highly rated schools that offered courses in town planning, architecture and the history of art: Harvard, Columbia, NYU, Princeton[150], Yale and MIT which he initially referred to as 'Boston Tech'. Constrained choices, then, saw him select the Massachusetts Institute of Technology (MIT) in 1945 to undertake a course in town planning as a 'special student' paying $300 for his fees with living costs estimated at $600 – he and his family stayed at the eminent Miles Standish Hotel in Boston[151].

Alomar may have won the prize for his town plan for Palma but he had little experience in this field. At this time there was no university in Spain offering a full course in planning. What planning higher education there was formed part of the curriculum of schools of architecture and engineering. It would appear, then, that he went abroad to receive some instruction in what was a relatively new field in his own country, despite Cerdá, Castro and Cort's inspiring beginnings. It would be interesting to know if he was encouraged in this venture by the authorities in Palma's city council. However, even in the USA town planning was still in its infancy as a free-standing academic subject although that country had a longer history of it as part of architecture programmes. The first American school offering bachelor degrees in town planning was that at MIT but this course had only begun within the Department of Architecture in 1934. The Harvard School of City Planning had had to close in 1936 due to a lack of funds[152]. By 1945 – the year Alomar attended – the MIT school had produced only 17 graduates in planning; there was a longer history of Master's degrees in City Planning with 159 being awarded between 1921 and 1945. It should be noted, however, that Alomar did not take a full degree programme, indeed he was able to attend for only part of one term in the Spring of 1945; he arrived late for the start of term hoping to perhaps make up for lost time in the subsequent Summer School. That proved not to be possible[153]. In an earlier letter to P. M. Chalmers at MIT from Puerto Rico Alomar had said from the beginning that, *I am not after academic grades as I do not intend to practice in the US, (I) just wish to get familiar with the last word in architecture and city-planning in which 'Boston Tech' is so famous*. All he wanted, he said, *'was a simple certificate for attending such courses'*[154]. He took only parts of course IV-B which began in Year Two after undergraduates had taken a general first year based on architecture. The course catalogue for 1945 describes the curriculum succinctly:

> . . . *Course IV-B includes preparatory subjects in engineering and in the natural and social sciences with the object of developing in the student an understanding of basic principles and relationships. The content of the third and fourth years is primarily technical in character with emphasis on the economic and administrative aspects, but with considerable time given to the working out in the drafting room of actual problems in the field of city and regional planning*[155].

His curriculum contained units in urban sociology, economics, law, statistics and business management as well as city and regional planning. There was a possibility of writing a dissertation but there is no record of his having done so. He was enrolled as a 'special student' in the department, the only one in that year and the only Spanish student at the University! In fact, under war-time conditions, the faculty at MIT elected to restrict the entrance of overseas undergraduate students to 130.

In his annual report for 1944-45, the Head of the School of Architecture and Planning drew attention to the visiting lecturers at the School. The Calendar of Events for the Cambridge Discussion Group and MIT students for April/May 1945 included a most influential figure in the American town planning movement, Lewis Mumford, who spent the week of May 7 1945, at MIT. He gave two seminars – one for architects and one for planners – and gave two lectures on city planning and population[156]. In addition, he met with students on an individual basis, a unique opportunity that was to impress Alomar; in his later work, he was to refer to Mumford with some enthusiasm. Another figure was Charles-Edward Amory Winslow, the eminent bacteriologist who had founded the Harvard School of Public Health; he also gave some lectures which, given Alomar and Palma's concern for urban sanitation, may have proved insightful. David Lilienthal, chairman of the Tennessee Valley Authority, was another influential visitor[157]. Throughout his life, Alomar claimed he was influenced by the work of these figures but his contact with them must have been rather meagre.

It would be misleading to think that Alomar 'graduated' in Town Planning despite this note in his autobiography: *'En junio o julio me gradué (sic) en City and Regional Planning, con la calificación, muy amable por parte de Adams, de H, o sea, passed with honor'* – his emphasis. (In June or July I graduated in City and Regional Planning, with the qualification, very kindly given by Adams, of H, or that is to say, passed with honour). This 'qualification' is not quite what it appears. The Records Office of MIT confirmed his non-graduate status:

> '... we can say with certainty that he did not attend within any degree program nor did he continue on to earn a degree from MIT. It is very possible (highly likely) that the notation "qualification...passed with honor" could have referred to the grading system in place at that time. A grade of "H" was a shorthand reference to "passed with honor", and is equivalent to the letter grade of 'A' as we know it now. This grading system was replaced with the more familiar (in the United States) "A, B, C, D, F" etc letter-grading system in January 1951'. (Personal email to author from MIT Archive Service, 28 April 2014).

It is interesting to speculate as to why Alomar referred to himself as 'graduating', a notion that unfortunately many subsequent writers have apparently accepted and which Alomar does not seem to have disputed[158]. In 1948 Alomar published a study he had undertaken while at MIT on planning in the USA, probably a class project, certainly not an award-bearing thesis or dissertation[159].

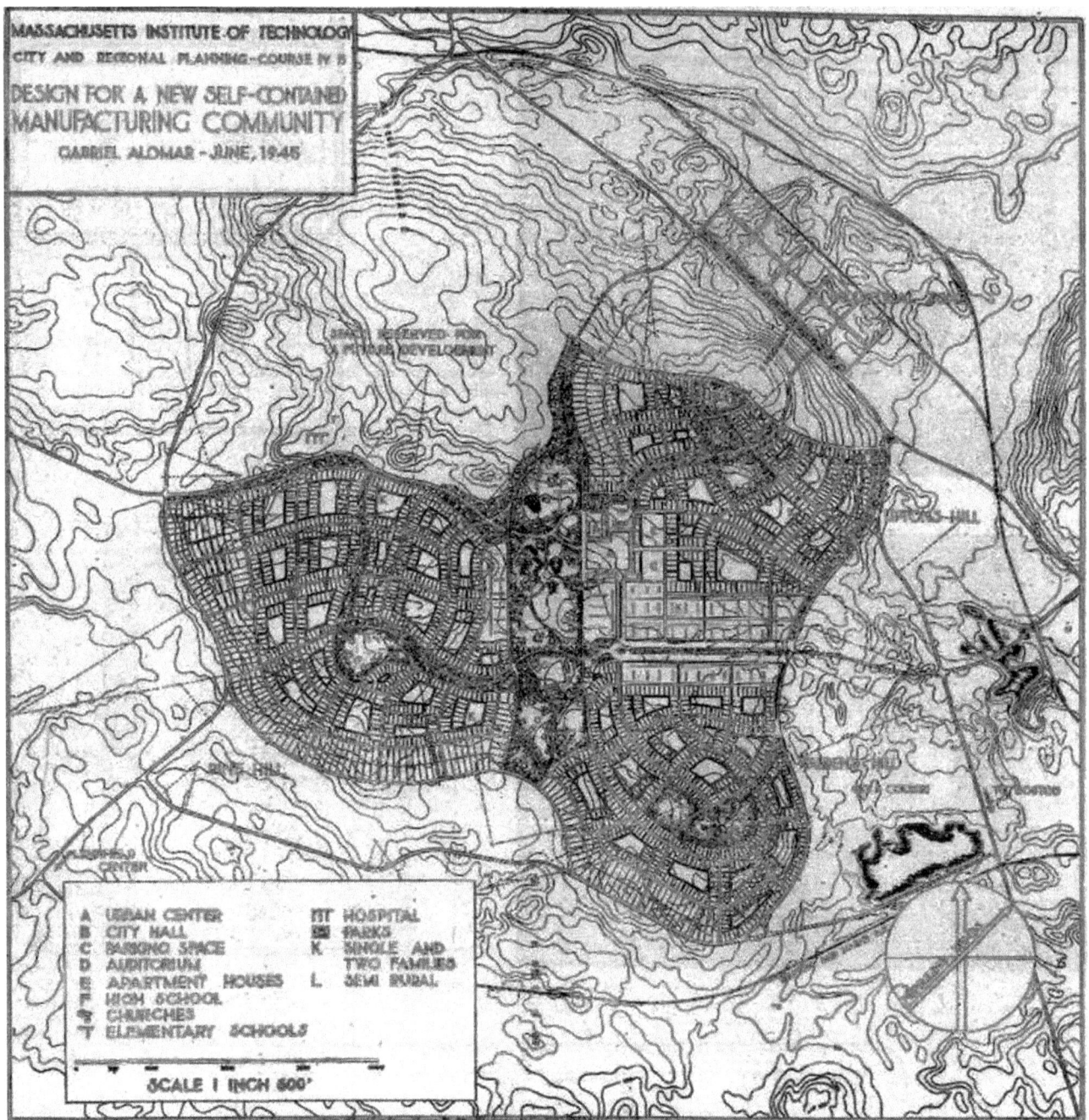

Fig 23   Alomar's plan for a manufacturing community drawn when a student at MIT, 1945. Source: Revista Naciónal de Arquitectura, 1948, 74, 56-59.

What was the effect of this sojourn in Massachusetts on Alomar's thinking? It was certainly a very active period in the development of planning ideas and practice in the United States at that time. To what extent was he aware of the searing differences of opinion on the planning of New York between Thomas Adams, the regional plan's director (and father of his tutor at MIT, F J Adams) and the Regional Planning Association of America and especially the opinions of Lewis Mumford – with its essentially Fabianist outlook?[160]. In his biography, he spends quite some time describing the cultural life of the Boston area in the Spring of '45, its art and music and conversing with students of the *rooseveltiano-socialista* persuasion. The Head of the School of Architecture and Planning during Alomar's short stay was William W. Wurster[161] but the tutor to have most influence on him was the director of the planning section, Frederick Adams (1901-1979) whose remarkable father, Thomas Adams (1871-1940), was a pioneer in the garden city movement and the first manager of Letchworth, later helping to found the British, Canadian and American Institutes of Planning[162]. His son, Frederick Johnstone Adams, had studied at the Architectural Association in London in the 1920s and graduated from Columbia University, New York in 1928. He served at MIT until 1964 helping to establish its first professional course in planning, later serving as Head of Department. He became a leading figure in American town planning. In addition to F. J. Adams was Draveaux Bender (1910-1986), who had graduated in architecture at MIT in 1933, held a Masters degree from Harvard, and gave classes in planning. Later he was to become an important planning consultant. Clearly, Alomar was influenced by these, especially in the urban sociological aspects, a theme he was to develop in-depth some years later in his book *Sociología urbanística* (1961). In the case of Lewis Mumford, it is difficult to assess his influence as he was, of course, a stern critic of the New York Regional Plan drawn up in the 1930s by Thomas Adams.

Although Alomar states that this interlude was to change his life, on balance, his experience at MIT can only have been somewhat limited insofar as the technical aspects of town planning were concerned. Admittedly he supplemented his classes with a programme of reading both at MIT and later in the New York Public Library but his exposure to the more up-to-date ideas that he desired before he set out for the USA can only have been relatively superficial. In 1968 the Dean of the Graduate School at MIT undertook a survey of graduates of twenty years ago. Alomar replied – rather late – in 1970, it is worth quoting:

> *The value of my experience at MIT in the years 1945-60 (sic) has been immense. When I arrived my ideas of city planning were only physical. With our admired and loved professor Frederick Adams, I followed a course on City and Regional Planning... At the same time, without any official qualification, I attended lectures of urban sociology (Prof Greely?) and I discovered a new field. This was the basis of my three books... these rather modest books it has been recognised contributed substantially to a change of mind of city-planners in Spain and South America*[163].

As we shall see, it is more likely that there was a large element of autodidacticism in Alomar's planning education in the United States that also came from many visits in later life.

But ideas from the United States were not the only ones to influence Alomar at this time. Many outsiders have referred to the rather poor level of central administration under Franco. It was said to have been characterised by inefficiency, cronyism and a need to please El Caudillo and his satraps. In the next chapter, when Alomar had been recruited to the civil service, there is some contrary evidence in the contents of *La Revista de Estudios de la Vida Local*. This would appear to show that those in the Institute of the Study of Local Administration – in the field of town planning and housing at least – were kept well informed of developments abroad and in all parts of Spain[164]. Conferences were regularly held, for example. One of the frequent and most pressing problems in the 1940s and '50s was that of post-war reconstruction in the damaged *regiones devastada*. Another topic that demonstrates the improving spirit of the time was a concern for the quality of housing in urban areas, linked to the age-old problem of overcrowding and public health. All of this is evidence that the Franco regime was slowly responding to the social needs of the country by developing a more technocratic bureaucracy, replacing, at this early stage some of the influence of the more ideological Falange[165]. Alomar's papers on planning in Puerto Rico, which are discussed in the next chapter, are clear evidence of the benefit of his North American and Caribbean sojourn widening his Spanish experience.

It is difficult to judge if the modernizing influences at the centre (Madrid) were translated into action at the periphery (Palma). Spain, after all, had few disposable resources at this time for such things as urban planning but like many totalitarian regimes, it had a penchant for the large-scale project, the most notable of which were the schemes for barrages, reservoirs and water supply which were increasingly 'municipilised' in the regulatory framework established by the Franco regime. Town planning appears to have been similarly attractive politically but most of its energy went into the restoration of the war-damaged areas of the principal cities. Although many major cities brought forward plans for their re-development, few were put into practice on the ground, partly the result of the continuing focus on their local authorities, part of what Juan Dávila has called the dialectic between the municipalities and the state in designing national urban structures[166].

Nonetheless, the 'state' in Franco's Spain under Falangist influence especially in the early years, was attracted to the idea of 'planning' in general. For example, the Instituto Nacional de Colonización (INC) was established during the Civil War itself to reorganize rural settlements in relation to agricultural production; good examples were the New Villages in the La Vera district of Extremadura with a focus on the development of tobacco growing, part of the move towards autarky. A second aim was to try to prevent drift from the land, reducing the rate of urbanisation. The 'rural man' was the idealised Spanish Man of the Falangists[167]. The destruction of large parts of Spanish cities by both sides in the Civil War gave rise to two post-war committees for the devastated regions and for reconstruction. In the urban realm, the 'centre' may have encouraged the large-scale reform of many of Spain's cities – a symbolic as well as practical move – often via their local 'controllers' such as Civil Governors – but the 'local' town hall had access to very finite design and material resources. Despite paying lip service to centralisation, the local authority retained much of its political primacy but there was a distinct tension between the centre's hopes and aspirations – hardly amounting to an ideology – and a municipality's competence in this field. Many urban plans were drafted but translating 'ideology' into concrete built forms created considerable anxiety. The urban authorities were dependent upon private capital from the construction sector for any progress and without a powerful and flexible banking sector credit and loans would not be forthcoming. In Mallorca, much of the poor design and layout of the new coastal resort settlements built from the late 1950s onwards was as much attributable to the lack of a decent planning technocracy and infrastructure as to corruption. As we have observed in Palma only three of Alomar's twelve project proposals received support initially.

8
Alomar in Madrid

Alomar's attraction to Madrid is, at one level, easily understood. It represented recognition of his experience in Palma, Puerto Rico and the United States. Few young Spanish planners of his generation would have had direct contact with their American contemporaries, for example. Such a move would give him access to the 'national stage' and an acknowledgement of his undoubted talents. One assumes that his invitation to join, what was in effect, Spain's civil service was flattering to his ego as well as his perception of it as an advance in his career. However, in 1950s Spain we are dealing with a highly politicised State in which certain forces, originally emanating from the Falange, that may have conflicted with his own more liberal views. Paul Preston tells us that it was almost obligatory to join the Movement if one joined the country's bureaucracy, rather as it was at that time in the Soviet Union to be a member of the Communist Party. We shall see that tensions between Alomar and his new employers would prove difficult for him to reconcile especially towards the end of the 1950s decade. At times his loyalty to the Falangist philosophies would be questioned. Perhaps *his* interpretation of the Catholic faith which allegedly was at the heart of much of Franco's Spain was at odds with that of his employer.

During the early years after the publication of his Palma plan in book form, his return from the USA and following the publication of the *Theory of the City* in 1947, Alomar was in communication with Carlo Ruiz del Castillo, the head of the local administration department in Madrid's central government among whose many functions was responsibility for *urbanismo* at the national level. The establishment of its *Instituto de la Vida Local* had been applauded at the 1941 conference on planning and housing. Alomar was already part of a wider group of planners and civil servants that included Carlo Ruiz del Castillo himself and the influential Pedro Bidagor, the *jefe* of the planning section[168]. They formed part of what may initially have been an informal group of specialists to examine the need for planning legislation that would cover the whole of the country to counteract the historical role and responsibilities of the plethora of municipalities. A second pressing issue for nearly all the cities of Spain immediately after the civil war was that of *chabolismo*, the growth of slums particularly on the edge of cities, similar to the *bidonvilles* of France. A policy for housing was to dominate town planning for the next fifty years.

It would appear that from these common interests Alomar was recruited to the Institute for the Study of Local Administration[169]. Here his duties would focus on the study of town planning, the dissemination of its modern ideas throughout Spain and the education and training of town planners. He always maintained, however, that his main interest was in the social aspects of urban development; eventually, he had the title of Professor of Urban Sociology in the Institute according to the title page of his book on this subject. He was well connected socially and at this stage had sympathy for certain aspects of the post-Civil War regime. He was, for example, at that time more committed to the idea of the nation-state and to Spanish nationalism with much less sympathy for the 'political regionalism' that had, and still does, dog Spain. He can be seen as one of the growing numbers of technocrats recruited by the Civil Service. However, there was considerable pressure to recruit those in sympathy with the regime and who were even more likely to be friends of politicians and the military. For example, Pedro Muguzura – who was head of the architecture section of the technical services of the Falange and of the committee for the defence of national artistic heritage – was a personal architect to Franco and a friend of General Jordan. Such influential people ensured that the 'correct' persons were appointed:

> *En la seleccion de los arquitectos que no accedian a traves de los cupos reservados puede observarse que tienen importancia los criterios de familiaridad, amistad, lealtad y recomendaciones personales. Un guia esencial de todo el proceso de seleccion de tecnicos llevado a cabo en la posguerra.* (In the selection of architects who were not recruited through reserved posts, it can be shown that the criteria of familiarity, friendship, loyalty and personal recommendations are important. It is an essential guide to all the process of selection of technicians carried out in the post-war period)[170].

Muguzura saw that recruiting the 'right' sort of people to the service of the State was the best means of winning the peace after winning the war, particularly in areas of priority such as reconstruction in the Devasted Regions.

Perhaps an even more important figure was the emergence of José Luis de Arrese y Marga (Arrese), a hardline fascist and devout Catholic, who had qualified with a doctorate in architecture in 1923 but who had rarely practised; Alomar saw him only as a politician.

Fig 24   José Luis Arrese Marga, a leading figure in the Falange, a hard-line fascist supporter of the Nazis, made Minister of Housing by Franco in 1957. Source: Reconstrucción, 1940.

Azpilicueta believes he reduced the profession and its work to *'mascara propagandista'* (disguised propaganda) subordinated to the needs of the New State[171]. We shall see his perverse influence when we consider the development of national planning legislation later in this chapter. Bidagor and Alomar acted as a counterweight to these once-powerful Falangist cadres, not that the Caudillo took much interest in such matters[172].

Alomar's 'theory' book had been published in 1947 so that his work was becoming well known on more than the provincial scene. In the first half of the 1950s, he began publishing a series of articles in the Institute's *Revista de Estudios de la Vida Local* (REVL) in which the benefit of his earlier stay in Puerto Rico soon became apparent. Such publications were an opportunity for Alomar to demonstrate his first-hand knowledge of some American planning ideas. Published in 1951 his first article draws attention to the history of planning in those countries affected by the Second World War, noting the importance of the role of the State, a notion that resonated in Franco's Spain but with a different frequency[173]. For a small island like Puerto Rico, it was the colonial experience – Spanish, and American after 1898 – that was to form the context for any planning. For Alomar this kind of historical setting was always important; a long preamble on the island's history provides this, although he says little about the many insurrections by Puerto Ricans against the colonial rule of Spain – and the USA.

His second context was the demographic history of the island especially the tremendously high density of population at 247/Km2 in 1950; at this time Belgium's figure was 270, the highest in the world, and UK's was 189 – all underpinned by a very high birth rate of about 40/1000 (France's figure was 14. 6/1000). Citing poverty and the divisive social structure as probable causes, Alomar demonstrates the influence of Lewis Mumford to whose ideas he had been exposed at MIT. Indicative of a traditional Catholic view, however, Alomar points to the importance of *'la noble institución familiar monogámica'* rather than birth control as a means of limiting population. While emigration had relieved pressure somewhat the main response to population pressure was urbanisation: 14. 6 per cent were living in urban areas in 1899 but this rose by a factor of three to 42. 1% by 1950. By the 1930s four large American corporations owned half of the good sugar lands and introduced American methods of production, reducing the demand for labour. Given the terrible working conditions and low wages, it was little wonder that city life and its economic and political advantages were seen as solutions to the poverty of rural areas[174]. Among the many disadvantages of overcrowding in the island's cities, especially in the capital Sant Juan, Alomar saw the lack of social space as significant. For many Puerto Ricans, the answer lay in emigration to the United States[175].

In reviewing previous planning statements of the 1930s he notes the significance of Rexford G Tugwell as governor of the island, a specialist in economic and urban planning and advisor to Roosevelt[176], and of Alfred Bettman[177] the defender of zoning policies in the United States. Tugwell had been Director of the New York Planning Commission whose recommendations had been defeated by Robert Moses (New York's most influential urban and highway developer) because of their advocacy of green open spaces in city plans. Perhaps he was given the governorship by Roosevelt as compensation. It would appear Alomar met Tugwell whilst in Puerto Rico and was to be influenced by some of his ideas. Although Tugwell had created the Puerto Rico Planning, Urbanization and Zoning Board in 1942, he was a centralist as far as the island was concerned and refused to accept ideas for the delegation of planning matters to provincial cities. One of the more intransigent aspects of progress in town planning in Spain since the 1920s was the conflict between the *municipios* and the central government in Madrid. Maybe Alomar drew a parallel here between the primate position of San Juan and his native Palma and Mallorca.

Alomar accepts that to some, 'planning' might be seen as a socialist concept -'...*una coaccion positiva y un control de las actividades en el uso y desarrollo de los bienes de su propiedad*' ('positive coercion and control of the activities in the use and development of the value of your property ') but, of course, such centralism is antithetical to the American federal political system. How, then, to introduce planning laws into Puerto Rico, an American colony? On the other hand, for Alomar rural/urban planning is not to be confused with Marxian centralist planning – '*El planeamiento urbano-rural es una necesidad cientifica por encima de los vaivenes de las ideas politicas circunstanciales.*' (Urban-rural planning is a scientific necessity of greater importance than the vagueries of current political ideas'), something of a naïve view perhaps, particularly at that time in Spain when nearly all policies were highly politicised[178]).

Alomar saw as important the distinction between American (as in Puerto Rico) planning practices and those of, say, France, Spain and their former overseas territories, with Americans suspicious of restrictions on personal freedoms. However, urban planning has to be seen in the context of national spatial organization that is, the integration of urban and rural spaces for planning purposes (a geographical continuum) whereas in 'Code Napoleon' countries distinctions were drawn between 'urban' and 'rural' spaces as separate identities. American control of Puerto Rican space (technically ruled by the American military until 1952 when it became an 'Estado Libre Asociado' or commonwealth) it adopted approaches to planning that could be different from those in the mother country but without taking sufficient account of history and culture: there may be a parallel here with experience in British India. One might also ask if the American 'colonial' authorities saw urban planning, particularly of the principal and primate city St Juan before the 1930s, as one approach to quelling local political aspirations.

Lastly, Alomar sets out a trilogy that will figure significantly in much of his future work: '*Ciudad, Barrio y Hogar – un habitat digno, es decisivo en la formación del indivíduo.*' (City, neighbourhood and home – a worthwhile habitat, is decisive in the formation of the individual'). He sees the modern city as massive and complex, not built at the human scale – another idea he pursues – together with his socio-ecological ideas that link home, neighbourhood and the wider city. He is critical of the impact of North American planning concepts on what is essentially a Spanish colonial city (St Juan de Puerto Rico) where the '*sentimiento de comunidada*' (community loyalty) is an important cultural element. He warns his Spanish colleagues of the possible danger of applying American models to the wider Spanish urban environment. In his writings about Puerto Rico, Alomar seemed unaware of the deep resentment of many islanders to American control of nearly all aspects of life, that is, the treatment of Puerto Rico as a colony.

Similarly, Alomar was also concerned that Spain should learn from other experiences elsewhere, particularly from its European neighbours who shared a similar culture. In 1952 he attended the 21st Congress of the International Federation of Housing and Town Planning held in Lisbon[179]. Although this organization had existed for 30 years this was the first time in ten years that Spain had been represented, largely for political reasons. It is important to note Spain's participation: it was slowly being accepted again amongst the international community. It was also an opportunity for him to express his conviction that urban places should be distinguished from rural ones, a theme he was anxious to put at the centre of the *Ley de Suelo* that he helped draw up for the Spanish government in 1956.

The main theme of the conference was *política del suelo urbano* (policies for urban land-use) and in particular housing types and neighbourhood planning. For Alomar, as *rapporteur* for Spain, what he brought away was the need for Spain to have proper planning laws like those developed or being developed in most European counties by revising its existing legislation. In particular, Alomar argued for Spain to shift its focus from housing towards planning the environment in which houses are to be located, something sadly missing from the then current regulations. This was probably the result of right-of-centre ideologues who saw housing as central to their view of the city. A land-use law would help avoid the current development of suburbs in what were, in effect, rural environments avoiding what he terms *zonas híbridas* (hybrid places), neither urban nor rural, then emerging in the ensanches in Spanish provincial cities.

To reinforce our view that the Spanish bureaucracy, at least, was more knowledgeable about international developments in planning than previously thought, we find in the same issue of this journal (REVL) reports on two significant activities: a review of the 1947 Town and Country Planning Act in the UK and of a visit in 1952 of 37 members of the British Town and Country Planning Association to Spain led by Frederick Osborn[180]. Although this group undertook field visits to eight Spanish cities it did not include Palma[181]. This was the beginning of a long period of association between Alomar and the planning system and legislation emerging in post-war Britain. He saw in the two town planning associations of the UK, organisations whose principles were in harmony with many of his own. He became a frequent correspondent of Frederick Osborn and many of the planners associated with the New Town movement.

In his role as one of the important figures in town planning in the Instituto de la Vida Local, Alomar was at the forefront of trying to disseminate ideas about town planning through Spanish national and local government. We have seen the influence of British, French and Austrian ideas on his own work in Palma and the ways in which he was later influenced by American planning theory. What he advocated, in particular, was Spain's need for a clear planning code, a set of 'rules' that had legal status to guide individual cities' planning aspirations within a national context, clearly influenced by Britain's Town and Country Planning Act of 1947, French ideas of 'amenagement' and American zoning laws. From the late 1930s, he was in communication with the International Federation for Housing and Town Planning, a body dominated by British interests including George Peplar, C. B. Purdom and Donald C L Murray, its general secretary. It was an organization like many scientific bodies of its time that had been in contact with planners in Nazi Germany. He possessed a copy of the Regional Plan Bulletin of the Regional Planning Association of New York of 1944 on urban expansion and he attended the international congress on the plan for Lisbon held in 1952 to which notable Swedish and British contributions were made. Equally noteworthy was his correspondence with Frederick Osborn, publishing an article praising British town planning, especially the early garden-city movement, in Town and Country Planning in December 1956 which Osborn edited[182]. In 1955 he had met with Frank Laing of the London County Council's planning division to discuss New Towns. In parallel with these international connections, Spain had begun to develop its network for town planning via its Federation for Housing and Town Planning founded by César Cort which was referred to earlier[183].

Given his experience and these contacts, together with his position in the Instituto, it was not surprising that Alomar was invited to be involved with the commission for the *anteproyecto* (blueprint) that was to draw up the ground rules for a new national planning law for Spain. In a hand-written note Alomar gives his original title for such a law – *un ley regimentu del Suelo su lo ga??* (illegible) *se verificere en la Edificacion*, indicating the need to link 'plan' with 'building'[184]. Members included Carlos Ruiz – the Director of IEAL, Pedro Bidagor – Jefe Nacional de Urbanismo (Head of national planning), and Gaspar Blein the director of planning for Madrid, the last two having been influential in the approval of Alomar's 1943 plan for Palma; Alomar had one of the lesser roles as one of four members of the secretariat. He felt that many of his planning ideas found in his 1947 theory book would be used and adopted by the eventual Commission set up to approve the land use law of 1956[185].

The Ley de Suelo was finally published in the *Revue de Estudios de la Vida Local* in 1956. The minister Blas Perez Gónzález set out a preamble at the beginning of the document emphasising Spain's slow increases in population, especially urban population, and its likely future growth, noting that at that time only 37% of Spain's population lived in towns of more than 10, 000, considerably below the proportion in more northerly European countries. Spain would need a planning system that reflected its own, unique geography and history. He also reminded his readers that a section of his ministry, the Jefatura de Urbanismo, had been created in July 1949 to bring forward a national plan for urbanisation. He wrote:

> *El cambio de los tiempos, en su eterno acaecer,va impondiendo a los hombres que tienen la responsiblilitad del Poder la obligación de afrontar los problem que la realidad nos ofrece para encauzarlos hacia una meta común: el major bienestar posible de la comunidad que riger* (In these ever changing times, as is always the case, it is the responsibility of men in power to deal with the problems that reality sends us, to steer them towards a common goal: the best welfare of the community they serve)[186].

In the conflict between private property and the collective needs of society referred to earlier he noted that the former is, *una institución básica en la concepcion cristiana de la vida* (an institution basic to the Christian view of life) The key proposal was the division between urban land and rural land to regulate the spread of built-up areas into the countryside while giving special consideration to the needs of Las Grandes Ciudades.

When later reviewing past attempts at previous legislation in 1969 – including the 1956 Act – Miguel Ribas i Piera, the author of the laws that succeeded it – noted that town plans in the decade after 1949 had two characteristics: an element of *racionalismo* that was widely resented and secondly, an emphasis on conservation and traditionalism – even folklore – that highlighted localities, neighbourhoods and organic groupings in cities, as exemplified by Alomar's 1940s plan for Palma. When Bidagor and the team in Madrid came to draw up the Ley de Suelo he was obviously influenced by its historical evolution. After all, he, Bidagor, had been advocating the need for national legislation since the late 1920s. It was inevitably a product of its time reflecting the political economy of Spain under Franco before the structural reforms of 1959. Legislation could be laid down but who was to pay for the town plans and the cities that would emerge from them under its aegis: Centre or Periphery?[187]

Much depended on how the *Ley* was to be administered. A typed copy in his archive suggests that Alomar may have been partly responsible for devising this structure[188]. Unsurprisingly a hierarchical structure was proposed arranged provincially with the civil governor at its head, followed by local representatives and administrators below which would be the town councils (*ayuntamientos*) who would be responsible for classifying land (urban and rural, with potential for development), formulating plans at five-year intervals and issuing building licences. Compensation for land compulsorily purchased – a serious criticism locally of Alomar's 1943 plan for Palma – remained a major issue until the law's reform. The act encouraged the development of vacant land within the city or town boundary and at its administrative edge thus recognising the need for expansion. Development i. e. actual building was to be in the hands of the private sector.

A second problem was to be the relationship between housing and planning. The post-civil war era recognised once again the need for additional housing and improvements in hygiene as Spain's birth rate and the drift to the towns accelerated and cities became ever more crowded. However, the political situation of the '40s and '50s meant that housing design was subject to political ideology with the Right insisting on socially mixed structures rather than zoning based on price, something Alomar had sought to address in his 1947 book, The Theory of the City. In fact, housing and planning remained somewhat separate entities until the mid-1970s (see below). This arose largely because of the influence of José Luis Arrese whose position in the hierarchy waned as the far right's influence on policy gave way to the emerging technocracy[189]. However, his friendship with the Caudillo persuaded Franco to establish a new Ministry of Housing in 1957 with him as its head. There were to be four *direcciones generales* each with its own leader, together reflecting the then-current tension between the failing Fet y de las Jons and the growing influence of the technocrats. Housing was to be led by Vicente Mortes Alfonso, a member of Opus Dei with close ties to the private sector. Architecture was headed by José Manuel Brujas Vega, an old compadre of Arrese. Construction had Antonio Carrea Véglison in charge; he was a veteran Falangist, a *vieja camiseta* (lit. an old shirt i. e one of the original members). Lastly, planning was to be headed by the most qualified of the four in his field: Pedro Bidagor, by this time a supporter of Arrese, who had been in charge of urban planning in Madrid in the immediate post-war period and head of the Jefatura Nacional from 1949. In the latter post, he had been embroiled in the controversy, even corruption, over the building of the first skyscrapers in Madrid. This was the directorate with which Alomar was to be associated. He may have been an old friend of Bidagor but he worked with him '*actuaba en el Ministerio con alas muy recortades*' (with very clipped wings)[190]. In retrospect, it is clear that mistrust between the various factions within the directorates – between the far right and the 'new men', many of whom belonged to Opus Dei – helped fashion the Ley de Suelo, one of the reasons why it never received the political support many believed it deserved. This was a time when industrialisation was increasing with a resultant growth of the major urban settlements. Corruption was rife and many green and recreational spaces in cities were taken over by developers for the building of low-quality housing in the ensanches. New forms of town planning were the last thing that builders wanted. Alomar was highly critical of the resultant law and foresaw many of the weaknesses that future critics would point to.

In the 1980 edition of *Teoria de la Ciudad,* Alomar expounded at some length on why the law did not resemble the one he had hoped and worked for. The *anteproyecto* (blueprint) which he had worked on, when raised to a full project for approval, was undermined by lawyers. The Fet y de la Jons members and the corrupt old guard (by this time the remains of Falange influence) shared common opposition to the original *Ley*. He drew an analogy with the making of a motor car: if various parts are changed during design and manufacture, a different model will result. The lawyers who dominated the Cortes had different political agendas, from each other and the law's originators: *Entre sectores confabulados se encontraban el de los notarios y registradores, el de ingenerios civiles, el de los arquitectos y el de los funcionarios locales* (a conspiracy between the lawyers, the civil engineers, the architects and the local officials)[191]. Alomar put much of the blame for its failure (in his opinion) at the door of Arrese, the former Falangist leader who demanded a law that reflected his national socialist ideals rather than the social-democratic culture of the Republic with an emphasis on the Movement's attitude and priority for housing instead of addressing the changing economic and demographic shifts going in Spain's cities at that time. One significant change in housing policy made by Arrese was to transfer more responsibility to the private sector which until then had lain with public authorities[192]. Alomar's ire was particularly reserved for his fellow architects whom he felt *se hicieron los mayores cómplices de la especulación* (became the greatest accomplices of [property] speculation)[193]. His relationship with Pedro Bidagor, the head of the new directorate of planning, had cooled and his vehemence was aimed at him and more especially at the fascist Arrese as Minister.

Alomar became bitterly disillusioned with the national government's failure to adopt this new law and its legal framework in the spirit which he and his planning colleagues intended. Later (1969) he was to write:

> *Regional planning, in Spain, has as its legal basis the Law instituted in 1956 on Land-Ownership and Urban Planning. If this law had been correctly applied, it would have shown itself to be appropriate, effective, up-to-date and capable of solving present-day town planning problems. The trouble is that it provides for a certain number of special regulations, and these, though more than fifteen years have elapsed, have yet to be drawn up. Who is responsible for the delay? One is tempted to accuse the pressure-groups whose interests lie in the direction of chaotic urban development and laisse-faire. No less pernicious is one particular clause whose wording was fatally amended by the Cortès at the last moment. This clause, which, for the 'destroyers of towns,' serves as a convenient Achilles' heel, makes it 'legally possible to approve' areas of special dispensation or in other words exemption from town planning regulations or bye-laws, particularly those regarding scale and proportion...*[194].

Even later in 1980, he thundered:

> *...cuidades que han crecido sin orden ni control, en las cuales unas condiciones de vida verdaderamente humanas son imposibles; muchos de los lugares de nuestras geografia privigilados por la naturaleza, sistematicamente destruiudos; gran parte de nustro patrimoni arqutectonico urbano desaparecido o devalorizado; y el entorno vital de nuestro pueblo, tanto el entorno natural como el entorno construido, irreversiblemente degradado* (... cities that have grown without order or control, in which truly human conditions of life are impossible; many of the places in our geography favoured by nature, systematically destroyed; large parts of our urban architectural heritage disappeared or devalued; and the vital environment of our towns nearly a quarter of a century later, both the natural environment and the built environment, irreversibly degraded[195].

To counterbalance this rather despondent view Fernando de Térán does point out that the Ley de Suelo once adopted did lead to the introduction of a new town planning element, namely the idea of zonification which in turn led to the expansion of the ensanches and the construction of *polígonos* (industrial estates), today a significant land-use in all Spain's major cities[196]. Curiously, Alomar was probably exposed to these peripheral industrial and commercial estates and their associated road systems during his sojourn in the USA in 1945 although they did not begin to appear in his native city until the 1970s and '80s.

Disillusioned, and despite his considerable reservations, Gabriel Alomar undertook to broadcast the new law as widely as possible to other European countries, especially those whose own burgeoning legislation in planning had influenced the 1956 Law. In a resumé entitled 'A new planning Act for Spain', and in which he already describes himself as ' Professor of Urban Sociology' as well as 'architect and town planner', he lists in some detail the major sections of the Ley de Suelo of 1956. This work appeared in a variety of European journals and magazines including the British *Town and Country Planning*.

But soon Alomar decided to turn his attention away from the wranglings within the government and amongst the ranks of the Falange and their competing bureaucracies and to concentrate on his study of the social aspects of planning and the training and education of a future generation of planners who might accept and implement his theories of town planning. Perhaps his lack of patience was to do with the fact that Spanish bureaucracy throughout the 1950s was characterised by too many different ministries being involved in planning, leading to competition and secrecy in the various institutions created in addition to his own, including rural colonization, housing and local administration – and, of course, considerable endemic corruption[197]. The result was that the disparate approaches made the formulation of any national planning almost impossible – *amparada por encargos de ayuntamientos que, por razones personales o politicoas, estaban viniculados a ellos* (as a result each city began to provide its own idiosyncratic plans), for example, Toledo, Zaragoza, Burgos etc[198]. And beneath this factionalism lay the disrupting hand of a declining Falange movement. Nonetheless, slowly Spain began to develop national legislation in which Alomar had played an important part.

Although the preparation for and the drafting of the 1956 Act took up a lot of Alomar's time in Madrid it was clear that he saw his role in the *Instituto* as something more than that of bureaucrat or administrator. His title of professor ensured that teaching and writing were of equal if not greater importance to him. As one of his functions, he identified the need to increase the number and quality of planning staff at all levels so that the objectives of the 1956 Act could be properly implemented particularly at the local level. The IEAL had already begun courses that could lead to the Diploma de Técnico Urbanista in the 1940s, indeed Alomar may have attended one himself in 1944. The First National Congress of Planning (Urbanismo), held on the 3rd November 1959 – a body that Alomar had helped to establish – and was the first such meeting since the signing of the Ley de Suelo in 1956; it was chaired by the national director of planning Pedro Bidagor Lasarte. Alomar welcomed this legislation as the 'the Magna Carta' of planning in Spain. Rather than dwell on the political and legal infighting that lay behind the law, he chose to give a paper outlining what was now required including teaching topography, the need to establish a *fomento* (a professional promotional body) at the national level to integrate all disciplines that planning embraced, the need for a planning journal, the importance of holding regular conferences such as this first one and the need to include planning in the private sector construction industry[199]. Also, he undertook a series of visits to international conferences and congresses, mostly in Europe, a part of the world to which he was drawn, thus broadening his knowledge of comparative town planning in different cultures. He became a prominent figure in this landscape which in turn would see him developing many more links internationally.

Assessing the contribution of Alomar to the Ley de Suelo is not easy as he was part of a team of distinguished architects/planners. His pioneering plans for the reform of Palma, his books on planning, his experience in Puerto Rico and the USA, his numerous contacts abroad had made him an attractive figure to the Instituto and the Franco administration. There were political and critical attacks on the *Ley*, in particular, following the creation of the Ministry of Housing headed by the Falangist Arrese, whose influence was soon waning, which saw many aspects of the law undermined. After some success with a law that led to the clearing of the shanty towns around Madrid and other cities José Luis Arrese faded from his once-influential position in the Falange and in the government. It might also be said, not unreasonably, that the failure of the Ley de Suelo saw the marked decline of Alomar's devotion to town planning. He realised increasingly that the kind of ideological rationale demonstrated by amongst others Juan Luis Arrese was incompatible with his own more liberal philosophy. The Falangist attachment to housing provision over comprehensive town planning made his position in government impossible. Just as he had looked beyond his native Mallorca in the mid-1940s in his search for a broader planning education so by the 1960s he appears to have tired of the political in-fighting in the Civil Service. The struggle between the military's influence and that of the Falange, the Carlists and the monarchists may have declined considerably since its peak in the 1940s and '50s. There was little logic in Franco's appointments and he continued to reward his favourites at any one time with government posts – such as making Arrese Minister for Housing. There was rarely any consistency in the leadership of departments including those concerned with planning and housing. It was not until the emergence of the new technocracy after 1959's Stabilization Plan that a more reasonable set of structures appeared. But by then Alomar had lost a lot of his original enthusiasm for planning in Spain. Much later, in 1968, the Dean of the Graduate School at MIT undertook a survey of the graduates of the previous twenty years. Alomar's eventual late reply in 1970 included the phrase that 'by the '60s I considered myself overpassed by new ideas and planning instruments and I passed to work in my old hobby of ancient architecture…'[200]. It was time to move on. From the early '60s, his work turned more toward particular aspects of the urban environment including the provision of green spaces and conservation. In 1963 he began to work for La Comisaria General del Patrimonio Artístico Nacional; by 1969 he was appointed as its head. A wider European setting attracted him more and he became Spain's representative on many architectural and conservation bodies including the Committee for the European Year of Conservation (Europa), 1973 and, with a wider remit, ICOMOS (International Council on Monuments and Sites)[201]. His contribution to these bodies will be dealt with in the next chapter.

9
ALOMAR AND URBAN CONSERVATION

> Not being able to forget my urban training, I was concerned not only to save the monuments of the past but to save the urban complexes in which the monuments are integrated. This, which today everyone defends, in those years was considered almost utopian... Today, something that I defended in the forties is now understood...that is, that it is necessary to conserve not only the monumental buildings but the districts in which they are set.
>
> Interview of Gabriel Alomar Esteve in the series 'History of contemporary urbanism'. COAM (1989) Biografia de arquitectos urbanistas, *Revista urbanismo,* 105, 8, 91-97

In the second edition of his *Teoria de la Ciudad* (1980), Alomar looked back on planning in Spain and its relation to the broader environment and the historical origins of cities in a highly critical manner covering the thirty-three years since its original publication, clearly indicating that his early feelings for the role of the historic in the urban environment had largely been ignored. And yet, he became one of the pioneers of the urban conservation movement in Spain, a movement that for him was *not* anti-modernist but one which has been 'a central supporting part of the transformation of the built environment in the modern age'. This transition can be traced from an early concern for the preservation of monuments, through restoration to conservation. Its anti-modernist stance initially arose in much of Europe as support for such movements as the Arts and Crafts' endeavours and as part of the opposition to highly functional architectural forms. There was, for him, a linked movement from concern for the condition of monuments to individual buildings to a concern for areas of cities and in some cases for whole cities or towns – the city as monument – as found in the work of Geddes in Scotland and Sitte in Austria, for example. By the second half of the 20C the conservation of buildings, areas of towns and indeed whole landscapes, had become built into emerging town planning regimes[202].

In early 1953 the Institute for Local Administration (IEAL), where Alomar worked, ran a series of courses in the history of urban planning. In the introduction to the text that followed from these courses the authors wrote:

> *Toda agrupación urbana, no nos canseramos de repetirlo, es una creación esencialmente histórica. El técnico urbanista que desconozca o no sienta tal axioma está expuesto a grandes errores: reformará o ampliara la ciudad a caprichio, con grave menosprecio por su pasado. Interrumpida entonces la tradición, se alterará su fisonomia y el ambiente que los siglos la han ido imprimiendo lentamente. No aludimos tan solo a la conservación de sus edificios antiguos, de sus calles y rincones mas bellos y típicos, adjetivo éste del que tanto y tan tópicamente se abusa... busca la continuidad, armonizando los residuos vitales de la existencia préterita con la necesidades del momento presente, y aun con las del futuro, integradas*

en un nuevo y complejo organismo que tenga por sí mismo posibilidades de viabilidad. (Every urban entity, we will not tire of repeating, is an essentially historical creation. The urban technician who does not know or does not feel this axiom is susceptible to making large mistakes: he will reform or expand the city capriciously, with serious contempt for the past. Interrupting tradition will alter its physiognomy and the atmosphere that centuries have shaped over time. We do not allude solely to the preservation of old buildings, streets and the most beautiful and 'typical' corners, often poorly described and therefore so abused… (the planner) seeks continuity, harmonizing the vital remains of the past with the necessities of the present-day, and even with those of the future, integrated into a new and complex organism that has possibilities of new life)[203].

Gabriel Alomar Esteve's work as an architect and a town planner was from the very beginning permeated with this concern for the historic. One of his first forays into conservation was soon after he qualified as an architect in 1934 when he objected to the construction of military barracks near the Baluard de Princep in Palma that would have destroyed the ancient gateway Porta des Camp. The city council decided not to intervene and fortunately, the arches of the bridge were buried intact so that later, if and when the army buildings were demolished, they could be successfully exhumed. Today they form part of an attractive public open space[204]. Another early action was to write a brief text on the place of historic churches in the townscape which, while describing their evolution, also pointed to their significance in the contemporary scene and the need to conserve them. In 1935 he wrote:

El fet que la part nova de la nostra ciutat estigui actualment en periode actiu de formació, ens ha duit a publicar aquest assaig, resum i concreció del nostre estudi del tema… sinó per cridar l'atenció de tots els que d'una o altra manera hi intervenen, començant pels meus companys de professió urbanistes i arquitectes, sobre un dels elements que fan més belles les ciutats. (The fact that the new part of our city is currently active in this stage of its development has led us to publish this essay… not because it hopes someone might take advantage of it directly, but rather to draw attention to all those who, in one way or another, intervene, starting with my fellow planners and architects, in one of the elements that make cities more beautiful), another early indication of the importance of conserving the historical in the townscape of cities[205].

It was also written at a time when the anticlerical movement was increasingly vocal. During the Civil War, many churches were burnt.

As his career progressed in the world of the civil service and his representation of Spanish interests internationally so this aspect of his work was to increase and would, in many ways, help to define him. This does not mean his work was dominated by designing or conserving particular architectural historic models such as the Gothic or the Palladian but rather we might see him as being part of a much later part of planning theory – modern, even before the Modern movement had barely started! A man out of kilter with his times within a closed Spain, but not perhaps within a wider Europe. For him, the ideal city would contain appropriate elements of the past, conserved, not simply for their own sake, but because through them, citizens become rooted, helping them to understand their place in the history of where they live. Alomar's concern for the ecological also embraces his notion of the past in the present, as though, perhaps, cities in times past were more in balance with nature. When speaking of Spain Alomar recognised that at the core of the conservation problem in his country was the rapid urbanisation taking place after the Civil War and its immediate aftermath:

> '...The answer to the challenge of urban concentration would normally be appropriate and timely town and regional planning programmes. But this solution has unfortunately proved unsuccessful during these last twenty years, for reasons which include over-rapid development on the one hand and the influence of pressure-groups on the other. What we are faced with are symbols of growth whose progress has not been arrested by remedial action. In the race between planning and the material progress which brings with it the growth of towns, building development and the wholesale tourist invasion, it is planning which invariably gets left behind'[206].

The relationship between his architecture and conservation derives its inspiration from regionalist ideas too, perhaps a natural product given his provincial, island origins and his training in Barcelona. He did not follow the same intense path in Catholicism as his co-worker José Farragut whose religious philosophy certainly influenced his designs. Alomar's emergence as an architect/planner in the 1930s to 1960s began at a time of Falangist politicisation until it was swept away by the growing influence of a new technocracy after the Civil War, but its admixture of spiritual teachings and political aesthetics can perhaps be detected in the monumental heaviness of many of his buildings and plans. Carrer Jaume III, which he and José Farragut designed, is the prime example but which is rarely seen today as pedestrians pass unconcerned under the arcaded façade of Palma's most fashionable street. Alomar's architectural philosophy was summarised by him in an important article in 1948, *Sobre las tendencias estilísticas de la arquitectura española actual* (Stylistic trends in present-day Spanish architecture) in which he believed Spanish architecture, in general, was conditioned by three things: a fondness for everything Spanish and ancient, a shortage in the post-civil war years of the materials required by modern building styles (e. g. glass, steel and cement[207]) and a certain cultural isolation such that... *'la arquitectura de este periodo no fue realmente un Clasicismo Imperial como en el siglo XVI, sino un Reaccionarissmo tradicional de cualidad romántica'*. ('...' the architecture of this period was not really an Imperial Classicism as in the sixteenth century, but a traditional reaction with a romantic quality'). This statement supports Carlos Sambricio's later view that it is difficult to identify a particular, state-sponsored 'fascist' architecture: a *melange* of styles as described by Alomar was much more common[208]. Alomar and Ferragut's new Gran Via, Carrer Jaume III, perhaps exemplifies this combination of 'plan' and 'building' in its traverse from the open land to the northwest to Plaça Tortugas at the head of the Born. Constructed in large part in Santanyí sandstone, a reference to perhaps the most traditional material on the island for historic buildings such as the Llotja (the Exchange on the original quayside) and La Seu (the Cathedral). This architecture has been described by Ferrer as, *'El historicismo y monumentalismo que pretendre dotar de carácter y estilo a la ciudad se extenderá a la nueva aquitectura a través de los denominados elementos de caracterización urbanística como la calle porticada. Para Alomar el, 'orden arquitectrónico debe supeditarse al orden urbanístico'* ('... historicism and monumentalism attempt to equip the city with a character and style that extends to the new architecture through the chosen elements of the porticoed street that characterise his urban plan. For Alomar the, 'architectural order must be subordinated to the urban order' (See Figs. 9 and 10).

As we shall show below, this part of the plan of the reform of Palma has within it the seeds of the concept of 'conjunto' something akin to the British 'conservation area' – in particular, that any new build should *enhance* the existing historic setting. In this, he moved away from the dominant theme in Spanish architectural conservation that was exemplified by the work of Luis Menendez-Pidal y Alvarez (1896-1975) who in 1937 had been appointed as the head of the national service for the defence of national artistic heritage[209]. His approach was essentially one of the restoration of single buildings i. e. *monuments*, much of which involved conservation but was less concerned with the spatial or townscape context of such works. It would appear that its main aim was to restore and enhance buildings of national historical significance in support of Nationalist ideals. From 1941 much of his work was concerned with overseeing the restoration of key buildings in the so-called First Zone in northern Spain, restoring buildings damaged during the Civil War[210]. In the case of Palma, many early planners drew attention to the importance of the historic in the built environment but it was Guillermo Forteza in the 1930s who had tried his best to articulate its rationale for Palma[211]. In his work, Forteza combined his political ideology with his extensive historical knowledge of architecture.

In October 2011 La Societat Arqueològica Lul. liana (SAL) held a seminar devoted to *La protecció del patrimoni immoble de Mallorca: els Conjunts Històrics* (Historic aspects of the protection of the built heritage of Mallorca: a united or holistic approach). Although it sought to cover areas other than Palma, much of it was devoted to Ciutat. It aimed to include several contemporary approaches to conservation including an examination of the success or otherwise of the current legislation, the drawing of special plans, the need for interdisciplinary teams in this field, the appreciation of heritage among local people and the impact of tourism – both good and bad, all based on a profound understanding of the urban morphology of the island's settlements. Catalina Cantarellas Camps assigns a key role in this policy and planning field to Gabriel Alomar Esteve in the 1960s. This, in turn, had its origins in his plan for the reform of Palma of 1943 but not finally expressed until his declaration of Palma as a *conjunt históric-artístic* in 1964.

Despite his scathing criticism of national town planning legislation after and including the Ley de Suelo, Alomar did admit that there were good examples of conservation planning at the local level: '*There are a great many ancient towns where more sensitive minority opinion has prevailed and has persuaded the majority on the local council to adopt its criteria, so that, with government aid and the support of one sector of public opinion, the landscape has been preserved or even improved. This has occurred in Santiago de Compostela, Toledo, Segovia, Palma, Cáceres, Ubeda, and Ronda, to name some of the most outstanding examples*[212].

In our earlier analysis of the growth of Palma and its changing morphology, we drew attention to three important elements: the historic core characterised by narrow streets and high building densities, the corset-like effect of the encircling walls and the growth of informal extramural suburbs. As the population increased from the 18thC onwards and the likelihood of external attack diminished, the socio-economic effects of these broad morphological features saw the rise of a tightly constrained city in which disease, mortality rates, congestion and pollution brought enormous pressure on housing and public open space. The late 19thC added a pressing need for industrial spaces. By the 20thC this was compounded by the rise of traffic into, out of and across the city, especially motor traffic after the 1930s, which coincided, roughly speaking, with the rise of new tertiary and quaternary economic activity, especially tourism. All the plans that we have referred to from Eusebio Estada's (1890) to PGOU (Plan General d'Ordinacio Urbana) in the early 1980s drew attention to the need for an outward expansion of the city and the need to modernise the core to accommodate modern economic activities but with the obvious contradiction that any such schemes could involve the destruction or at least serious modification of the historic areas of the city and their significant architectural/artistic buildings such as the Porta de Camp described above. The early plans we have described, and the probable influence of Cerdá upon them, while drawing attention to the question of the cultural significance of the built form, most had a technological focus based on an overarching concern for accommodating changing transport systems: railways, trams, motor traffic, ports. It was not until Alomar's Plan of 1943 that the conservation of the historic environment was seriously addressed. At this point, it is worthwhile reminding ourselves of Alomar's three or four key areas that his plan would need to address. It is difficult to rank them in order of importance but Alomar knew that modernising the city was vital. Any new streets or zones that he wished to put into the plan – it was after all called a *reform of the existing structure* – would need to minimise their impact on the historic environment. This was well demonstrated in his concern for his new thoroughfare Carrer Jaume III which drove through parts of the historic core. Medieval streets and buildings, especially houses, would have to be destroyed but he was anxious to ensure that both the new road itself and the new streets and houses that were both designed to reflect the historicism of the area. He was at pains to point out in his *Theory of the City* (1947) that he was not following the modernism of Sert and Le Corbusier but more the ideas of Sitte and the notion of 'community'. Within this older paradigm, he felt that his materials and architectural designs should reflect local geology and wood and not glass and concrete and that their scale should be 'human'.

Later in the 1960s to achieve his aesthetic objectives, he believed it would be necessary to draw up a catalogue of all buildings and areas so affected and rank them according to the priorities attached to them. As he wrote in his published plan for Palma in 1950:

> *... the basis for 'Special Ordinances of Historic-Monumental Areas', which constitute a chapter, is part of our Plan... These Ordinances are founded on two bases: the cataloguing of the existing monumental treasure and the operation of a Board or 'Board of Trustees', formed by a certain number of life members, people with recognized prestige in matters of history and architecture that ensure the preservation of the traditional spirit of these old neighbourhoods. As for the previous work of cataloguing, there is no doubt that it is of great importance. If we want our historical-artistic treasures to last, first of all, we must understand them and make them known. The work already begun in the 'Monumental Catalogue of Palma' to collect and make an inventory, in an orderly and systematic way, the description of each of our civil monuments, from the sumptuous palace to the simple and modest window, each example to be noted and described in a corresponding file.*

Recording in detail the history and architecture of the 'monuments' became something of an obsession with Alomar, resulting in the publication of his plea for a policy for architectural and urban conservation in the Balearic islands, jointly produced with his son Antoni in 1994[213]. Much of the archive of his endeavours has recently been brought to light by Tomas Vibot[214].

Here we begin to see Alomar's identification of the classic tension in the conservation movement: are buildings and /or areas to be retained *in tacta* i. e. *preserved* or the extent to which they may be modified and hence *conserved*? This, wrote Alomar, would need a code of practice to be enshrined in legislation. Although there was something of a tradition of the historic areas of cities to be given special protection – Granada had declared for a *ciudad artística* as early as 1926, for example – the national legislation was weak and it was left to local government to manage this aspect of urban planning[215]. In Palma certain by-laws to manage conservation had been enacted in 1944. By the 1960s Alomar had served various departments of the central government in Madrid and knew the importance of obtaining for Palma some greater kind of legal security for the conservation of its urban environment.

Under his influence, the ayuntamiento was successful in obtaining a *decreto* for the *conjunto históric-artistico* for the city from the Ministry of Education in Madrid. This identified three zones for protection: the historic core, a 'zone of respect' where the size and volume of buildings would have to reflect the city's silhouette or outline and a zone with special planning requirements for the setting or context of historic buildings and urban open spaces. Regrettably, these zones were never clearly delineated[216]. The local authority would have powers under existing legislation relating to 'artistic treasures' to manage these zones but under the auspices of the national Ministry of Education that was responsible for such matters as the central government was always wary of too much devolution. In a notebook in the family archive, there is clear evidence that Alomar was influenced by British experience in dealing with 'monuments'. He refers, for example, to the Ancient Monuments Consolidation and Amendment Act of 1913, noting at this relatively early date the responsible minister (of Works) had powers to conserve significant historic monuments and to take account of their setting, an idea Alomar was to develop later under the heading of *conjunto*. In greater detail, he notes that the Town and Country Planning Act of 1947 develops the idea of listing buildings of historic and architectural interest (Part III, Section 30 of the act) noting the possibilities for local authorities to take conserving action. Alomar was later to be influenced by British policies concerning conserving spaces in cities and towns as well as buildings[217]. It is worth noting again the apparent similarity between the notion of a *conjunto* and the British term 'a Conservation Area' defined as *'areas of special architectural or historic interest, the character or appearance of which it is desirable to preserve or enhance'*. The latter reached the British statute books via a Private Members Bill put forward by Duncan Sandys, founder and President of the Civic Trust, and later enshrined in the Civic Amenities Act 1967. He was a man with whom Alomar was later to have close dealings in connection with the Council of Europe's Europa Nostra which Sandys chaired during 1968-9, and whom Alomar described as 'mi amigo'. Is there a possibility that Alomar knew of the contents and intentions of the forthcoming bill? Did he, at this early stage, have any contact with the Civic Trust and those drafting the bill, or more likely, that this topic – parts of cities and towns in need of protection – was already being circulated amongst planners and architects in Europe? The term *conjunto*, like *conservation area,* embodies an important inclusive spatial element, not simply a set of 'monuments' to be protected. Alomar was well aware of the destructive effects on many Spanish cities of development in the later years of the Franco era. He had almost certainly experienced such legal concepts from his exposure to ideas at MIT in 1945 where one of his tutors was the influential F J Adams.

In the American notebook in the archive referred to above it would appear that Alomar was planning a book on monuments and their conservation in Spain, to be called El Patrimonio Monumental de España, setting out chapter headings on the current legal aspects, the cultural value of monuments including their style and character, the restoration of monuments addressing the need to retain style (perhaps according to the doctrines of Sitte), a catalogue of Spanish monuments and their settings, their appeal to the Spanish people, concluding with an appendix on new official legal structures that would be required to protect and conserve them. The book would be profusely illustrated. He even sketched a possible cover.

Fig 25   Sketch of the title and cover of a book proposed by Alomar. Source: From his American notebook at MIT, 1945. Arxiu Municipal de Palma.

These notes suggest once again Alomar's academic interest in his professional life and practice and the need to communicate his ideas to a wider public and potential policymakers.

His concern for monuments and urban historic areas was by no means his only interest in popularising ideas about the past in cities and towns; he could see their potential in leisure activities too. Referring to two previous UNESCO conferences on conservation and tourism, Alomar, at the 1969 ICOMOS conference on the same topic held in Oxford, UK, drew attention to:

> *'the concepts 'monument' and 'site' natural, historical or artistic, were put on the same footing. Yet, in my opinion, in reality, the problem of 'sites', the importance of which in this respect has considerably increased in comparison with that of 'monuments', is not yet properly considered; 'sites' are considered, too, now as values in themselves. We must begin by clarifying the true meaning that we give to the term 'natural, historical and artistic sites': these are 'geographical areas, large or small extension, which since they contain values of a 'bionatural' order: scientific, aesthetic, historical or ethnological, all deserve to be effectively protected with all their characteristics'*

> *'The doctrine of the conservation of the cultural heritage has undergone an important evolution, with regard to its very purpose. Half a century ago, we were concerned primarily with the preservation of a*

limited number of high-quality materials (sic), to which was given the emphatic name of "national monuments", considered as values in themselves. This idea has been largely overtaken...'

'From this idea of a monumental setting, we have come to recognize the aesthetic value of historical and artistic urban ensembles, so that the problem of their restoration has become more complex, with its social, economic and urban implications. The value, as a tourist attraction, of a well-developed old town, even if it does not contain world-class monuments, is extraordinary. The relationship between the monuments and the landscape is also extremely important. As a castle cannot be aesthetically separated from the rock or the hill on which it is seated, the presence of a monument reflects the landscape by giving it a ladder...'

'I come to the conclusion that the time has come to start the planning of cultural tourism, at the European level first and soon at the universal level. Such planning is essential to create new tourist centres and to protect traditional tourist sites from destruction. It will oppose the destruction that can come from speculation[218] (Author's translation from French).

In the 1970s Alomar was asked to represent Spain in the Council of Europe. Later much of this thinking was to be enshrined in its Convention for the Protection of the Architectural Heritage of Europe signed in Granada in October 1985. Alomar was an influential member of the committee and working party that eventually drew up the laws and regulations that were to be followed by member states at that time – and later under the Treaty of Lisbon of 1990 – that applied to all 28 European Union states. After defining architectural heritage the treaty addressed three principal elements: historical monuments, groups of buildings, and sites, clearly following Alomar's concerns for the spatial and geographical settings of architectural heritage. The signatories agreed to establish records of these three elements and to integrate architectural heritage into urban and regional planning, supported by appropriate fiscal measures and training. The Convention contains many phrases now familiar to British legislators: *'the combined works of man and nature', 'to maintain inventories', 'to prevent the disfigurement, dilapidation or demolition of protected properties', 'compulsory purchase of protected property', 'to encourage private initiatives', 'new uses for old buildings', 'an element of cultural identity'* etc. but which at that time may have been less well known to some other European states, perhaps including Spain where the traditional emphasis had been on 'monuments', often seen in isolation. As has been shown, under the Franco regime, 'monumentality' figured significantly in heritage planning and in its contemporary application. Today in Spain one of the most politically contested parts of townscape heritage is the preservation or removal of Civil War and post-war monuments. In Madrid, for example, such monuments were built toward the middle part of the Franco regime, clearly designed to be reminders of its ideology and meant to be everlasting; today they are seen by many observers as an embarrassment and unwanted anachronism in the city's townscape[219]. In Porto Cristo in east Mallorca was the monument celebrating the defeat of the Republican landing in 1936; it was demolished in 2002, while arguments about the monument in Sa Faxina, in Palma to the sinking of the Nationalist cruiser, 'Baleares', rumble on[220]. It was inaugurated in 1947 at an enormous fascist ceremony. It is set in a park, ironically originally a play space for a school designed by Alomar's contemporary Guillem Forteza in 1935. For

Sóller, as early as 1945 Alomar designed a memorial to the fallen in a garden setting in a small plaça. So far (2021) it has survived demolition.

Fig 26   Monument to Nationalist cruiser 'Baleares' sunk by the Republican navy in the Spanish Civil war, Ses Faixent, Palma. Source: Author's photo.

Fig 27   Sóller Monument to the fallen, designed by Alomar. Source: Author's photo.

10
Alomar and *Espaces Verdes*

Early theories and policies

In one of his earliest ventures into planning theory in 1947 Alomar stressed the need for a national planning policy for urban *and* rural areas. As part of this, he advocated the inclusion of open spaces in any urban plan, something he had already included in his reforms of Palma. In his sociological writing, Alomar linked gardens and green spaces with ideas of recreation, that is the use of non-work time. He drew on evidence from the medical practitioners of his time[221]. It was part of his ideas for the humanistic city emerging even at an early stage of his career:

> *Y sin embargo, el contacto con la naturaleza le es necesario al hombre, tanto por razones físicas e higiénicas como por razones psicológicas, para que sus pulmones puedan de tanto en tanto respirar el oxígeno puro, como para dar a su espíritu la ocasión de sentir la emocion única del espectáculo natural, siempre renovado en el ciclo de las estaciones.*
>
> *El volver a introducir el elemento verde dentro de la ciudad, un grado suficiente para renaturalizarla, así como el proteger y abrir al público zonas naturales extensas y asequibles fuera de los cascos urbanos, es dificil. Tambien lo es el poner un límite decisivo al crecimiento urbano. Sólo puede conseguirlo una politica inteligente de planeamiento decidido.* (And yet, contact with nature is necessary for man, both for physical and hygienic reasons and for psychological reasons so that his lungs can from time to time breathe pure oxygen, so as to give his spirit the opportunity to feel the unique emotion of the natural spectacle, always renewed in the cycle of the seasons.
>
> Re-introducing the green element within the city, enough to 'green' it, as well as protecting and opening large and affordable natural areas away from urban centres to the public, is difficult. It is also going to put a limit on urban growth. Only an intelligent policy of resolute planning can achieve it.)[222] (Author's translation).

In any urban plan a variety of green spaces should be provided, he said, including *'la pequenia plaza, paseo o espació libre para festejos y el jardin para juegos de párvulos'* (the small plaza, *paseo* or open space for games for children)[223], all part of his avocation of harmony and ecological balance that he referred to in his *Teoria de la Ciudad*[224]. He also believed that each of the neighbourhoods (*barrios*) he proposed in his plan for the reform of Palma should have ready access to open, green spaces. This did not mean, however, that all open spaces in cities were sacrosanct. In one significant example, the construction of Carrer Jaume III, the Paseo de Mallorca and the new associated apartment blocks were eventually to be driven through the ancient *huerto d'en Moranta*[225]. It was precisely these suburban or semi-rural spaces at the edge of the expanding city that could then be developed providing green spaces, not only gardens but cemeteries, sports grounds and public parks, allocated in the area beyond, but on a planned rather than a historical evolutionary basis as in the fringe belt theory developed by MRG Conzen, Jeremy Whitehand and Michael Barke and others at a later date [226]. In his early textbook on urban theory, Alomar identified these edge green spaces with the need for the urban citizenry to have access to the more distant open countryside beyond a city's boundaries for recreational purposes including days out and fiestas for the workers, daily travel for the middle classes and even second homes and weekend cottages (*casitas*) for the better off. But, he concludes with a plea: '*Por qué no ir extendiento las ventajas que esto proporciona, más o menos paulatinamente, a las classes trabajadoras, especialmente en las ciudades medias*'[227] ('Why not go on extending the advantages that this provides, more or less gradually, to the working classes, especially in the medium-size cities'). Harking back to the longstanding concern for hygiene, in more direct planning terms he was at pains to emphasise the need for a variety of open spaces as a benefit to health helping to offset the disadvantages of high density living in so many of Spain's largest cities. For children, they were an opportunity to unite the urban child with Nature, part of his emerging ecological philosophy of *un urbanismo humanista*. Following British and American theories of the 1940s, he also advocated the use of green belts (*cinturas verdes*) to constrain urban expansion and provide 'lungs' for the dense urban population[228]. He was less clear about their function to separate one city from another and to avoid the growth of conurbations. As with 'garden cities' his understanding seems to have been coloured by Mallorcan experience, dominated as it was by a most primate city. The concept is better understood in Mallorca today.

In the post Civil War period one of the most influential Spanish organisations to which senior town planners and urbanists belonged was the Federation of Town Planning and Housing first established in 1939 to which we have drawn attention before[229]. At its seventh and final meeting, actually held in Palma in 1954, Alomar in his address to the delegates chose to concentrate on green spaces in cities, calling for their greater provision in plans and in the townscape. He repeated his plea, expressed in *Comunidad Planeada* (1955), for plans to include social as well as 'play-space', pointing to their health and community developmental benefits, reiterating César Cort's ideas quoted elsewhere for the ruralising of the city. In conclusion, he addressed the need for the notion of park-ways to serve as routeways between and within cities and for Spain to have national parks – no doubt calling on his North American experience in both cases[230].

Alomar's contribution to green space schemes

Against this general background of planning policy and theory it is appropriate to examine now some of the specific 'green spaces' schemes that Alomar was associated with, sometimes as an employee, sometimes as a promoter.

Given his early experience at Sa Vall, and like many influential town planners such as T. H. Mawson, [231] it might justifiably be said that Alomar came to urban design via garden design. As we shall see much of his approach to garden design was, like his architecture, strongly historical with references to earlier periods. Especially significant were Italian styles from the late 14C to the 19C, largely because over those centuries Mallorca had strong trading and economic links with Florence, Rome and Naples, part of the circuit of trade in the Mediterranean[232]. For Alomar, public gardens were an essential element in the design of cities in such places as *ramblas, plaças* and *avingudas* adding a biological or vegetal contribution to the hard edges of the built form, places of retreat from the commercial world of the city and, being derived from nature, a complement to the human scale that he sought in his plans. In the case of his native city, he was conscious of the role historically of the large open spaces in Palma particularly between the medieval and Renaissance walls, in the Rambla and the Born once the Riera had been diverted to the west of the city in the 17C, and in the 'squares' of the 18C. In his 1943 plan he proposed a series of new parks across the city including San Magi park, a park at the Institut, Amanecer park, Can Canals park and a park in the suburb of Soledad[233]. In this, he was seeking to amplify the Calvet plan of 1901 by creating a semicircular but discontinuous zone of green spaces across the city, partly between the historic core and the eixample. He was anxious to avoid what he called *pseudo urbanizaciónes* or *urbanizaciónes salvajes*, the principle being to distinguish the urban from the rural, a notion that was later to underpin much of the Ley de Suelo of 1956. Sadly, few of these proposed open spaces were developed; such *espaces verdes* and parks were more the product of later plans especially those of 1968 and after[234]. According to a census carried out by the municipality at the beginning of the year 2000, 280 green spaces were counted in the built-up area of Palma; these included the *plaças*, the principal roads that were planted, the wooded areas (mostly on the outskirts) and gardens. By 2019, , according to Biel Alomar Garau,

> *el verde urbano de Palma ha suprevivido mejor en el radio externo de la ciudad. Pero si la expansion del espacio urbano hace precedentei sobre el medio rural, en las barriadas prifericas y ya rururubanas se enfrantan dos culturas,la de la ciudad y la del campo, confrontacion que normalment se saticface a fafor de la primera y en predjuicio del secondo.* (The green spaces of Palma have survived better in the external radius of the city. But if the expansion of the urban space takes precedence over the rural environment, two cultures, the city and the countryside, confront each other in the rural and rururuban neighbourhoods, a confrontation that normally satisfies itself in favour of the first and prejudicially to the second)[235].

His grandfather's observations on the earlier Calvet Plan included a statement that there was insufficient green and open space in the eixample and in his 1943 plan further parks were included. However, any such open/green spaces were to be part of his ideas for *communities* within the suburbs: they were not to be solely landscapes of housing with occasional greenery but planned communities with schools, parks, kindergarten and public open spaces. He identified eleven such spaces in his 1943 Plan, in this way helping to lower the intensification of the urban environment with a strong social purpose[236].

Alomar certainly loved gardens if not the actual dirty hands' aspect of gardening. He loved designing gardens for himself as at his house in Sa Calatrava and for many of his clients, both public and private. His very first commission was to design the gardens at Sa Vall (sometimes recorded as S'Avall), one of the largest estates in Mallorca bought by the magnate Juan March Ordinas in 1919. Here he was responsible for all aspects of the estate's development in the 1940s from demolition, new build and water supply to garden design. He redesigned the ancient defensive tower that stood at the heart of the estate and then laid out new gardens on a large scale into the 1950s. This was a tremendous undertaking for someone with so little experience. It included engaging, on March's instructions, the building firm Construcciones Salvá from Soledad. How and why he was given this contract is so far unknown; it may have been through the good offices of the Bishop Miralles of Palma. As noted earlier it was March's faith in him, backed by his enormous wealth, that gave Alomar his first and most lucrative contract. In November 1941, for example, he received 725, 000pts for his work on the gardens to date. In addition to the well-known cactus gardens, Alomar tried to reflect in his gardens the landscape of south-east Mallorca – an area of the very dry *marina* famous for its *marès* stone for building and noted for its pine trees (*pinus halepensis*), tamarix and cistus[237]. He was not able to complete the extensive works at that time because in 1943 he was already considering going to Puerto Rico and thence to the United States with his family, but clearly, he retained oversight of the project into the 1950s[238]. Later he was to design many of the additional buildings on the estate including

> *'a series of buildings around the tower: a large dining room with its loggia and terrace, large kitchens and another home for another part of the family, all in the northern part and in the first stage. In the western part: rooms and bedrooms for the children and governesses. Closing the southern part, a slender loggia which overlooks the library, bedrooms and living rooms. The part on the east, that is, the façade, was completely demolished in its entirety and was brought forward some five metres, decorating it with large windows "de columnetes" or "colonelles" in the style of the conquerors. Work continued into the 1960s with more buildings: employees' houses, garages, warehouses, electricity station, stables, doghouses, dairy farms, stables, straw warehouses, barns, water tanks, etc., wide avenues and extensive gardens. All of this forming a large group that might be called call 'The town of Sa Vall'.* [239] (Author's translation)

Fig 28 Alomar's initial design for Lloseta gardens. Source: Cuardanos de arquitectura, 6, 1950.

A second early scheme was for the house and gardens of the Palacio de Ayamans in Lloseta, also for the March family who feared that if the Second World War embraced Spain then Palma might be subject to aerial bombing[240]. Although there was a paucity of records concerning the original mansion, Alomar tried to ensure that his changes respected the previous architecture. Originally an *alqueria* (Muslim estate from the 10thC) on lands given by Jaume I to the Count of Béarn, Lloseta was developed by the Tagores family who inhabited the changing mansion until the late 19C when it was modernised again. According to Alomar, this latest rebuilding did not respect its history – the Count of Ayamans had a fondness for cement render – losing most of its Mallorcan characteristics, turning it into an Italianate villa[241]. In what was essentially a new building, Alomar attempted to combine the acceptable Italianate aspects with traditional Mallorcan building styles and materials. It was the wife of Juan March who employed Alomar to remodel the gardens; work began in January 1942 and was complete by May 1944[242], yet another example of his early work linking garden design to its urban plan setting, somewhat different from his work at Sa Vall, an isolated mansion in the countryside. These gardens presented a quite different challenge, first to design them along contemporary lines and secondly to integrate them into the townscape. The former were to be laid out on that part of the property that was by 1900 an orchard; in effect, Alomar had a blank canvas upon which to design his garden. It consisted of a series of Mallorcan style terraces descending from the east side of the house , connected by stairways separated by Italian style balustrades, the whole planted with tall, Italian cypresses and Mallorcan myrtles. Fountains, pools (*piscenes*) and rectilinear planted parterres completed the scene. Meanwhile, the original garden in front of the house retained much of its original form[243]. Of course, at the time, and indeed until recently, this was a private house belonging to the powerful March family so that by definition it was isolated from the town surrounding it, essentially a private space to which local residents had only occasional access. Its plantings, its gated entrance and its external railings marked it off from public view. In 2014 the local authority, having acquired the property, began proceedings to change its protection under Spanish law so that both the house and gardens might be open to the public and to integrate the whole into the small town of Lloseta, surely a planning move that Alomar, with his concern for *espaces verdes* in towns, would have approved seventy years after his original work was completed[244].

Following the decision to expand the Spanish national tourism industry, despite Franco's serious misgivings – he favoured the growth of industry – Mallorca sought to play a leading role. Expansion meant increasing the island's infrastructure to service tourism, particularly in terms of hotel provision and transport. Such infrastructure required land, land in close proximity to the sea. The early planners of the 1950s expected growth to occur to the East and West of Palma. To the east lay land of low agricultural value but with great tourism potential in the form of beaches. Developers saw the potential of what was to become known as the Platja de Palma stretching from the outskirts of the city to the low-cliffed land near Cala Blava that included seafront lands in two administrative areas, Palma and Llucmajor. Along this line was to be built Coll d'en Rebassa, Sometimes, and Merivelles, culminating in a new resort – S'Arenal[245]. The expectation was that much of the development would be for the middle classes both Spanish and generally European and that much of it would be in the form of summer residences. This notion was soon to be overtaken once mass tourism expanded enabled by aircraft and the building of Son Sant Joan airport.

Fig 29   Gardens of Ayamans in 2019 at Lloseta designed by Alomar. Source: Author's photo.

Fig 30   Alomar's gardens at Lloseta, 2019. Note proximity to town. Source: Author's photo.

One particular urban planning scheme that Alomar designed initially lay to the east of the developing resort of S'Arenal in Llucmajor. When the estate of Son Verí de Marina came up for sale in the late 1950s land was allocated for additional tourism infrastructure and Alomar was asked to draw up a plan for part of its development[246]. The site had the sort of historical origins that attracted Alomar. Originally a large 15thC estate that stretched from the outskirts of Llucmajor to the sea[247], its geography also suited Alomar's rather romantic ideas: an area of pine woods and *garriga*, gently sloping its way down to a line of low cliffs that gave superb panoramic view across the whole of the Bay of Palma with few accessible areas of beach, an area not unlike those he was to plan in the northeast of the island around Cala Ratjada. This was not the sort of location for the burgeoning mass of tourists but one more likely to appeal to the more genteel summer visitors.

Turning his back on the rigidities that can be found in his 1950 plan for the eixample and Jaume III in Palma or the formalities of the Lloseta gardens, he focussed instead on a plan that had more flexibility, more sinuosity, an idea that he had probably absorbed following his time in the USA in 1945, influenced by the teachings of Frederick Adams at MIT[248]. His plan is sometimes wrongly described as a 'Garden City' (*ciudad jardin*) but it exhibited many of the design characteristics of a garden *suburb*; it would be a misunderstanding to describe the settlement as 'urban' because it lacked the economic and social rationale that Ebenezer Howard and Parker and Unwin had for Letchworth or Welwyn Garden City. We have seen that some Mallorcan writers seem to be unclear about the role and purpose of 'garden cities'[249]. This may be because Howard's original work was not translated into Spanish. The early adoption of some of them was mostly associated with social reform, not town planning. It was not until the 1930s that Howard's ideas were taken up in Spain and then mostly by anarchist reformers.[250] In this case, it was more an adaptation of the garden *suburb* models that descended from Norman Shaw's Bedford Park, Parker and Unwin's plans for Brentham in Ealing, West London or Hampstead Garden Suburb, with, in Alomar's case, the defining characteristic being space for coastal tourism as a quasi-suburban if rather distant, adjunct to the city of Palma[251]. Thus, his plan was to be irregular of outline with a curving road layout and with about 25% of the total area devoted to *espaces verdes* between the building blocks. By 1968 Antoní Galmes believed that Alomar's plan for Son Verí ...'*volgué i li dona una personalitat propia amb les verdós deis seus pinars i l'in teres pintoresc i encantador del Hoc, en una páranla, que Son Verí seguís essent Son Verí*,' ('kept its own personality with the green of the pine trees and picturesque and charming characteristics, so that Son Verí was still Son Verí')[252]. Its houses are for the most part individually designed, some showing modernist influences, some harking back to *Ibicenco* (Ibizan) tendencies. Alomar the architect designed few if any of the houses. Originally there would have been low rise, almost cottage-type *chalets* immediately facing the sea with more substantial villas built on the rising ground behind. Present-day land values, heightened by the need of the more crudely affluent to be on the land's edge, has sadly seen most of these early buildings replaced.

Alomar's contribution to this still verdant landscape was his plan, not for an urbanization as local residents are keen to point out, but for a set of suburban detached houses that still permit short distance commuting to Palma's offices and banks or when the working life is concluded, a safe and secure refuge from the city.

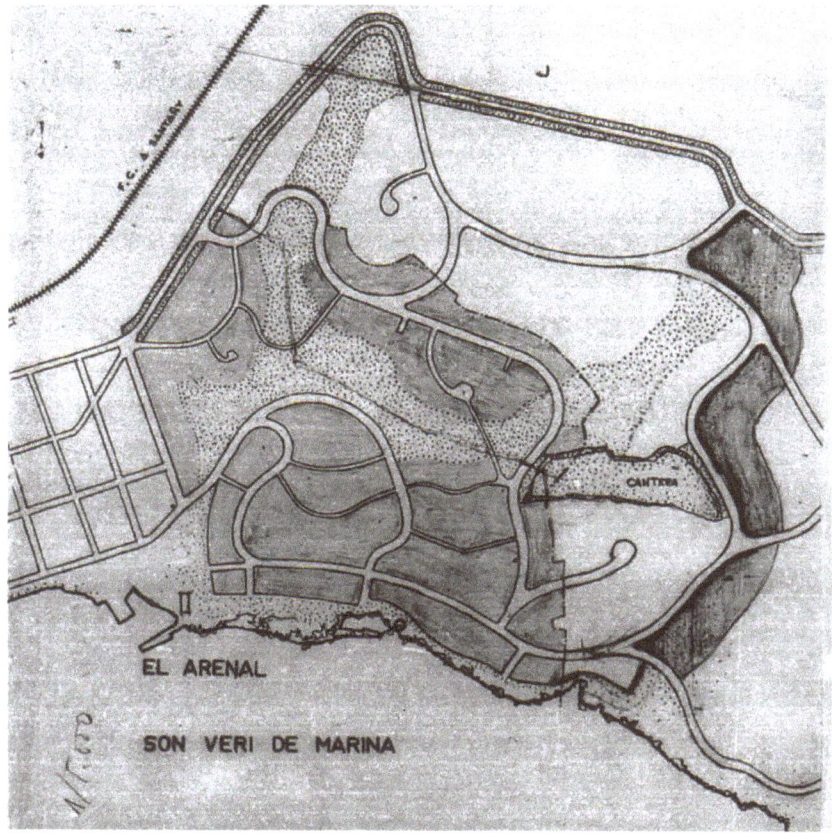

Fig 31   Alomar's original plan for the garden suburb of Son Veri. Source: Archivo planeamento Govern Balear (after Horrach).

Fig 32   Curved roads showing perhaps the American influence on Alomar's design for the garden suburb of Son Veri, 2018. Source: Author's photo.

Fig 33   Alomar's Son Veri. A detached house from 1960s on a large plot. Note trees of former pine woods, 2018. Source: Author's photo.

One theme that runs through much of Alomar's professional life is his work for Juan March Ordinas and his family and their presence in the northeast of Mallorca. We have already drawn attention to Carrer Jaume III, Lloseta and Sa Vall. Further involvement with the family was for the gardens of Torre Sa Cega, the four-square mansion that acted as the family's summer home near Cal Ratjada. This was built primarily for March's wife, Leonor Servera, who came from nearby Capdepera[253]. She had a keen interest in gardens and employed the well-known English landscape architect Russell Page (1906-1985) to design the gardens around the house's prominent site in the 1960s. The gardens were later partly refashioned by Alomar (and Leandro Silva) but it is difficult today to identify his contribution. Because of his association with the growing resort of Cala Ratjada he was also invited to design a new parish church for the town.

Another scheme nearby, that actually involved laying out a plan, was for a seaside urbanization, Son Moll, adjacent to Cala Ratjada in Capdepera. This had begun with a few houses in the 1930s followed by two hotels overlooking the beach built in the 1950s. For Alomar, a commission to build two elegant villas (Marbella (no13) and Sa Caleta (no. 21) in Avenida Arquitecto Alomar), for members of his own family, was expanded into a larger settlement when the ayuntamiento of Capdepera proposed a plan for a suburb of Cala Ratjada on the Son Moll estate in 1962. This was to be a well laid out series of tree-lined streets – rather like Son Verí de Marina at S'Arenal but more rectilinear – with views of the sea and close to the small beach. Plots were initially allocated for individual detached houses with extensive gardens affording privacy for the expected middle-class purchasers. Some of them were for members of his own extended family including his daughters Mari Carmen and Nani. Alomar was honoured by having the principal street of his plan named after him.

Fig 34   Street name plaque, Son Moll. Source: Author's photo.

Today, sadly, much of his plan has been overtaken by rather mundane seaside architecture built on the original wooded landscape. His villas, however, have retained their original charm, one is now part of the international holiday rental market, another in a rather dilapidated state, often let to visiting groups, and his daughters' houses used by them as weekend retreats.

A small development to the north of Cala Ratjada at Cala Guay was for the German Dr Otto Schlandt on a steep slope of pine woods running down to the *cala*, now known as Cala Lliteras.

Once again, we see Alomar taking full advantage of the site in his plan for the development of both seaward views and the morphology of the valley. Two types of house were proposed, a larger detached model and smaller houses arrayed in a staggered terrace with small private gardens to front and rear. It is difficult to appreciate the Scandinavian influenced design since they have been much modified since the 1960s. Indeed, the whole site is currently being 'upgraded' and completely surrounded by architecture of the second decade of the 21st century. Of Alomar's original plan nothing remains: while the original views out to sea remain, the wooded landscape has long gone with only relict features of one set of his terraced houses barely discernable.[254]

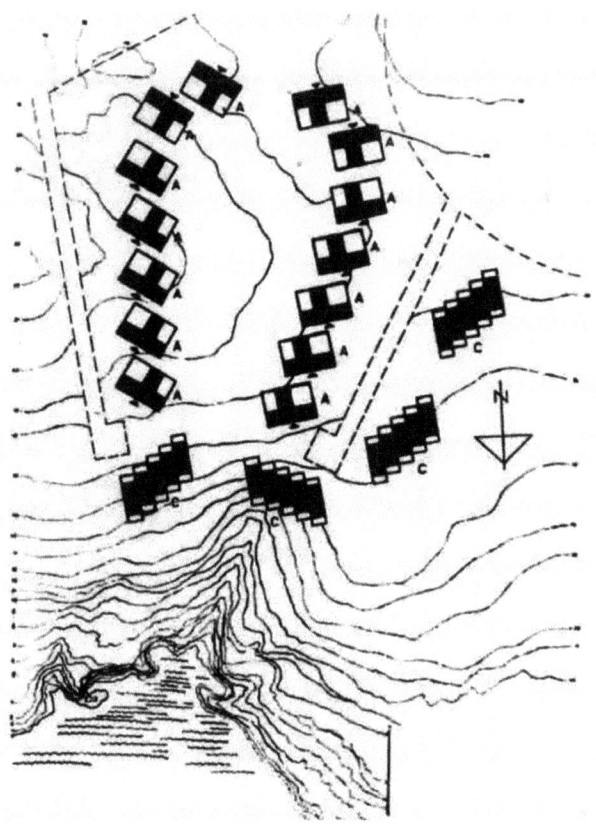

Fig 35   Alomar's plan for Cala Guya in North East Mallorca for Dr Otto Schlandt. Source: Cuardenos de arquitectura, 57, 1964.

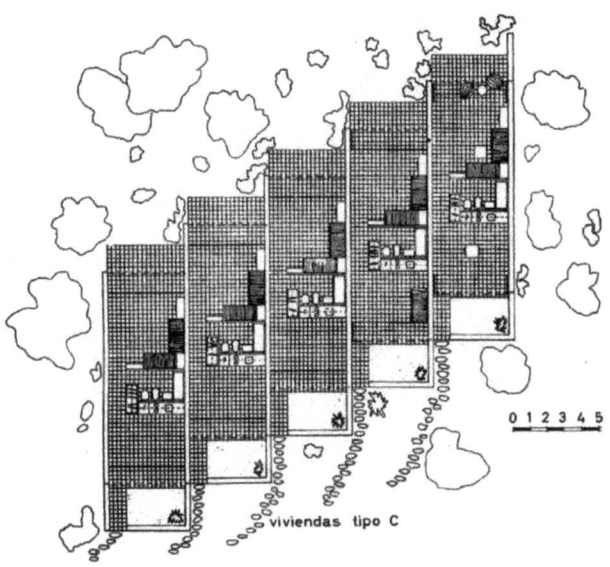

Fig 36   Proposed layout of housing at Can Guya. Source: Cuardenos de arquitectura, 57, 1964.

Perhaps his most famous work in garden design in an urban setting was for the S'Hort del Rei alongside the Almudaina in Palma. This scheme is particularly noteworthy because it called on Alomar's skills and knowledge in all his fields of interest: architectural history, conservation, garden design and town planning. Of further interest is the fact that although researched and designed by Gabriel Alomar, who by this time was vice-president of ICOMOS, it was his son Antonio who oversaw the construction of the gardens in 1969-70[255]. This was to be a local scheme funded by the ayuntamiento, and not a state-funded scheme, even though Alomar had helped fashion national policies for this approach to the enhancement of the urban environment. Nonetheless, it would appear that the city council had to be convinced of the importance of this work as a national monument (see the arguments regarding 'sites' and 'monuments' in Francoist ideology, cited above) before funding became available, an example, perhaps, of centralism even though its influence was declining by this date[256]. The *alcalde* (mayor) of Palma during the mid-1960s was General Máximo Alomar (no relation), a native of Mallorca but a Franco appointment since the military remained powerful in the city at that time, whose support for Gabriel Alomar's scheme was vital in obtaining national approval[257].

Fig 37   Demolition of important buildings, including the Lírico Theatre, to make way for S'Hort del Rei designed by Alomar and his son Antonio, c. 1968.

In his planning for these gardens, Alomar made, with the help of Prieto-Moreno, an architect with a strong interest in the history of architecture and gardens, a detailed narrative and account of the origins of this aspect of the Almudaina[258]. Tracing its development from its beginnings to its modifications under the Almoravids, it involved unearthing the origins of the original *horta* that served the Almudaina as part kitchen garden/part leisure space so loved by Arabic culture with its irrigation and water features. Alomar's plan called for the demolition of large parts of the Arabic/Berber wall, the exposure and reconstruction of the sea gate and the creation of a large open space on which to build the new garden. In the post-Arab/Berber centuries, medieval Mallorca had used this area for a variety of purposes and by the 18th and 19thCs a hotel and the famous Lirico theatre had been built there; they too were demolished but only after attracting considerable local opposition and securing promises to build a new theatre, promises, that, sadly, were never fulfilled. Herein is enshrined the essential contradiction faced by all developers and planners between preserving certain beloved elements of the then-contemporary townscape and the desire to replace them with something new but sympathetic. Another of the contradictions, typical of the politics of planning, is the fact that simultaneously Alomar was General Commissioner for National Artistic Heritage from 1963-69. Some cynics might argue that perhaps that is why the work on the gardens was carried out by Alomar's son. In addition, the site proved to be difficult because of the need to at least echo the shape of the original Arabic gardens that resulted from their proximity to a new main road – Carrer Maura – and the Almudaina walls being restored. Originally designed as a series of four *riads* or terraces with a central canal and running water and with no large trees, as was the Hispano-Arabic ideal, Alomar sought a degree of intimacy in his garden with gateways limiting access. But he was conscious of it being a public space unlike those of Sa Vall, Lloseta, Torre Sa Cega and Can Bruy. Alomar was also aware of the growing urban tourism industry and the need to improve the city's appearance for visitors as well as a general public benefit. In this sense S'Hort des Rei is clearly another *proyecto* emerging from his wider town plan of the 1940s.

Fig 38   S'Hort del Rei nearing completion c. 1971: Source: Courtecy of Bartolomé Ramón Construcciones archive.

A final garden scheme must be that of Alomar's own house in the Sa Calatrava district of Palma. A private rather than a public space, its site and the house and gardens closely reflect Alomar's own theories of urban design: human scale, historically sympathetic, use of local materials and in some ways 'monumental', although that may not have been the architect's original intention! It was, of course, designed by Alomar for himself and his family. He had been able to acquire a considerable tract of urban land within the southeast corner of the Renaissance walls – one of the parts of the city his 1943 Plan had highlighted for reform. He was able to obtain planning permission that involved the demolition of the existing properties and the construction of a large townhouse, indeed a *palacio*, along Italo-Spanish lines looking out over the wondrous Bay of Palma to the rear and with fine views of the east end of Palma's gothic cathedral and the Bishop's Palace. Unlike the late renaissance palaces and patios at the core of medieval Palma, it did not front onto the street, Carrer Alonso; it retained an enclosed curtilage of about 5 hectares to include house and garden, only approached via a short tunnel guarded by iron gates.

Fig 39   Alomar's 'palacio' in Sa Calatrava built in the 1950s in the Italianate style. Source: Author's photo.

Fig 40   Part of Alomar's garden. Source: Author's photo.

In the last twenty years, a more radical view of the process of the historic planning of towns has emerged in western society in which 'nature' (cf. gardens and public open spaces) in cities is seen as an effort by developers and later town planners to ameliorate the generally deleterious effects of city-building and urban life, a deliberate attempt to offset the effects of poor housing, pollution, noise and traffic, as a means of deflecting demand for radical change, especially from the working classes. From our analysis of Alomar's labours in this field, it is more likely that his perspective owes more to the City Beautiful movement of the earlier 20th century than to a class-oriented view. In many ways, Alomar's own garden typifies his approach to town planning – relating built form to nature – but it also encapsulates his dilemma when he retreated from the political world of *urbanismo* that had emerged in the late 1950s with which, finally, he could not agree and which was not aligned with his philosophy and indeed, his taste. Behind its Arab-style entrance off a quiet street and surrounded by a garden he had designed Alomar felt safe, able to entertain his family and friends, able to lead the life of an educated gentleman but by no means a recluse, researching the history and art of Mallorca until his death on Christmas Day, 1997.

11
Alomar's legacies

It is now almost eighty years since the acceptance of Alomar's plan for the reform of Palma, his first venture into town planning. In attempting to assess his legacies one is faced with the obvious fact that both planning in Spain and the cities being planned have changed dramatically so that any surviving features are most likely to be the physical ones in Mallorca, especially in Palma itself. If his successors in Spain and elsewhere have absorbed any of the philosophies of planning set out in his books and academic papers they have almost certainly been modified by firstly, the changing patterns of urbanisation since the 1970s by which time he had virtually ceased to be directly involved in town planning and secondly by the nature of town planning itself as the profession and its political context has reacted to the first point. *Legacies* (plural) is a deliberate choice of title; it will be important to see if his view of town planning is a holistic one, embracing physical planning, social planning, urban conservation and the role of 'nature' in cities.

One can also set the development of his ideas against a theoretical background. Nearly thirty years ago the radical theoretician David Harvey identified the simple purpose of urban planning as seeking to maintain or restore social harmony by using the technology of planning and its pervading ideological context as a means of balancing capital and class interests. Improving the physical environment ('nature') was seen as compensation for the (poor) quality of life found in rapidly industrialising and urbanising cities, those living and working there being increasingly alienated and looking for redress[259]. As this chapter advances, we shall see if Alomar's ideas about planning and urban living reflect in any way this kind of analysis, given the setting of the 'failed' Second Republic in Spain and the rise of a fascist regime, the times in which his life's work in *urbanismo* is to be found.

But any assessment ought to start with a consideration of five areas of professional specialisation remembering that any retrospective view must take account of the times Alomar lived in and through. First, would be his reforms for Palma: What was the cultural and political context that might have conditioned his design ideas? Were they successful? How much has survived? To what extent was his plan original? How much of his reforms reflected the earlier work of his predecessors? Secondly, was his relationship with the magnate Juan March Ordinas – tobacco smuggler, industrialist, a supporter of Franco and the Nationalist cause, financier and banker, and above all for our narrative, patron of Alomar whom March supported in many of his early endeavours. Thirdly, would be his concern for planning policy and legislation that came from his time in Madrid and later representing Spain abroad; this would include his advocacy for a national planning framework and his contribution to urban conservation. Fourthly, is his lifelong interest in open spaces and gardens in cities, the 'nature' referred to by Harvey although this was probably not Alomar's interpretation. Lastly, something should be said about his interest in the training and education of planners, including his own experience in the United States of America and Latin America and the books he wrote to encourage others. We have tried to show that while there may be a stream of continuity in these phases, his progress through his professional life was marked by clear breaks of slope: training in Barcelona, involvement in the Civil War, his exposure to Nationalist politics, his plan for Palma, his time in Puerto Rico and at MIT, his time at the Institute in Madrid, the frustration with post-war philosophies especially the ideological conflicts in the regime between planning and housing, his wider European experiences including his move into urban conservation leading to his break with the regime and his final withdrawal into history and art.

While it may be true to say that 'planning' in Spain was – and to a certain extent still is – different from that which developed in more northerly European countries such as the UK ('town planning') and Germany (*stadtebau*) it did not emerge in isolation and Spain has always been well connected with practice and theory in the wider world. Certainly, from the 1920s Spanish planners, although trained in schools of architecture or engineering, were often in contact with their peers elsewhere. In the case of Gabriel Alomar Esteve, we have shown that the training he received in *urbanologia* as part of his architecture degree drew in part on the work of Cerdá in Barcelona, Haussmann in Paris and Sitte's work in Austria and Germany and Castro's and Cort's work in Madrid. Since town planning was initially seen from a perspective of architecture and building design it is not surprising that it was perceived as a contribution to a city's beauty as much as its functionality. It would be true to say that few cities other than Madrid had planners and plans from the 1920s in the way we have come to understand them today. From the archive material available it is difficult to see how far Alomar was directly exposed to some of the early 20thC city plans that were produced elsewhere in Spain, such as the Zuago-Ribas-Navarro plan for Zaragoza of 1928, as he was drafting his plan for Palma. In his scheme for Palma the maps produced for the competition in 1942, the final draft of 1943 and his 1950 book certainly reflect the artistic style of a previous era[260]. He was also acutely aware from his own experience of the social and economic needs of his native city – housing, sanitation, traffic and tourism – the first three of which were evidence of the neglect of the city to develop beyond its walls over 100 years despite the early plans of Calvet, Bennàzar and others. The earlier pioneers of planning in Palma that we examined were, perhaps, more influential on his own plans than many might accept, especially those of Bernat Calvet. That overused phrase of Isaac Newton's, 'If I have seen further, it is by standing on the shoulders of giants', certainly has some resonance when we examine the degree of originality in the Alomar reforms. On the links between planning and economic development, Alomar seems to have had little to say in his Palma plan.

Together with his concern for the 'ecology' of cities, his theories were soon to be overtaken by new, modernist and more practical planning philosophies. Might it not be the case too, that, inevitably, he was drawn into the ideological tensions between the Falange and the modernisers which manifested themselves in the former as advocacy for fashioning cities around the theme of housing provision as promulgated by Serrano Suñer the movement's early leader, in the 1940s:

> *The reconstruction does not aspire to leave the people of Spain, to whom it is targeted, in their previous state. It aspires to improve their situation, bringing to them the breath of the national revolution… We truly hope that the new houses meet the requirements of hygiene and joy, so that the children of those who sacrificed themselves, appreciate the huge scale of the effort undertaken*[261] (Author's translation).

Alomar's 'reforms', then, certainly alleviated some of the more negative symptoms of the rapid growth of Palma but on reflection, they were soon to be transformed by the new demands created by rapid urbanisation in the 1960s and '70s. If his plan had powerful architectural elements perhaps they reflected the monumentalism of the early Franco era as well as his concern for neo-classicism. Perhaps the best survival from his planned reforms – Avenida Jaume III – is indeed as much a piece of monumental architecture as an example of 1940s town planning *per se*. Some would argue that Alomar's reasoning for the style of Jaume III (historicism) sounds a little like a posthoc rationalisation for the somewhat old-fashioned look of the street. It could also be argued that many of his reforms simply resulted in real estate gains with Jaume III, essentially a new shopping street and Mercat de l'Olivar, an additional market. Even the Plaça Major has become, together with Carrer Sant Miguel another retail complex mostly aimed at tourists. Many of the modernist architects and planners of the early 1930s, who at one time might have been numbered among his colleagues, had either gone into exile or been killed in the war. Was Alomar simply a 'survivor', espousing values that were soon to be swept away, as in Madrid? Against this might be set his 'Avenida' tower completed in 1941 which harked back to his 'rationalist/modernist' ideas of the Republican 1930s. As Rodrigo Almonacid Canseco points out: '*Evidentemente, la principal censura a 'lo moderno' es de orden poltico-ideologico. Al imponer un regimen dictatorial, nacionalista y autarquico, la modernidad de Ios años 30 se asocia a Ios arquitectos del bando perdedor de la Guerra Civil*'. ('Evidently, the main censorship of 'the modern' is of a political-ideological order. By imposing a dictatorial, nationalist and autarchic regime, the modernity of the 1930s has become associated with the architects on the losing side of the Civil War')[262].

On the other hand, is it more accurate to see Alomar's planning not simply in a technical, problem-solving way but as a demonstration of his somewhat romantic-rationalist- localist perspective?

In attempting to make some kind of judgment or critique of the twelve elements of his reforms for the historic core of Palma one is faced with the inescapable fact that only three of them were executed. First, Jaume III and the construction of the housing and the Paseo de Mallorca associated with this phase was the first to go ahead. Ultimately, the price paid for the highway was the sacrifice of his housing scheme to the apartment blocs like Carrer de Bonaire. Building the new market nearly did not take place as it proved most difficult to persuade local construction companies to accept the financial risk; twice the project was put out to tender but without success. It was only when March's financial muscle was put behind EUSA, the company originally established by Alomar, that progress was made[263]. Similarly, the construction of the massive stairway to the north of the Plaça Major linking it to the Via Roma or Rambla was finally funded in the same way. The examination we have made of these reforms – both executed and not undertaken or incomplete – demonstrates clearly the limitations of Alomar's success but as *proyectos* rather than part of a comprehensive city-wide plan. Jaume III is certainly a most striking addition to Palma's townscape in functional and aesthetic terms but his actual contribution to the architecture demonstrates the work of Ferragut as much as his own, just as Juncosa and Vicente Valls Gadea made a more significant contribution to the Mercat de l'Olivar area which, when completed, enabled the market activities in the Plaça Major to be moved and Alomar's fifth project to be at least partially constructed as planned. The proposed reforms to the two southerly corners of the city, Puig de Sant Pere and Sa Calatrava, had a mixed reception at the time and what reforms have been achieved in these two historic areas came long after Alomar had retreated from the planning of his native city.

Was he more successful with his proposals for improving movement within the historic core? Here, the inner ring road (the *avingudas*) following the line of the old city walls – and first proposed by Bennàzar – has had to be expanded to accommodate a massive increase in car-borne traffic, public transport and delivery vehicles. Alomar – as were his predecessors Calvet, Bennàzar and Forteza – was conscious of the need to connect the low town with the high town, a problem derived from the physical geography of the city planned in Project 4. Similarly, another planned road (Project 7) was to run from Carrer Sindicat to the St Antony Gate and then on towards the Manacor road. Behind all these traffic-based road schemes was the general idea that as much movement as possible was to be kept out of the old historic core by confining it to the new roads. Thankfully perhaps, none of these projects was completed and in any case, would have involved the demolition of many buildings. Later planners in other European cities would have had no such scruples![264]

It is difficult to see from a 1940s perspective if Alomar could or should have foreseen increases in road traffic. He did not have at his command the sort of mathematical, statistical and other modelling tools that became available to future generations of planners. Much of his plan, then, was overtaken by events shortly after it was published in book form in 1950; not only increases in traffic but shifts in the nature of the urban economy, demographic increases that would have surprised him and, following *autonomia* in 1986 and Spain's accession to the European Union in the same year, all changed the parameters within which his plan might have worked. But above all, was the explosion in the tourism industry after the mid-1950s that transformed Mallorca's socio-economic structures so dramatically and so quickly[265]. The islands' capital city's urban structures had to accommodate equally rapidly all of these forces. Alomar's prize-winning plan, so elegant, so clear in its exposition, was soon swept aside by political and economic forces the scale of which he could not have foreseen. The failure of the local authority to complete all of his twelve projects might also be ascribed as much to the failure of the ayuntamiento in the late 1940s and '50s to persuade local developers to undertake many of the projects as to the cultural and political factors to be found in the make-up and power of the council where members had to consider their position in relation to pressures from Madrid. Mallorca may have been an offshore island in the mental maps of many but it had supported the Nationalist cause, fought off an invasion by Bayo's forces and adopted the ideologies of the Movement. As these characteristics waned with the onset of modernising forces – in the case of Mallorca associated with the rise of mass tourism from the mid-1950s – so the need for new plans for Palma soon became evident. Perhaps it was in the *eixample*, the 'new city' beyond the line of the city walls – that space that César Cort identified as the meeting of rural and urban land uses in Spanish cities – where Alomar made his only mark of space for future development, although even here his predecessors had laid down the idea initially. Alomar hypothesised a road system but it was to be private sector developers who built what we see today. Nonetheless, suburban and edge-city expansion since the 1990s has shown the limits of his vision. The *cintura*, the *polígonos*, the shopping malls, the expansion of the city along its coastline to the East and the West, would surely have amazed him.

Since Alomar's plan of the 1940s, there have been several major plans for the city of Palma under the general heading of Pla General d'Ordinacio Urbana (PGOU). While it is true that they have built on Alomar's foundations – as he built on those of Calvet et al – they have had to deal with a changed and changing set of constraints, most of which were beginning to emerge soon after Alomar's plan was completed on paper. Although such plans of the 1960s attempted to address city-wide planning, most have also been *proyectos*, directed at specific areas and/or problems beginning with an area Alomar identified, Puig de Sant Pere, in 1980, followed by el Jonquet (1985), Sa Calatrava (1989) and La Gerreria (1995). Unsurprisingly projects in the following decades have concentrated on the more peripheral parts of the administrative area of Palma, and today have embraced the challenges of the wider Palma city region – Marratxi to the north, Calviá to the west and Llucmajor to the east. These post-Alomar developments clearly illustrate the shifts in planning theory from the sort of whole city approach to the more piecemeal plans of limited scope, to the planning of the city region of Greater Palma. The question now being asked is: who is responsible for planning the city and its region as a whole?[266]. Palma appears to demonstrate something Teresa Franchini wrote in 2014:

> *Since the establishment of a planning system in the mid-1950s* (i. e. following the Ley de Suelo – author) *the planning process in Spain is characterised by an emphasis on zoning, master and detailed plans for infrastructure development. There is no spatial planning profession per se and planning in Spain is predominantly led by architects who have specialised in urban design and larger-scale planning. Deregulation policies in the 1990s and early 21st century, together with a lack of clarity in administrative policies, have led to widespread sprawl, development scandals and rampant real estate speculation, which have in turn reflected negatively on urban and spatial planning and brought the planning profession into disrepute*[267].

Early in his period working in Madrid, Alomar wrote to his friend Gaspar Blein in late 1946, lamenting that in an American bibliography of planning around the world he could find not one reference to Spanish practice[268]. While engaged at the Institute in Madrid he produced two more important books to encourage and direct the education of planners that he had first emphasised in his pioneering Theory of the City in 1947. In *Comunidad Planeada* (1955), in what is perhaps his best book, he presents for planners the latest thinking on the social aspects of their profession, much influenced by what he had learned in the USA. Here he advances his personal philosophy on the concept of the *city as community*, contributing through the medium of planning the notion that the object of planning would not solely be to focus on the material structures of cities and towns but on the '*nuevo el spiritu de cohesión y de fraternidad, reorganizando entre les hombres los groups biológicos, ya que la especie humana, como tantas otras especies natural, ha sido creada para vivir formando comunidades* (the new spirit of cohesion and fraternity, reorganizing biological groups among men, since the human species, like so many other natural species, has been created to live in communities.) The book begins with the principles of ecology, moves through chapters on the spatial organization of the human habitat, the varieties of types of social organization – including an especial concern for 'the masses' in cities and before moving on to social problems. The fourth part of the book develops his theory of ecological planning. His concluding chapter is one that reflects his own rather moralizing thoughts about a planned society, particularly a Christian one, noting the need to be aware of the possible conflict between liberty and planning and planning and property, all of which reflect his post-USA reading. In his notebook started while at MIT, there are extracts and observations from Hayek's *Road to Serfdom* (1945), Clement Attlee's *The Will and Way to Socialism* (1935) and John Jewkes' *Ordeal by Planning* (1946), all part of the debates going on internationally about the rebuilding of the world after the Second World War[269]. Hayek's neoliberalism, which is very much about the tyranny of State planning and Socialism and became well-read throughout the era of Soviet domination. Later some European countries saw the only way to economic growth being via capitalist market forces, a view not so very different from Jewkes'. Hayek might have seen Franco's version of development in the same light. Attlee's *The Will and the Way to Socialism* (1935) set out a counter view and certainly helped fashion policies in Britain's Labour Government (1945-51) which favoured the nationalisation and planning of strategic industries, and of course, included the Town and Country Planning Act of 1947, which many saw as the nationalisation and planning of land-use. Curiously, there appears to be no mention of Beveridge's texts that led to the foundation of the Welfare State, of which aspects of planning, including town planning, were part. Spain under Franco, and especially under the policies of autarky, would have been much less conscious of these movements because of its isolation in the 1950s, seeing them as socialistic but to some, including Gabriel Alomar Esteve, and therefore indicative once more of his more open internationalism. It is difficult to say when looking back on this era whether Alomar's ecological and social approaches to planning had much effect on the wider development of Spanish town planning. Sadly, Spanish cities were soon to be swamped by massive and rapid urbanisation, including coastal tourism development. In the 1960s the arrival of a more liberal economy, itself so often accompanied by corruption and favouritism, reduced the possibility of any meaningful land use planning in urban and rural areas.

But here we are talking of Alomar's textbook writing designed to guide Spanish planners, part of their education and training. To what extent has an apparent lack of progress in planning in Spain since then in any way been attributable to the subject's place in the country's higher education system? We shall try to assess the influence of Alomar on planning education in modern-day Spain below but one can only say that his pleas for a separate system of training for planners have only partially come to fruition. Education and training in planning are likely to be a response to demand, and as we have shown, national and, to a lesser extent regional governments, have been negligent here. Perhaps things are changing under forces such as sustainability, equality and diversity but Spanish planning remains bound strongly to its traditions.

In the case of Mallorca while the proportion of total land area given over so far to urban expansion is limited – built up and urbanised land is only about 5-6% of the total (it is 11-12% in the UK), it is highly concentrated in Greater Palma, along the *raiguer* and in the atoll of largely tourist urbanisations around the coast except to the north and west. It is in these areas that the DOT (Spatial Planning Guidelines) identified as areas under the greatest pressure in 1997[270]. Clearly, despite the founding national legislation, Spain remains with only a weak national framework for planning policy and practice. Following autonomia, from the 1980s the provinces of Spain gradually increased their own planning policies and appointed staff to implement them, but it is still the case that it is the local authority, the *ayuntamiento/ajuntament*, that is responsible for managing old and new urban developments and the use of rural land. In Mallorca the land-use laws of 1975 and 1990 defined the urban areas, restricting development in the non-urbanised parts but its implementation remained largely in the hands of the municipalities. In the case of the Balearic Islands and much of Mediterranean Spain, it is the coast that has come under the greatest pressure in the last sixty years and until the mid-1980s it was this zone that suffered the greatest ravishes largely because of the tourism developer's perception that sites nearest the sea ('front line') were the most valuable. In the Balearics, the Law of the Coasts of 1988 restricted development within 100 metres of the coastline but like so much legislation this was only 'honoured in the breach'. It took a national law in 2009 (Article 118) to enforce this much more strictly[271]. In more recent years the Govern (the government of the Balearic Islands) and Mallorca's government – the Consell – have imposed somewhat greater control on land use and its planning, employing a better-equipped bureaucracy to manage the island's development.

Perhaps the greatest of all the pressures on landscape derives from the rising number of people on the islands – visitors and indigenous – that is associated with what might be called *late-urbanisation* (cf. late-capitalism). The demographics have been analysed and described elsewhere with Mallorca's population now estimated at just less than one million, onto which must be grafted an annual visitor population of over 15. 0m, the latter spread over the year but with a marked concentration in July and August[272]. While the concentration of this population is to be found in Greater Palma and in the coastal tourism settlements, the effects of late-urbanisation are increasingly ubiquitous, fuelled by such mechanisms as rising housing demands quantitatively and qualitatively, counterurbanisation, residential tourism, second- homeownership, longer distance commuting, new industrial/business locations, agricultural decline and changing on-coast and in-the-countryside leisure patterns. Much of coastal Spain and certainly much of the island of Mallorca especially can bear witness to this. Alomar was acutely aware of the need for *regional* planning, mostly as a result of his American and European experiences, but Spain was not ready for it. In Spanish culture, *regions* have meant competing political spaces, not sub-sections of the national geographical system.

In the field of urban conservation, which became one of Alomar's principal interests, authorities have established registers for individual buildings (including gardens and monuments), archaeological and geological sites in a series of registers (*catalogos*) which record architectural details and historical significance but the legislation that should assist their protection has proved difficult to enforce. Such registers are arranged hierarchically with the national *Registro General de Bienes de Interés Cultural y el Inventario General de Bienes Muebles* (BIC catalogue – *Bienes de Interés Cultural*) at the head[273]. For historic areas of towns and villages, there is no equivalent to British Conservation Area policy but municipalities can implement controls using town planning legislation such as in the *casc antich* in Palma. Each municipality maintains a catalogue of its patrimony but lists are not a substitute for determined action.

What of the cultural landscape, perhaps best expressed in Spanish as *el patrimonio cultural*? Here, in theory, at least, recognition and protection are given via another series of registers of ethnographic and archaeological features which include '*naturaleza y el paisaje, muebles e inmuebles, costumbres y creencias que no son incompatibles con la vida moderna*' (natural features and landscape, buildings and real estate, customs and beliefs that are not compatible with modern life). While these recognize the richness of Mallorca's landscape characteristics, the accompanying legislation seems aimed at protecting or conserving specific artefacts and less with 'the totality of landscape that would emphasise the almost ecological interdependence of all such features in a historical context in geographical spaces'[274]. It is in this regard that a holistic approach mirrors much of Alomar's early concerns for the totality of landscapes.

Over and above these details relating to zoning, land use and the need for planning control of development lay Alomar's continuing concern for the aesthetic in the urban environment:

> *El valor urbanístico, estético y humano de nuestra ciudad nueva, menos que mediocre, más que a la poca calidad de su trazado o de sus edificios, se debe al la falta de i una reglamentación que imponga un mínimo de orden en la conjunto. . . de crear una ciudad buena y hermosa.* (The urban, aesthetic and human value of our new city, whose mediocrity, rather than the poor quality of its layout or its buildings, is due to the lack of a regulation that imposes a minimum order on the whole . . . And then, our children's generation will be able to create a good and beautiful city.')[275]

Alomar's concern for the education and training of planners appears to have had little impact. City planning courses are subject to the vagaries of university administration as well as demand and certainly not need. By the first decade of the 21stC only three institutions had free-standing planning departments with their own degrees at the undergraduate level: the former 'polytechnic' institutions of Granada, Valencia and Madrid. The comparative figures for Germany, France, the Netherlands and the UK were 10, 20, 9 and 29. Even the Irish Republic with a population of 4.74m had three planning schools and neighbouring Portugal, with a population of 10.3m, had nine schools. Today, Spain has the lowest ratio of planning schools to the population of any country in Europe at 15.7. The vast majority of planning education today remains in the schools of architecture just as it did in Alomar's day; there may be about seventy such schools today compared to the handful in the late 1930s. Here the content can vary from a few modules at the undergraduate level to a greater proportion in a variety of masters degrees which are often aimed at only certain aspects of planning. In addition, there are now modules in several related social science disciplines such as geography, economics and law. From the titles of these modules, it is difficult to see the influence of Alomar other than as a historical figure. This does not mean he has no legacy in planning education because many of the causes which he espoused such as ecology, urban sociology and community development now figure prominently in a country in which sustainability and diversity are political forces to be reckoned with. Nonetheless, it would be true to say that in Spain the emphasis still lies on buildings and real estate and not on their spatial context. In these circumstances, it is perhaps not surprising that many of Spain's Master's degrees in planning focus on the city as commodity with graduates looking for employment not in the public sector with national, regional or local government but in the private sector as technocrats and consultants serving property developers. This is not unique to Spain; in the UK planners, more especially in the large cities, have been reduced to protectors of the public interest against the advances of international capital, often undermined by changing government policy which seeks fewer regulatory controls in order to loosen ties to capital investment[276]. To date in Palma the advances of capital have been in three principal directions: the building of prestigious iconic buildings such as the new conference and hotel centre in the sea-front district, the development of large scale edge of town retailing schemes such as Festival Park and Al Campo accessed from an expanded *cintura* (outer ring road) and the related high-speed road network, and in the gentrification of some parts of the *casc antich*. The first of these appears to have been done without proper market research and could well become a 'white elephant'; its development has been mired in possible corruption that may have resulted in the imprisonment of important political figures. The second might be seen as part of the planned expansion of the city following plans of the 1970 and '80s and is more typical of European urban growth generally. The final item is currently undergoing considerable opposition from those concerned with the old city as a living space with Palma's own residents being priced out of their traditional environment by foreign inward investment, and rapidly rising rents exacerbated by such movements as Airbnb, processes witnessed in many other Europen cities. Will the current generation of Palma's planners and those of the proximate future be able to withstand these forces of late capitalism? Does the 1943 plan for Palma drawn up by Alomar have any lessons at all for today's planners?

Alomar's plan was designed to deal with the problems the city inherited from the 19th and early 20thCs. In this sense, it is not so very different from the earlier plans of Calvet and Forteza. It was not really a plan to deal with even the contemporary challenges of the 1940s and '50s. Alomar, rather than leading new advances in the planning of Palma and in Spain at that time, might be better seen as among the last of an older school of planning.

His success in contributing to national planning and policy proved to be less significant than he had hoped. Despite the enthusiasm that he brought with him to Madrid in the 1950s when he was full of lessons he had learned from his experience in Palma, matched by the absorption of American ideas from his short stay at MIT and complemented by later visits in 1948 and 1949 and from his knowledge of British planning policy enshrined in the 1947 Act, it was frustratingly difficult for him to translate his ideas into action on the national scene. It would appear that he was only appointed to somewhat minor roles in the formulation of the Ley de Suelo, for example, as a member of the secretariat. His claims for a more central position appear a little exaggerated. More importantly, he clearly found much of the politicking in Franco's government distasteful at one level, and being unable to influence more important figures than himself, at another. His lack of exposure to the nastiness of political in-fighting – after all he had never held elected political office – must have left him as something of an outsider, the provincial architect/planner from a distant off-shore island that barely figured in the geographic perceptions of Madrid's bureaucrats and civil servants. Did he have a somewhat naïve view of what Nationalist politics might achieve? Only latterly has much of Franco's rule been seen for what it was: inefficient, corrupt, riddled by ideological conflicts with no clear sense of where it was headed, dependent upon the whims of a steadily weakening and more distant leader who preferred hunting and fishing to directing his country into the second half of the 20th century. Nonetheless, and despite its alteration in the Cortes by lawyers representing the interests of property and business, the 1956 land-use law (LS56) and the subsequent reforms of 1975, 1990 and 1998, remains an important beginning to the formulation of national planning legislation. Alomar should be seen as one of that group of planners and lawyers who pioneered the idea of a national system for his country. Sadly, its final promulgation by Pedro Bidagor for largely political reasons led to the loss of the friendship of a close colleague.

Perhaps, too, he might be seen – and maybe he saw himself – as more of an academic figure, a teacher, a writer of books and academic papers, more at home in the *Instituto de Estudios de Administracion Local* (IEAL) where he has been described as a 'professor' (although he held no university post) than in a government department or the Ministry of Housing[277]. While at ILEA one of his main tasks was the dissemination of modern ideas in town planning, particularly to the architects and planners at the level of the ayuntamiento. In addition to the courses he gave for these more senior officials, he also saw that it was necessary to develop a somewhat lower level of practitioner, what in Spain became known as *técnicos urbanistas*, equivalent to planning technicians in the UK, that is, trained to a higher diploma level but not graduating with a university degree. His pioneering work here eventually evolved, after post-Franco reforms in the 1980s, into the *Centro de Estudios Urbanos del Instituto de Estudios de Administración Local* which acted as a forum for professionals engaged in urban studies as well providing training courses, including validating some university programmes at Masters level.

Throughout his life, Alomar was always an active publisher of books and papers most of which have been referred to during the writing of this monograph. Beginning with essays on his native city and published locally he moved quite early to writing what became a standard textbook *Teoria de la Ciudad* published in 1947 by ILEA, a work he had begun while in the USA and the draft of which helped him secure the post at ILEA that he was to occupy for the next decade[278].

Of his five principal books on planning, three were of a pedagogic nature perhaps the most successful ones being those that dealt with urban sociology where he tried to introduce to planning policies and practice in Spain some of the ideas he had been exposed to at MIT in 1945. Later in life, he was quite happy to describe himself as an urban sociologist. In the introduction to one book he laid out his ideas clearly:

> *El urbanismo, como ciencia, arte o tecnica de la organización de los ambientes en los cuales el hombre desarolla su vida, ha sido inevitablemente superado al descubrirse que la ciudad como realidad ecologica no puede independizarse del campo, del medio rural. Se empezó planificando a la ciudad y hoy se planea la region y la nación entera, dentro de la cual la ciudad no es mas que un punto singular, punto de interes concentrado, pero solo un punto, un lugar geometrico. Habiamos pensado en nombres mas aparopridados, como el de 'fundamentos sociales del planeamiento regional y urbano'.* (Urbanism, as a science, art or technique of the organization of the environments in which man leads his life, has been inevitably overtaken by discovering that the city as an ecological reality could not become independent from the countryside, from the rural environment. At first it was the city that began to be planned and today the region and the entire nation are planned, within which the city is but a singular point, a point of concentrated interest, but only one point, a geometric location. We had thought of more appropriate names (for this book), such as the 'social foundations of regional and urban planning'.)[279]

Lastly, we have to consider the relationship between our protagonist and Juan March Ordinas. This figure has probably attracted as much attention from Spanish and other historians and biographers as Franco himself. The question to be asked is, to what extent was Alomar aware of March's illegal and corrupting activities in Mallorca and on the Peninsula? While it may be true that the evidence of the scale of his misdeeds has only come to light in recent years, there is no doubt that on the island at least, his 'history' as smuggler, owner of the tobacco monopoly, landowner and banker was no secret, even if that secret was not widely broadcast for fear of retribution. When Alomar returned from his studies in Barcelona before the Civil War his political acumen and that of his family must have known something of March's role in attempting to undermine the Republic. To quote Paul Preston 'the Republic had acquired a fabulously rich enemy', devoted to waging war on Azañas' government[280]. He had been imprisoned in the Cárcel Modelo for corruption in 1932 but was elected from there to the Tribunal of Constitutional Guarantees![281] He escaped in November, returned to Mallorca where he was elected – almost certainly by bribing electors – to the Cortes which immediately gave him immunity from prosecution. As early as 1935 in the Cortes, Teodomiro Menéndez called him the Sultan of Spain, saying the people of Spain were his subjects[282].

March's role in the Civil War is well known, ranging from the infamous Dragon Rapide flight that brought Franco from the Canary Islands to Morocco to the direct subsidy of rebel forces via the purchase of Italian aircraft. Overall, it has been calculated that March covered 8 to 10 % of the cost of the Nationalist war effort. In Mallorca, it was March's money that funded the rebels' defeat of Alberto Bayo's invasion and the cruel repression of legitimate forces and the passing of the island into fascist control, including, as we have shown, local government. Little of this financial support was altruistic; March emerged from the war with his wealth at least doubled.

To give some idea of his financial influence after the war in the early 1950s – at an early stage of Alomar's professional practice – March deviously gained control of the Barcelona Traction, Light and Power Company (BTLP), an action that yielded him as much as six billion pesetas. This one aspect alone of his continuing enormous wealth shows that any investment in Alomar's plans for Palma was trivial – and even here, the investment in Jaume III, the Olivar market and the Plaça Major was viewed by March as a profit-making and controlling venture.

What was Alomar's relation with March? Was it purely a business relationship or were they on more intimate terms? Examination of Alomar's initial contract for the rebuilding and reform of March's enormous hacienda and gardens at Sa Vall might lead us to see the young, newly qualified architect as somewhat naïve but how were the two men thrown together in this enterprise? Was it through family connections? Alomar's father was known to be on terms with March and March's son with Alomar junior. What was the family's stance on the Civil War? Alomar served in the Nationalist army as we have shown even if it was in a rather cushy billet. What were the pre-War relations between his father/family and March? Alomar has been able to show his bona fides for support for Catalan culture and language but did this extend to support for Catalan independence? If the former, would not Alomar have been aware of this man's rise to notoriety initially in their shared space in their native Mallorca and its capital city and later nationally and internationally? His pernicious influence on Spanish governance was surely felt everywhere. Would Alomar not have had to confront the moral issue of accepting finance from such a tainted source? Or was he bound by the disinterested mores of any capitalist entrepreneur?

There is also the delicate matter of Alomar working under the Francoist regime, for the ayuntamiento of Palma who approved his plan for the city in the immediate post-war period and later when he worked in a variety of roles for central government – in the Institute, in the Ministry of Housing, and for Spain's conservation movement both at home and abroad. In all locales, he was clearly a respected figure, able to contribute to important areas of government urban policy. Rather, as in the case with his work for Juan March, the key questions are: how much did he know of the evils of the regime, how did this knowledge influence his decisions, what was the extent of his sympathies for the non-political and technical aspects of the regime's objectives- questions that could be asked of almost any Spaniard at that time?

What of Alomar's own education in town planning? We have detailed the courses he took as an undergraduate noting that the Barcelona curriculum in the 1930s contained few units devoted to town planning. Alomar sought to rectify this by going to the United States but the time he spent at MIT was very limited as we showed in an earlier chapter. He obviously derived much from his very brief sojourn there and from subsequent visits to the USA despite the constraints of World War II. One has to conclude that in many respects he could be described as self-taught in town planning although he certainly absorbed much from his regime of wide reading. In addition, whilst at the Institute in Madrid, he was able to undertake research and the act of writing textbooks for publication exposed him to many ideas as revealed in his footnotes and references. Might he be better described as a theoretician or a philosopher of town planning? After all, after the plan for the Reform of Palma, he designed no detailed city or town plan.

Much of what he wrote about planning seems to lack the technical detail of converting plan into action, even in Palma much of the detail was left to architects and builders. He also seems less concerned with the social and economic contexts of how they would be interpreted by those implementing his plans. There is not the detail in statistical analysis for example that one might have expected nor is he particularly conscious of the political environment within which planning takes place. Was it just not wise in the Franco era to say much about the ideological drivers behind Spanish planning? And what of his experience of Puerto Rico? His papers show little appreciation of the repressive regime of the United States to its colony and the desires of the local population for independence. The whole of the '30s in Puerto Rico was characterised by the tension between workers and the authorities resulting in wage reduction, increasing poverty and a series of strikes – and worse – massacres, most of this occurring under the Presidency of Franklin D Roosevelt, the advocate of the New Deal. Presidents appointed the governors of the island, of which there were many post-1898, who were rarely competent, often corrupt and saw their appointment by Washington as an opportunity for self-advancement. Amongst the greediest was Blanton C Winship (1934-39) who invested vast sums of state money in militarizing the island and its repressive police force. Alomar was surely aware of the massacres during his reign. He was fortunate that on his arrival the governor was Rexford Tugwell (1941-46), a Roosevelt New Dealer, liberal in contrast to most of his predecessors, who created the Puerto Rico Planning, Urbanization and Zoning Board in 1942. Alomar appears to have been able to write a critique of some of his ideas while failing to see their application to an island under a repressive regime with strict social divisions. Did Tugwell's advocacy of island-wide planning influence Alomar's own thoughts when he came to contribute to the Ley de Suelo a decade later?

Many of the questions raised in this review of Alomar's work and its legacies are difficult to answer. This book is not a biography and it is not until his personal and family archive becomes available to scholars and the public generally, that they might be fully answered. From the perspective of the second decade of the 21st century, what can be said of the three or four proyectos of his plan for Palma that were completed? The recent somewhat more radical interpretation of the Alomar townscape has emerged that focus on property development in Palma, something that does not seem to stem from Alomar's thoughts or writings. Designing a city and its buildings as a means for investors to make money was distant from his rather idealised thoughts and yet the whole process of town building in Spain early in his career was predicated on returns on capital. As we have shown there was little construction by the state, local or national. Turning plans and projects into built form was the business of the private sector.

The historic core of Palma on which Alomar's plan was focussed has recently been the subject of intensive study by the city authorities and pressure groups (such as Palma XXI), primarily because tourism and well-heeled more permanent immigration have together been exerting considerable pressure on the inner city's structure, appearance and social composition[283]. This revealed that in the 143 hectares of the historic centre the tourist impact is concentrated on the area between the Parc de Mar, the Cathedral and the Plaça d'España including the Plaça Major, Calle St Miguel, El Borne, Oms and Jaume III, all spaces that are familiar to tourists. Here hotels have increased from 38 in 2014 to 101 in 2017, many in converted historically important buildings. Car ownership and use by residents and visitors have increased, assisted by the proliferation of car parks, many underground. Bus data shows the city-region nature of Palma as Alomar predicted, with over 16000 passengers per day arriving in the city from all parts of the island. Pedestrian concentration can be found in key areas such as the Plaça Major; footfall can average 2500 to 3000 per hour in Calle St Miguel for example in August. Seven per cent of Palma municipality's population is located in the historic core; accommodation for locals has become a political issue with house prices and rents rising markedly by as much as 30-40% in the years since 2012. Rentals have been exacerbated by the rise of Airbnb and by sales of apartments to foreign investors – over 30% of the historic core's population is foreign-born. Finally, the retail and commercial property market has been transformed to satisfy the demands of tourists with the ground floor buildings of many streets converted to seasonal retailing of goods few locals require. In the case of Jaume III under its arcades were developed high-class retail establishments, offices, hotels with exclusive apartments above that could command high rents. Similarly, in the Bonaire zone that was built to the east of the avenue and in Paseo de Mallorca parallel to the Riera, Alomar's scheme for individual townhouses was soon abandoned by property developers whose sights were on high density, high-grade apartment blocks that would yield much higher income in both equity value and rents in the future.

The urban policies of the city government that began in 2012 were focussed on the 'entrepreneurial city' that was designed to develop Palma as a new engine of growth in the tourism industry on the false understanding – as it turned out – that the sea and sand coastal tourism economy had reached its apogee. Sònia Vives-Miro, Onofre Rullan and Jesus M. Gonzalez-Perez have sought to show that market forces working within this policy ('there is no alternative') have produced in recent years quite large-scale evictions of people and small businesses unable to pay rent or meet payments on mortgages in the historic core and, indeed, some of its penumbra. The land-use zones established in the post-Alomar city-wide plans of 1973, 1985 and 1998, together with the myriad of local projects that dealt with many parts of the historic townscape, were overtaken by policies to encourage tourism-based activities such as boutique hotels, Airbnb accommodation, expensive apartments many used by foreigners only seasonally, retailing establishments often national or internally owned to sell imported goods to the high-density flow of pedestrian visitors. The impact of this 'revolution' has had a serious impact on Alomar's townscape[284]. A recent study by Palma XXI et al has mapped ground floor land-uses and pedestrian flows in the tourism season – now lengthened to include most of the year – that occupy much of at least two of Alomar's *proyectos* – Jaume III and Plaça Major[285]. His vision for these areas was somewhat different but they have nonetheless provided the space and the possibility of adaptation to accommodate this new economy but an economy that is for the benefit of visitors and only marginally for residents. If his Reform no. 8 had been built no doubt that would have suffered the same fate. Alomar's Palma of the 1940s has become *Marca Palma* – the Palma brand – of the 2020s.

How can Gabriel Alomar Esteve's contribution to Spanish town planning be best summarised? First, his provincial beginnings in his native city remain just that. Not entirely original, leaning heavily on at least one of his predecessors, Bernat Calvet, his schemes for the historic core were only partially successful; he contributed little to the detail of the outward expansion of the city via his scheme for the eixample. Too much of his plan was left to builders and property speculators – perhaps a product of the corrupt and inefficient times of the Franco dictatorship. Second, his plan vision was too romantic relying heavily on what had become outdated theories often derived from other cultures such as German and British. It might also be said, perhaps playfully, that his plan for Palma was the product of an artistic rather than a technological mind. After all, it was first exposed at the Expocisión Nacional de Bellas Artes in Barcelona in 1942 as a series of architectural drawings, some reproduced in his autobiography, and won a prize for its artistic design in the architecture section, only later being converted to a plan on the ground with all its potential economic and sociological implications, which as we have seen were rather thin. Remember that he employed at least one graphic designer to draw many of his convincing maps in his 1943 plan and 1950 book. The same may be said for the views expressed in his books. His perception of society based on community and Catholic beliefs was overshadowed by the State's right-wing ideologies. Soon, Spain was to be transformed by industrialisation, rapid and extensive urbanisation and of course, mass tourism. His retreat from town planning in the late1950s and 1960s into the world of urban conservation suited him much better. Here he could indulge his desire to accumulate and add to his and his country's international experience with a strong European flavour; Western Europe was a more attractive stage on which to act. Similarly, his concern for open and green spaces within cities that we have explored fitted in so much better with his desire to bring about environmental improvements in citizens' lives. In some, if not many, of these areas perhaps Alomar's time has come again.

In Mallorca, there is a strong movement to reverse much of the emphasis on economic growth that is still underwritten by mass tourism, both in the coastal resorts and Palma itself, and which made Mallorca one of the richest places in Spain. Palma's encephalic position in the island's urban hierarchy has surely reached its peak. The whole island is increasingly being planned as an urban space with new policies required to address decentralisation, especially in the neighbouring municipalities, echoing Alomar's call in 1962 for regional planning. Nationally and in the Balearics there is strong support for a 'greener' economy and urban environment with a new set of secular social values based on community ideas. For most things urban, planning schools in universities are beginning to witness more emphasis on these issues in the town planning curriculum. The tension between construction and planning is moving slowly towards a concern for the aesthetics of the built environment in housing, in public transport and public open spaces and in the improvement of the quality of life, giving hope for the future of a healthier urban Spain.

References and Notes

Sources of Endnotes:

Principal archive

AA – The Gabriel Alomar Esteve Collection, Consell de Mallorca at Ciutat de Querètaro, 3, 07007 Palma. telefon-fax 971 219 550 / 971 219 639.

https://web. conselldemallorca. cat/ca/arxiu-general.

Email: arxius@conselldemallorca. net

AP – The city archives of Palma can be found at Can Bordils (Arxiu Municipal de Palma) Carrer de l'Almudaina, 9, 07001 Palma.

Email: arxiu@palma. cat

Newspapers

ABC – https://www. abc. es/hemeroteca/historico

Diario de Mallorca (including La Almudaina) – https://www. diariodemallorca. es/hemeroteca/. For some articles, this requires a subscription.

La Vanguardia – http://hemeroteca. lavanguardia. com/

Journals

Architecture, city and environment. (ACE)

Boletín de la Cámara Provincial de Comercio, Industria y Navegación de Palma de Mallorca. (BCCIN)

Cuadernos de arquitectura

Ciudad y Territorio

El Bolletí de la Societat Arqueològica Lul. luliana (BSAL)

Journal of the Royal Town Planning Institute (RTPI)

La Revista de Estudios de la Administración Local y Autonómica (REALA).

Revista de la vida local (REVL)

Mayurqa

Randa

Theses

Researchers on Spanish town planning are fortunate that many doctoral theses may be found online. Many are referred to in the references.

Video

A brief video on the work of Alomar was originally made by UIB shortly before his death and published in 2001 on line at

youtube. com/watch?v=FbOjI3ULM0k

References and Endnotes

1   Amengual B (1903): *La indústria de los forasteros*. Palma. Amengual and Muntaner.

2   Diario de Mallorca, 14 August 2019.

3   Fundació initiciatives del Mediterrani (2018): *Capacitat de càrrega turística; estudi al centre històric de Palma*. Consulted online at http://palmaxxi.com/informes/ October 2020.

4   Alomar Esteve G (1986): *Memorias de un urbanista 1939-1979*. Palma. Miguel Font.

5   Buswell R (2013): *Mallorca; the making of the landscape*. Edinburgh. Dunedin Academic Press, *xiii*.

6   In 1978 Alomar retired from private practice and said he would be 'in the Balearic Islands, working in historical researches and writing especially on subjects of medieval history, sometimes on historical city planning'. Letter to David Fryer, secretary general to R.T.P.I, April 22 1978. AA Box K.

7   Hall P (2000): The centenary of modern planning in: Freestone R (Ed): *Urban planning in a changing world*. London. Spon, 23.

8   Alomar Esteve G (1950): De la arquitectura al urbanismo y del urbanismo al planeamiento. *Cuadernos de arquitectura*,11-12, 22.

9   Martorell Fullana C M (n.d.): *Modernització, republicanisme i patrimoni a la ciutat de Palma a l'època del Sexenni Democràtic (1868-1874)*. http://ibdigital.uib.es/greenstone/collect/memoriesUIB/import/Martorell_Fullana_CatalinaM.pdf. Consulted 5 Feb 2014.

10   Hall P (1998): *Cities in civilization*. London. Weidenfeld and Nicholson, 683.

11   Sevillano Colom F and Pou Muntaner J (1974): *Historia del puerto de Palma de Mallorca*. Palma. Instituto de Estudios Baleáricos, 348-9.

12   Salas-Vives, P., & Pujadas-Mora, J. (2018). Cordons Sanitaires and the Rationalisation Process in Southern Europe (Nineteenth-Century Majorca). *Medical History,* 62(3), 314-3 Published online: 11 June 2018. Consulted 30 October 2018.

13   Pujadas-Mora, J.M. (2008): La producció científica d'Enric Fajarnés i Tur (1858 – 1934). (The scientific production of the physician Enric Fajarnés i Tur (1858-1934)). *Enric Fajarnés i Tur (1858 – 1934), entre la història i la demografia*. Palma.Consell de Mallorca, 35-78.

14   Pujadas-Mora, J.M. (2012): La cuantificación demográfica y epidemiológica en el higienismo balear, 1850-1930. (Demographic and epidemiological quantification in Balearic hygienism, 1850-1930). *Dynamis*. 32, 1, 166.

15   El Alcázar, 21 Feb 1940, quoted by García and Guerrero, 2014.

16   Barceló Crespí M (2012): *El raval de mar de la ciutat de Mallorca*. Palma. Lleonard Muntaner.

17   Sevillano Colom F and Pou Muntaner J (1974): *Historia del puerto de Palma de Mallorca*. Palma. Instituto de Estudios Baleáricos, 268.

18   Santaner Mari J (1967): *Historia del arabal de Santa Catalina*. Palma. Parroquia Inmaculada Concepcion, Espartero.

19   De Terán F (1999 Edn.): *Historia de urbanismo en España III; siglos XIX y XX*. Madrid. Cátedra, 56ff.

20   It was not until 1971 when the Instituto de Estudios Fiscales published the third volume of Cerdá's theory, with an introduction by the economist Fabiàn Estapé, that his work reached a modern audience. Estapé's introduction has subsequently been published as *Vida y obra de Idelfonso Cerdá* (2001): Barcelona. Peninsula. However, the monarchist town planner César Cort had promoted Cerdá as the founder of the discipline in the 1920s and again at the conference on town planning and housing held in Madrid in 1940 (See Garcia and Guerrero, 2014).

21 In recent years there has been a resurgence of interest in Cerdá not least among Catalunyans and Barcelonistas, much of it critical. For an early account see: Estapé F (2001).For a more recent and critical appraisal of his work see a series of articles in: *Barcelona quaderns d'història* 2008,14. *Cerdá i els altres.La modernitat a Barcelona,1854-1874* and Bonet Correa, A (2009): *Ildefons Cerdá y el Ensanche de Barcelona*, Madrid, Ministerio de Cultura – Sociedad Estatal de Conmemoraciones Culturales. See also Eduardo Aibar E and Bijker W E (1997): Constructing a City: The Cerdá Plan for the Extension of Barcelona. *Science, Technology, & Human Values*, 22, 1, 3-30.

22 Magrinyà, F (2008), El ensanche y la reforma de Ildefonso Cerdá como instrumento urbanístico de referencia en la modernización urbana de Barcelona *Scripta Nova: Revista electrónica de geografía y ciencias sociales*, Nº. Extra 13, 296, 2009 (Issue dedicated to: Globalización y modernización urbana: Lisboa y Barcelona). Consulted online 9 Oct 2014.

23 Aibar E and Bijker W E (1997): Constructing a City: The Cerdá Plan for the Extension of Barcelona *Science, Technology, & Human Values*, 22,1, 3.

24 Aibar E and Bijker W E (1997): Constructing a City: The Cerdá Plan for the Extension of Barcelona *Science, Technology, & Human Values*, 22,1, 10, 24.

25 López M (2009): Cerdá and the Local Planning Tradition. Reason in the city: the Cerdá Plan. *Barcelona Metropolis*. Autumn.

26 Ward S V (2000): Re-examining the international diffusion of planning in: Freestone R (Ed): *Urban planning in a changing world*. London. Spon,41.

27 Hughes R (1992): Barcelona. London. Harvill, 276-278.

28 De Terán, F (1999): Historia del urbanismo en España III; siglos XIX y XX, Madrid, Cátedra, 111.

29 De Terán, F (1999): Historia del urbanismo en España III; siglos XIX y XX, Madrid, Cátedra, 95.

30 Dávila Linares J M (1991): *La ordinación urbanística durante la primera mitad del siglo XX. Premisa para un tratamento integral de los espacios urbanos. Investigaciones Geográficas*, 9,102-5. On-line digital edition. Consulted 12/10/2017.

31 Bujosa y Homar F (2003): Eusebio Estada i la mentalitat higienesta in, Eusebio E: *La Ciudad de Palma.* facsimile edn. 2003,16-19.

32 Buswell R (2013): *Mallorca; the making of the landscape.* Edinburgh. Dunedin Academic Press, 154. See also: Penya Barceló A (1991): La Ciutat i les manufactures; aspects de la indústria urbanas al segle XIX in: Manera C and Petrus Bey J: *Del taller a la fàbrica*,67.

33 Seguí Aznar M (1985-7): Planteamientos teoricos y realización practica del Plan Calvet. *Mayurqa* 21,394.

34 Ladaria Benares, M. (1992): *El ensanche de Palma. Planteamiento del tema, problemàtica, construcción y valoración de un nuevo espacio urbano, 1868-1927,* Palma. Ed. Ajuntament de Palma, 69.

35 Seguí Aznar (1985-7): Planteamientos teoricos y realización practica del Plan Calvet. *Mayurqa* 21,396.

36 Seguí Aznar (1985-7): Planteamientos teoricos y realización practica del Plan Calvet. *Mayurqa* 21,400.

37 Seguí Aznar (1985-7): Planteamientos teoricos y realización practica del Plan Calvet. *Mayurqa* 21,395.

38 Buswell R J (2011): *Mallorca and tourism; history, economy and environment.* Bristol. Channel View Publications, 36-41.

39 Aleña J (1916): *Anteproyecto de Reforma de Palma.* Tipo-litografía de Amengual y Muntaner. Palma.

40 Seguí Aznar M (1981): Propuestas ubanisticas de Gaspar Bennàzar *B.S.A.L*,38,478

41 Sevillano Colom F and Pou Muntaner J (1974): *Historia del puerto de Palma de Mallorca*. Palma. Instituto de Estudios Baleáricos, 275-279.

42 Barceló Pons B (1963): El Terreno; geográfia urbana de un barrio de Palma. *BCICON,* 640,125-178

43 Forteza G (1921): *L'art de construir les ciutats i la reforma de Palma*. Palma. Amengual i Muntaner.

44 Seguí i Aznar M (1993): Guillem Forteza, arquitecte i urbanista in: Oliver i Jaume J and Seguí i Aznar M: *Guillem Forteza, Arquitecte escolar.* Palma. Conselleria de Cultura, Educació i Esports, 41-45.

45 Forteza G (1921): *L'art de construir les ciutats i la reforma de Palma*. Palma. Amengual i Muntaner,7.

46 Mayol Amengual, J (2010): L'arquitectura escolar de Guillem Forteza 1917-1943. Abstract of Ph.D thesis, Universitat Politècnica de Catalunya. http://hdl.handle.net/10803/77767. Consulted 17 Feb 2014.

47 Seguí i Aznar M (1993): Guillem Forteza, arquitecte i urbanista in: Oliver i Jaume J and Seguí i Aznar M: *Guillem Forteza, Arquitecte escolar.* Palma. Conselleria de Cultura, Educació i Esports, 44-45.

48 Buswell R J (2013): *Mallorca; the making of the landscape.* Edinburgh. Dunedin Academic Press, 182-4.

49 Cirer J C (2009): *La invenció del turisme de masses a Mallorca*. Palma. Edicions Balear. Chapter10.

50 Walton J (2005): Paradise lost and found; tourists and expatriates in El Terreno, Palma de Mallorca from the 1920s to 1950s in, Walton J (Ed): *Histories of Tourism.* Clevedon. Channel View Publications, 179-94.

51 Simón P (2004): Les muralles de Palma avui, in: Ajuntament de Palma (2004): *I centenari de l'enderrocament de les murades de Palma, 1902-2002. Palma,* 127-131.

52 Ladaria Benares, M. (1992): *El ensanche de Palma. Planteamiento del tema, problemàtica, construcción y valoración de un nuevo espacio urbano, 1868-1927.* Ed. Ajuntament de Palma. Palma,197-201.

53 Alomar G (1987): *Un poble i una nissaga; la vila de Muro i els Alomar 'de la Serra'.* Palma,19.

54 Alomar G (1987): *Un poble i una nissaga; la vila de Muro i els Alomar 'de la Serra'.* Palma, 30ff.

55 Alomar G (1986): *Memorias de un urbanista 1939-1979*.Palma. Miguel Font.

56 García-Ruiz Rossellò A (2000): *Gabriel Alomar: Arquitecto, historiador y humanista.* Inaugural lecture. La Real Academia de Belles Artes de San Sebastiàn de Palma,16. Consulted on-line 8 Oct 2014.

57 Alomar y Canyelles A (1989): Notes per a la biografia de Gabriel Alomar i Villalonga *BSAL*. 45, 403-405 ff. Alomar Esteve G. *Memorias de un urbanista,1939-1979.* Palma. 1986, 17. This Gabriel was Alomar's uncle but 26 years younger than his father. He was asked to tutor the young Alomar.

58 Writing from his wife's family home in Mayagüez, Puerto Rico in 1944 Alomar applied to a number of 'ivy league' schools of planning in the United States. Accompanying this letter is a list of the courses he took in Barcelona between 1927 and 1935. AA Seccio A Box 7.

59 *Exposició commemorativa del centenari de l'Escola d'Arquitectura de Barcelona 1875-76/1975-76.* Barcelona. Escuela Technica Superior de Arquitectura de Barcelona.1977, 140-145.

60 *Urbanologia*– a term pioneered by César Cort.

61 ABC, 19 July 1942,17.

62 Report on La exposición nacional de bellas artes de Barcelona. Proyectos ideóles y realizaciones arquitectónicos. La Vanguardia, 31 July 1942. See also: Review, National Exhibition of Fine Arts of Barcelona, 1942. *Cuadernos de arquitectura*, 1944,1,24-27. Consulted on 15/10/2016

63 Buckley H (2nd Edn 2013): The life and death of the Spanish republic. London.I.B.Taurus,145

64 Naturally there was also an equivalent Catalan group known as GATCPAC (Grup d'Arquitectes i Tècnics Catalans

pel Progrés de l'Arquitectura Contemporànea).

65   In his autobiography Alomar gives the impression that his location on the Pyrenean frontier was something of an easy posting yet at this time the leadership of the Nationalist army was increasingly concerned with neighbouring France's possible aggression towards Nationalist areas close to the border which was the main entry point for many of the armaments desperately needed by the Republican forces and had to be strongly defended.

66   For a useful summary of many of the organizations that participated in this movement see: García M.C. and Guerrero Lopéz (2014): The National Federation of Town Planning and Housing (1939-1954); a network of urbanism in the Spanish post Civil War period. *Journal of Urban History*, 40(6), 1099-1122.

67   Munoz-Rojas O (2009): Falangist visions of a neo-imperial Madrid. *Journal of War & Culture Studies*, 2, 3, 335-352.

68   Amongst other things he was the architect chosen by Franco to design the frightening Valle de los Caidos.

69   Lopéz Diaz J (2003): Social housing and Falange: Ideology and buildings in the '40s. *Scripta Nova* VII, 146 (024), August 1, 2003.

70   Seguí Aznar M (1981-84): Francisco Casas; arquitecto rationalista. *Mayurqa*, 20, 409.

71   Lopéz Diaz J (2014): La influencia de la ideología fascista en la recepción de la modernidad arquitectónica española durante el Franquismo. Comunicación presentada en el *Congreso Posguerras: 75 aniversario de la Guerra Civil española*. Universidad Complutense de Madrid. 3-5 de abril, 9. Consulted on line 19 September 2019.

72   Martínez Caro, C. (1998): La aportación de Gabriel Alomar a la formación de una nueva mentalidad urbanística en el ambiente de la Arquitectura española 1950/1965. In: *Actas del congreso internacional. De Roma a Nueva York: itinerarios de la nueva arquitectura española 1950-1965*, 283–291. Pamplona. T6 Ediciones.

73   Angela was two years older than and taller than her husband to be; a very determined woman. Personal communication Gonçal López Nadal, 11 January 2016.

74   Some of this report appeared in: Alomar, Gabriel (1935): *L'emplaçament Urbanistíc del Temple Cristià*. Francesc Soler. Ciutat de Mallorca. This is probably Alomar's first ever publication.

75   Alomar Esteve G. *Memorias de un urbanista. 1939-1979*. Palma. 1986,19-20.

76   Gabriel Riera Alemany had been the Nationalist military commander of Pollença in Mallorca during the Civil War.

77   Urbanismo España. *Revista de la vida local* (1947): 32. 241-244.

78   Seguí Aznar M (1981-84): Francisco Casas; arquitecto rationalista. *Mayurqua*, 20, 393-420.

79   Antonio Parietti was born in Palma in 1899 and died there in 1979. It was as a road engineer that he made his reputation in the early 20th century, when the population was much lower and there were hardly any motor vehicles but with excellent prospects as a tourist destination. As part of plans to improve roads in the '20s and '30s, he personally supervised two major public works projects in the Serra de Tramuntana: the 1925 road between Port de Pollença and Formentor, which gave access to Adan Diehl's famous hotel there, and the 1933 road to Sa Calobra. There is a monument dedicated to his memory, built in 1968, on the road to Cap de Formentor.

80   Seguí Aznar M (2000): *Urbanisme i arquitectura a les Balears*. Palma. Documenta Balear,35.

81   Roberto Homs y Gràcis was a well-known Barcelona architect and member of the Asociación de Arquitectos de Cataluña.

82   Enric Matas I Ramis (1887-1956) was a 'moderne' architect, the municipal architect of Calaf in Catalunya. He has a civic centre named after him in Horta, Barcelona.

83   I am indebted to Gabriel Alomar Garau for this information.

84   Alomar Esteve G (1986): *Memorias de un urbanista 1939-1979*.Palma. Miguel Font, 20.

85   Alomar Esteve G (1986): *Memorias de un urbanista 1939-1979*. Palma. Miguel Font, 19.

86   I am indebted to Gabriel Alomar Garau, grandson of our protagonist, for some of this information regarding the competition. See: Palma XXI – biography of the city, online at https://palmaxxi.com/llibres-de-palma-xxi/

87   Alomar Esteve G (1950): *La reforma de Palma; havia la renovacion de una ciudad a traves de un proceso de evolucion creativa*. Palma. Móssen Alover. Chap.3.

88   Alomar Esteve G (1947): *Teoría de la Ciudad*. Madrid. I.E.A.L. 1947. 2nd Edn. 1980, 40.

89   Ferragut became one of Mallorca's best-known architects. He was a devout Catholic. He was murdered in 1968 ostensibly for money but there was always a suspicion that he was killed for his homosexuality at a time of considerable repression. A.B.C. 27/02/1968, 36. Consulted 15/04/2016.

90   González Pérez J (2017): *Les ciutats de les Balears; process d'urbanització i urbanisme*. Palma. Muntaner, 50.

91   Terán F de: (1999): *Historia del urbanismo en España III, siglos XIX and XX*. Madrid. Cátedra, 50.

92   AA Secció N Box 9.

93   Letter from Alomar to Gaspar Blein, municipal architect for Murcia city. AA Box K.

94   The early ideas on compensation and value added that followed from urban development can be found in the works of Cerdá to whom we have referred earlier, again demonstrating his innovative qualities. As the growth of Spanish cities increased, the need for national legislation began to emerge. It was probably Cerdá's thoughts that found their way into Articles 9 to 11 and 35 of the General Law Project for the reform, sanitation, expansion and other improvements of towns under Posada Herrera of 1861 where they were codified. And these laws were not to be replaced until the Ley de Suelo of 1956 which, of course, Alomar helped draft. Vaquer Caballería M (2014): La distribución de beneficios y cargas en el urbanismo español. *Revista de derecho urbanístico y medio ambiente*, 5.

95   Soler G (2010): La modernización de Ciutat. *La Almudaina*, 484, 1-2.

96   Preston P (2012): *The Spanish Holocaust: Inquisition and Extermination in Twentieth-Century Spain*. London. Harper Collins.

97   Sambricio C (2015): On urbanism in the early years of Franco in: Bodenschatz H, Sassi P and Welch M (eds): *Urbanism and dictatorship: a European perspective*. Gutersloh. Bauverlag, 120.

98   César Cort Boti (1893-1978) qualified as an engineer and architect in Madrid where he founded the first school of town planning in Spain in 1922 – a subject he called *urbanalogia*. He became one of the most influential figures in his field. He drew up plans for Murcia (1928) and Valladolid (1938). He was imprisoned by the Popular Front during the Civil War but afterwards composed plans for Badajoz (1940) and La Coruña (1942-48). He made a fortune from tungsten mining in Galicia during the Second World War. Episodios Inmobiliarios: César Cort, *arquitecto, urbanista, emprendedor y visionario* http://urban-networks.blogspot.co.uk/2011/12/episodios-inmobiliarios-cesar-cort.html. Consulted 5 Jan 2017.

99   'Ruralize the cities and urbanize the fields' was the motto of the first Spanish planning book, written by Cerdá. César Cort: *Campos urbanizados y ciudades rurizadas*. Madrid: Federación de Urbanismo y de la Vivienda de la Hispanidad, 1941. Quoted by Sastre L (2016): El sol, la cal y la sal; arquitectura rural en la periodo de la autoquaria. 140-157, from the catalogue of the exhibition, *Campo cerrado; arte y poder en la posguerra espanola, 1939-53*. Museo Reina Sofia. Consulted on-line at www.scribd.com/document/310741010. 18 October 2018.

100   García M.C. and Guerrero López (2014): The National Federation of Town Planning and Housing (1939-1954); a network of urbanism in the Spanish post Civil War period. *Journal of Urban History*, 40(6), 1099-1122.

101   I am indebted to Maria Cristina Garcia Gonzalez whose doctoral thesis – *César Cort y la cultura urbanística de su tiempo* was the principal source of information on the life and work of César Cort. Consulted on-line at García González, María Cristina (2013): *César Cort y la cultura urbanística de su tiempo. Cuadernos de Investigación Urbanística* 87, 10 May 2019.

102   As another example of the continuity of aspects of the planning of Palma, a delegation from the City Council, headed by the mayor Emile Darder, went to Madrid as early as 1931to try to secure resources for important public works for the city, including the Mercat de l'Olivar.

103   Quotations from a letter to Gaspar Blein, 14 December 1946. AA Box K.

104   Hamer D (2000): Planning and heritage: towards integration in, Freestone R (Ed): *Urban planning in a changing world*. London. Spon,199.

105   Review of Alomar's plan in: *Revista de Estudios de la vida local*, 1947, 32, 244.

106   Soler G (2010): La modernización de Ciutat. *La Almudaina*, 484, Aug.

107   Alomar Esteve G (1950): *La reforma de Palma*. Palma. Mossen Alcover, 50.

108   Ferrer Forés J J (2015): La vivienda colectiva en la obra de José Ferragut Pou, in Ferragut Canals J: *El arquitecto José Ferragut Pou*. Palma. Olañjeta, 206 -209. See also: *Revista de la vida local* (1947) 32,241.

109   Bennàzar G (1921): *Reforma de Palma. Primera Sección: Plaza y Mercado del Olivar. Memoria núm. 1: explicación del Proyecto.* Palma. Amengual y Muntaner.

110   Forteza,G (1921) : *L'art de construir les ciutats i la reforma de Palma*, Palma, Amengual i Muntaner.

111   Letter from Alomar to Gaspar Blein. 24 October 1949. AA Box K. Gaspar Blein was the municipal architect of Murcia and had drawn up a comprehensive plan for the city on principles very similar to Alomar's for Palma. A detailed comparative study would pay dividends. Blein's plan (1942-49) involved linking the old Muslim city of Murcia to a new extension via a Gran Via, a circular plaza and links to new roads to Madrid and Alicante. Blein was having great difficulty finding finance for his scheme and wrote to Alomar asking if EUSA might be interested in investing in Murcia. See also: Nicolás Gómez D: Arquitectura y urbanismo en los inicios de la Murcia contemporánea. Consulted on line at: www.regmurcia.com/docs/murgetana.April 2019.

112   Enrique Juncosa Iglesias (Palma 1902-1975), graduated from the School of Architecture of Barcelona. Early in his career he was associated with Guillem Forteza; appointed municipal architect in 1931 and held office until he was removed from it in 1937. He was reinstated after the Civil War. Brother-in-law of Joan Míró. It would appear that Alomar had little respect for him while he was one of the city's municipal architects.: 'Juncosa brings shame on our profession in all regards' – letter from Alomar to Gaspar Blein, December 14, 1946. AA Box K.

113   Mendoza M (2021): Un anhel de modernitat: projeccio i construcció del mercat de l'Olivar (1914-51). *Ciutat, Revista de Palma, 6,12-14*. Palma XXI.Consulted online March 2021.

114   Copy of a letter (probably made by Alomar) from Bidagor to the mayor of Palma, 10th January 1950. AA Box K.

115   Letter from Alomar to Gaspar Blein, municipal architect of Murcia city. 24 October 1949 AA Box K.

116   Cañellas G: La reformas urbanas de nuestra cuidad; historia de un fantasma, *La Almudaina* 12 June 1949,5.

117   Mari Carmen, Alomar's daughter: personal communication, June 2019.

118   Alomar Esteve G (1980): *Teoria de la ciudad* (2nd Edn). Madrid. IEAL,50-53.

119   Colegio de Arquitectos Palma de Mallorca (1975): Exposicion Puig de Sant Pere. Palma. CAPM,16.

120   Joan Roca Cladera interview https://nanopdf.com/download/joana-roca-cladera_pdf. Consulted June 2020. (Author's translation).

121   Ajuntament de Palma (2004): *I centenari de l'enderrocament de les murades de Palma (1902-2002)*. Palma.139.

122   Joana Roca Cladera interview https://nanopdf.com/download/joana-roca-cladera_pdf. Consulted June 2010. (Author's translation).

123 *Realizaciones (1989)*: Palma de Mallorca: plan especial de rehabilitacion y reforma interior del barrio de Sa Calatrava. 10,31-32.

124 Franquesa J (2013): *Urbanismo neoliberal, negocio, inmobiliario y vida vecinal; el caso de Palma.* Barcelona. Incaria, 17-22.

125 Franquesa J (2013): *Urbanismo liberal, negocio inmobilaria y vida vecinal.El caso del Palma.* Barcelona. Incaria,177-181.

126 Pallol Trigueros R (2009): *El Madrid moderno; Chamberí (el sanche norte) simbolo del nacimiento de una nueva capital,1860-1931,* 58. Quoting Castro. Doctoral thesis, Complutense de Madid. Consulted on line 26 November 2020.

127 A valuable examination of the example between Calvet's plan of 1901 and Alomar's of 1943 can be found in Arquitectives (2019): Re-pensar L'Eixample: Passat, present i future. Palma XXI. Consulted on line January 2020.

128 Charles Edouard Jeanneret-Gris, better known as Le Corbusier (1887-1965) made a brief visit to Mallorca in March 1932. According to Alomar he was impressed by Gaudí's work on the Cathedral and by Mallorcan doorways. *Diario de Mallorca* 05/02/2009. Consulted on line 23/08/2016. Alomar noted the visits of Le Corbusier and Gaudí, Gabriel Alomar Esteve G (1987): Sobre las estancias en Mallorca de los arquitectos Gaudí y Le Corbusier, in *Massilia: anuario de estudios lecorbusierianos.* 2009,61-66.

129 Domenech D (2018): The national revolution in architecture: rooted modernism in the Spanish New State (1939-1959) *Brill on-line publications.*7, 2, 214.

130 Lejeune J F (2010): 1939-65: reconstruction and colonization in Spain. The modernization of the Spanish vernacular in, Bucci A and Moll L: *Regional architecture in the Mediterranean area.* Firenza. Alinea, 371.

131 Alomar Esteve G (1947): *Teoria de la ciudad.* Madrid. I.E.A.L, 55 and 88.

132 Alomar Esteve G (1947): *Teoria de la ciudad.* Madrid. I.E.A.L, 52-55.

133 For a useful summary of Sitte's ideas see, Jerram L (2007): From Page to Policy: Camillo Sitte and Planning Practice in Munich. *Manchester Papers in Economic and Social History,*57. Consulted on line 12 Aug 2015.

134 Alomar Esteve G (1948): *Teoria de la ciudad.* Madrid. I.E.A.L, 88-90.

135 *REVL,* 43,1949.

136 Nuñez Granes P (1908): *Ideas generales sobre la urbanización de los alredordes de las grandes urbes.* Madrid.

137 Benabent Fernández de Córdoba M (2006): *La ordinación del territorio en España.* Sevilla. Universidad de Sevilla, 87-102.

138 De Terán F (1999 Edn.): *Historia de urbanismo en España III; siglos XIX y XX.* Madrid. Cátedra,170-1.

139 García González M and Guerrero S: *El estatuto municipal de 1924 y la profesíonalización del urbanismo en España: el caso de Ceuta.* Consulted on line April 27 2019 at oa.upm.es/51212/1/MCGG.

140 Alomar Esteve G (1962): El urbanismo y las ciencias económico-regionales *Cuadernos de arquitectura* 47,45-54.

141 Company A (2008): *Emili Darder Canaves. El darrer batle republicà de Palma.* Palma. Ajuntament de Palma.

142 Later that month on 31 May 1937, a lone Potez 540, flown by the Czechoslovak pilot Jan Ferak, bombed Palma, causing about ten dead and about thirty wounded. On the return flight it was intercepted by Italian planes and it crashed near Andraitx. *Biplane fighter aces of Italy* http://surfcity.kund.dalnet.se/italy_lalatta.ht. Consulted 11 Aug 2015. On 7 December 1937 a raid of at least twenty Republican aircraft was made on Palma; 70 bombs fell on the poorest part of city with 15 killed and 40 wounded. Massot y Muntaner J (1995): *El cònsol Allan Hillgarth i les illes Balears (1936-39).* Barcelona.Publicacions de l'Abadia de Monserrat, 215.

143 César Cort: *Campos urbanizados y ciudades rurizadas.* Madrid: Federación de Urbanismo y de la Vivienda de la Hispanidad, 194. Quoted by Sastre L (2016): El sol, la cal y la sal; arquitectura rural en la periodo de la autoquaria. 140-

157, from the catalogue of the exhibition: *Campo cerrado;arte y poder en la posguerra espanola,1939*-53 Museo Reina Sofia. Consulted on-line at www.scribd.com/document/310741010. 4 February 2019.

144   Alomar Esteve G (1987): *Un poble i una nissaga; la vila de Muro i els Alomar 'de la Serra'*. Palma,9-16.

145   Alomar Esteve G (1978): *Urbanismo regional en la edad media:las'ordinacions' de Jaime II (1300) en la reino de Mallorca*. Barcelona. Gili.

146   García Ruíz Rosselló D (2000): *Gabriel Alomar, arquitecto, historiador y humanista*. Lecture to La Real Academia de Bellas Artes de San Sebastian de Palma de Mallorca,11.

147   Ginard Feron, D (1999): Els anys de la fam. Una aproximació a l'economia mallorquina durant la postguerra (1939-1951). *Randa*, 43.

148   Maria's father, Miguel Esteve Blanes, was born in Artá in 1876 and died in Palma in 1952. Her mother, Maria Rosario Bianchi Rosafa, was born in Añasco, Puerto Rico in 1879 and died in Palma in 1969. The family home located in Mayagüez in the west of Puerto Rico was a substantial mansion by the 1920s designed by Sabás Honoré one of Puerto Rico's most famous architects.

149   Much of his wife's wealth was partly derived from the Puerto Rican sugar refining company Central Coloso Inc. perhaps the largest one on the island until its decline in the 1970s when it was taken into State ownership only to be privatised two decades later. It ceased operation in 2003.*Enciclopedia de Puerto Rico*.

150   There is a copy of Professor J M Gaus's report to the Harvard Graduate School of Design published in 1943 on the education of planners in AA Secció K Box 7 which suggests Alomar had read it. In the event, Princeton informed him that they had too many staff on (military) service to be able to accept him as a special student. A similar response came from Yale.

151   This nine-story apartment hotel was built in 1925. It is located at the junction of Bay State Road and Beacon Street. It originally contained 225 suites, on 20,808 square feet of land. The exterior bottom two stories were made of limestone and the upper floors of brick. As was the case throughout the city, it was constructed to be fireproof. It was the first in a series of hotels to be sold to Boston University and converted it into a men's dormitory in 1949.

152   The Harvard Mail, June 5 1936. www.thecrimson.com. Consulted 29/04/2017.

153   Letter to Frederick Adams at MIT, March 17 1945. AA Secció A Box 7.

154   Letter to P M Chalmers, February 18 1945. AA Secció A Box 7.

155   MIT Course Catalogue 1944-45.

156   AA Secció A Box 7.

157   MIT President's Annual Report 1944-45, 138-9.

158   There is a very faint possibility that his tutor may have had in mind the concept of the *ad eundem* degree, that is, a courtesy title granted by one college or university to an alumnus of another. Usually this is given to recognise a person's status when he or she takes up employment in the new university. Oxford University retains such a notion know as 'incorporation', as does Harvard. But this is pure guess work.

159   Alomar Esteve G. (1948). Un trabajo escolar de Urbanismo en los Estados Unidos. *Revista Naciónal de Arquitectura*, 74, 56-59.

160   Usefully summarised in: Hall P (1998): *Cities in civilization*. London. Weidenfeld and Nicholson,782-791.

161   William Wilson Wurster was one of America's foremost architects. He was married to Catherine Bauer Wurster one of the founders of modern public housing in America and founding Secretary to the RPAA – a formidable partnership.

162   For details of Thomas Adams' life see: Michael Simpson (1985): "*Thomas Adams and the Modern Planning*

Movement: Britain, Canada and the United States 1900-1940. London and New York, Mansell. For a summary of his life and work see: http://www.kosmoid.net/planning/adams. Consulted 28/4/2014.

163   Letter to MIT Graduate School, June 1970. AA Secció A Box 7.

164   This journal began in 1942. It was aimed at a readership made up of academics, researchers, experts and generally at all those professionals interested in the field of government and local and regional administration. It was multidisciplinary, particularly in those disciplines that contributed to understanding the subject matter of the journal: law, administrative sciences, political science, public management, sociology and economy. In its early years it nearly always contained a section on *urbanismo*. In 1985 it adopted the title *La Revista de Estudios de la Administración Local y Autonómica* (REALA).

165   See for example the statement of the Falange leader Rámon Serrano Suñer:

We hope that these houses meet the demands of hygienic and cheerful homes, so that the children of those who sacrificed appreciate the fruit of so much effort. The work of the architect will continue the patriotic and Christian task of the women of Spain framed in the Women's Section of Falange, to bring a better idea of home and the highest idea of the Fatherland; and so that those who receive the benefit of our reconstruction no matter how many the amenities that in the new houses they find, their sensitivity in terms that could forget that the new houses and the new towns of Spain are founded on the exemplary lesson of those stones that the war removed.

in: *Reconstrucción*, 3, número extraordinario junio-julio, 1940. Madrid: Dirección General de Regiones. Devastadas y Reparaciones, 1940. Quoted by Sastre L (2016):El sol, la cal y la sal; arquitectura rural en la periodo de la autoquaria. 140-157 from the catalogue of the exhibition *Campo cerrado;arte y poder en la posguerra espanola,1939-53* Museo Reina Sofia . (Author's translation). Consulted on-line at www.scribd.com/document/310741010. 18 October 2018.

166   Dávila Linares J M (1991): *La ordinacíon urbanística durante la primera mitad del siglo XX. Premisa para un tratamiento integral de los espacios urbanos.* 9,101. Digital edition. Consulted on line, 21/08/2014.

167   Lejeune J F. (2010): 1939-65: reconstruction and colonization in Spain. The modernization of the Spanish vernacular in, Bucci A and Moll L: *Regional architecture in the Mediterranean area.* Firenza. Alinea. 366.

168   Pedro Bidagor (1906-1996) was perhaps the most influential figure in the development of modern town planning policy in Spain. Originally trained as an architect he became involved in schemes for the replanning of Madrid in the 1930s. In the Civil War he remained in Madrid during the Francoist onslaught and was interned by Republicans, to emerge as the head of the City's technical section responsible for its planning. Often against Falangist opposition in the Ministry of the Interior, he became the principal author of the General Urban Plan completed in1946. He was a correspondent of Alomar and they met frequently at conferences. Rodriquez Avila L (1970): History of contemporary Spanish urbanism: Pedro Bidagor Lasarte. *Urbanism* 2,71 andTerán, Fernando de (1983): *Pedro Bidagor. Quaderns d'arquitectura i urbanisme.* 157, 131-133.

169   Alomar Esteve G (1980): *Teoria de la ciudad.* Madrid. Instituto de estudios de administracion local,56.

170   Azpilicuerta Astarloa E (2004): *La construcción de la arquitectura de postguerra en España (1939-1962).* Ph.D thesis. Universdad Politécnica de Madrid. Esquela técnica superior de arquitectura. Consulted on line. January 2019,116.

171   Azpilicueta Astarloa E (2004): *La construcción de la arquitctura de postguerra en España (1939-1962).* Ph.D thesis. Universidad Politécnica de Madrid, Esquela técnica superior de arquitectura. Consulted on line. January 2019,128.

172   Preston P (1993): Franco: a biography. London. Harper Collins.

173   Alomar Esteve G (1951): El planeamiento en Puerto Rico. Un caso ejemplar del planeamiento urbano-rural de orden nacional en un pequeño pais. *Revista de la vida local.* 56 and 57, 224-244 and 416-430.

174   Denis N A (2015): *War against all Puerto Ricans; revolution and terror in America's colony.* New York. Nation Books.

175   Not long after Alomar's visit Stephen Sondheim was to epitomise relations with USA in the West Side Story song 'America'.

176   Tugwell served in FDR's administration until he was forced out in 1936. He was a specialist on planning and

believed the government should have large-scale plans to move the economy out of the Great Depression because private enterprise was too frozen in place to do the job. He was denounced by conservatives who said his government-imposed planning violated the values of individualism. He was the first director of the New York Planning Commission. *Wikipedia*. Consulted 21 June 2015.

177   To remove the primary source of the political graft, Bettman introduced a bill in the Ohio Legislature authorizing cities to create citizen-dominated planning commissions, permitting these commissions to prepare plans for their communities, and specifying that once such a plan is adopted by the commission, it cannot be violated by a city council, thus placing determination of public works expenditures in the hands of the planning commission. Enacted in 1915, this legislation became the basis for local community planning in America. 'Community planning' and 'the planning of communities' became central to much of Alomar's philosophy on town planning.

178   An account of town planning in Puerto Rico in the 1950s written in English shortly after Alomar's visit in 1945 can be found in Howell B (1952): The Planning System of Puerto Rico. *The Town Planning Review*, 23,1(3), 211-222. Consulted on line March 2020.

179   Alomar Esteve G (1952): El XXI congreso de la Federacion International del Urbanismo y de la Vivienda, celebrado in Lisboa. *Revista de estudios de la vida local* (1942-1984), 65,707-714.

180   Pérez Mínguez y Devillota L (1952): Urbanismo. *Revista de estudios de la vida local* (1942-1984), 65,715-722.

181   Osborn was disturbed by the high-density buildings and sprawl of Madrid and the failure to develop new towns as an alternative. These early study tours were largely designed for British planners to learn from foreign experience. But did Spanish planners learn anything from their visitors? Cook I, Ward S and Ward K (2015): Post-war planning and policy tourism: The international study tours of the Town and Country Planning Association 1947-1961. *Planning, Theory and Practice*, 16 (2), 184-205.

182   Alomar Esteve G (1956): A transcendental experiment. *Town and Country Planning*, XXIV, 58-59.

183   Many papers and letters pertaining to these points can be found in: AA Secció A.

184   AA Secció K Box 7.

185   Alomar Esteve G (1980): *Teoria de la ciudad*. Madrid. Instituto de estudios de administracion local,61-62.

186   Ley de Suelo. *Revue Estudios de la Vida Local*, 1956,88,461.

187   Ribas i Piera M (1969): La planificación territorial. *Ciudad y territorio*, 1,7-12.

188   AA Secció K Box 7.

189   '… José Luis Arrese, who had recently been removed from the ministry attached to the General Secretariat of the Movimiento (Spain's only political party) after his plan for the reorganization of power around this all-powerful party was blocked. This episode constituted the Falange's last attempt to reappropriate the regime; from this point on they were definitively marginalized…Arrese's appointment as head of the Ministry of Housing amounted, therefore, to a demotion to the periphery of political power.' Vorms C (2013): Madrid in the 1950s: The Issue of Shacks and Shantytowns. *Le Mouvement Social* 245, 4, , pages 43 to 57.Translated from the French by Cadenza Academic Translations. URL: https://www.cairn-int.info/journal-le-mouvement-social1-2013-4-page-43.htm. Consulted 21/06/2020,

190   Alomar Esteve G (1980): *Teoria de la ciudad*. Madrid. Instituto de estudios de administracion local,62.

191   Alomar Esteve G (1980): *Teoria de la ciudad*. Madrid. Instituto de estudios de administracion local,66.

192   Sambricio C (2020): Politíca de vivienda en el primer franquismo, 1936-1949, *Temporánea*,1,76.

193   Alomar Esteve G (1980): *Teoria de la ciudad*. Madrid. Instituto de estudios de administracion local,66.

194   Alomar Esteve G (1969): Problemes que presente la conservation du patrimoine culturel immobilier en Espagne. *Monumentum*. (ICOMOS). Vol. 3.English translation.

195   Alomar Esteve G (1980): *Teoria de la ciudad*. Madrid. Instituto de estudios de administracion local,68.

196   Téran F de (1999): *Historia del urbanismo en España III, siglos XIX y XX*, 237.

197   For example, see: Preston P (2020): *A people betrayed; a history of corruption, political incompetence and social division in modern Spain, 1874-2018*. London Collins, Chapter14.

198   Téran F de (1999): *Historia del urbanismo en España III, siglos XIX y XX*, 230-236.

199   Alomar Esteve G (1959): La gestión urbanistica en el orden técnico. Paper given at First National Congress de Urbanismo, Barcelona, November. AA Secció K Box, 7.

200   AA Seccio A Box 7. Shortly after the new Dean, Lloyd Rodwin, wrote to him soliciting contributions to the Alumni Fund Drive of $100 to $1000!

201   The Second Congress of Architects and Specialists of Historic Buildings, in Venice in 1964, adopted the Venice Charter and with the support of UNESCO provided for the creation of the International Council on Monuments and Sites (ICOMOS).

202   Glendinning M (2003): The conservation movement: a cult of the modern age. *Trans. Royal Historical Society. Sixth series*,13,359-76.

203   García A et al (1954): *Resumen histórico del urbanismo d'España*. Madrid. Instituto de estudios de administración local, x.

204   Diario de Mallorca: The prophecy of the architect Alomar, 22 March 2013.

205   Alomar Esteve, G (1935). *L'emplaçament urbanistíc del Temple Cristià. Palma.* Imprenta de Francesc Soler, 6. This is probably a privately published version of an essay that first appeared in *La Nostra Terra* (1935): 6, 6-10, but with illustrations drawn, presumably, by Alomar.

206   Alomar Esteve G (1969): Problemes que presente la conservación du patrimoine culturel immobilier en Espagne. *Monumentum*. (ICOMOS). vol 3.

207   A law of December 1941 *'annuls the use of rolled steel in building and greatly restricts the amount of steel in reinforced concrete. Unable to use modern structural systems – free structures with reticulated pillars, metal trusses in roofs of diaphanous spaces, or beams of large lights to open wide openings – the qualities of space were severely affected and the possibilities of modernity very reduced'*. Almonacid Canseco R (2017): La continuidad de 'la moderno' en la arquitectura española de los años 40 in: *Los años CIAM en Espagne: La otra modernidad*. C2C Proyectos, Editoriales de Arquitectura, 215.

208   Sambricio C (1959): La arquitectura española 1939-45: la alternativa falangista. *Arquitectura*,199, 7.

209   Martínez-Monedero, M (2008): Las restauraciones arquitectónicas de Luis Menéndez-Pidal: la confianza de un método *Arquitectura y urbanismo*,67.

210   Martínez-Monedero, M (2009): Luis Menéndez-Pidal y las restauraciones arquitectónicas de la 1ª Zona. *Loggia, Arquitectura & Restauración*, 20. Servicio Publicaciones Universidad Politécnica de Valencia, 8-23.

211   Forteza G (1931): *La urbanització de Palma. Ciutat antigua i ciutat moderna*, Estampa Soler Prats, See also: Seguí Aznar, M (1984): *Guillem Forteza: estudis sobre arquitectura i urbanisme*. Publicacions de l'Abadia de Montserrat, 1984.

212   Alomar Esteve G (1969): Problemes que presente la conservación du patrimoine culturel immobilier en Espagne. *Monumentum*.(ICOSMOS). vol 3.

213   Alomar Esteve G and Alomar i Canyelles A (1994): *El patromoni cultural de les illes Balears*. Palma. Govern Balear.

214   Vibot T (2015): *The art captured; Historic-monumental archive of the architect Gabriel Alomar i Esteve.* Pollença. El Gall.

215   La Llei de Defensa del Patrimoni Històric Artístic Nacional, May 1933.

216   Alomar Esteve G (1974): El Conjunto Historico-Artistico de Palma de Mallorca, Real Academia de San Fernando, 102-3

217   Tumbler University Note Book, family archive (nd).

218   ICOMOS (1971): Colloque sur les Monuments et le Tourism. Oxford, 7-11 juillet 1969. Reports by national committees *Monumentum*. Numero Special, 6. Alomar was Spain's representative at this conference.

219   Canosa Zamora E and García Carballo A (2016): Madrid Km 0. La intervención franquista en la construcción de algunos paisajes simbólicos de la capital. *Estudios Geográficos*, LXXVII, 281, 415-442.

220   Gonzalez-Ruibal A (2009): Topography of terror or cultural heritage? The monuments of Franco's Spain in: Forbes N, Page R and Perez G (Eds): *Europe's deadly century; perspectives on 20th century conflict heritage*. London. English Heritage.

221   Alomar Esteve G (1961): *Sociologia urbanistica*. Madrid.Aguilar,77.

222   Alomar Esteve G (1950): De la arquitectura al urbanismo y del urbanismo al planeamiento *Cuadernos de arquitectura* 11&12, 22.

223   Alomar Esteve G (1950): *La reforma de Palma*. Palma. Mossen Alcover,90.

224   Alomar Esteve G (1947): *Teoria de la ciudad*. Madrid. IEAL, 178 and 185.

225   Alomar Esteve G (1950): *La reforma de Palma*. Palma. Mossen Alcover, 50.

226   Pioneered by Louis's study of Berlin in the 1930s fringe belts received much more attention following Conzen's work on Alnwick and Newcastle in UK in the 1960s. See for example, Conzen MRG (1960): Alnwick, Northumberland: a study in town plan analysis, *Publications, Institute of British Geographers 27* and Barke M (1990): Morphogenesis, fringe belts and urban size: an exploratory essay in, Slater T R: *The built form of western cities*. Leicester. Leicester University Press, 280-288.

227   Alomar Esteve G (1947): *Teoria del Ciudad*. Madrid.IEAL, 146-8.

228   Alomar Esteve G (1955): *Comunidad Planeada; principios de Sociologica aplicada al Urbanismo y al planeamiento Rural*. Madrid. IEAL, 183.

229   García González MC and Salvador Guerrero S (2014):The National Federation of Town Planning and Housing, 1939–1954: A Network for Town Planners and Architects in Franco's Spain. *Journal of Urban History*, 40(6),1099-1122.

230   Seventh Congress, Palma, Mallorca, 10th to 17th October 1954. Referenced by García Gonzalez MC and Salvador Guerrero S (2014): The National Federation of Town Planning and Housing (1939-54): a network of urbanism in the Spanish post-civil war period,10. 14th International planning history society conference. Consulted on-line November 2019. URL http://www.iphs2010.com/abs/ID50.pdf.

231   Thomas H Mawson (1861-1933), originally a nurseryman and maker of private and public gardens, he was best known as a landscape architect. He became President of the Town Planning Institute in 1923. 'His strong social conscience led him to want the general public to be able to enjoy good landscapes, particularly urban, which until then had been the privilege of the wealthy few'. Surely, sentiments that Alomar would have shared. Mawson H (1984): T H Mawson (1861-1933), Landscape architect and town planner. *Journal of Royal Society of Arts* 132,190.

232   Alomar Esteve G (1993): Presentació in: *Jardins de Palma; història i imatges*. Murray D.G, Llabres J and Pascual A. Palma. Olañeta (2008 Edn),5.

233   Seguí Aznar M (1990): *Arquitectura contemporánea en Mallorca (1900-1947)*. Palma. Font,343.

234   For a more detailed analysis of Palma's present-day green spaces and their links to tourism and visitor attraction see: Saint-Martin Y (2002): La répartition des espaces verts à Palma de Majorque, *Rives nord-méditerranéennes* [on line], 12, placed on-line 28 January 2015, consulted 7 February 2019. URL: http://journals.openedition.org/rives/136 ; DOI : 10.4000/rives,136.

235 Alomar Garau G (2021): Urbanismo crítico, cartografía y evolución del verde urbano en los planes de ensanche históricos de la ciudad de Palma (Mallorca). *ACE: Architecture, City and Environment*, 15(45), 9039 10-11. Consulted online March 2021.

236 Alomar Garau G (2021): Urbanismo crítico, cartografía y evolución del verde urbano en los planes de ensanche históricos de la ciudad de Palma (Mallorca). *ACE: Architecture, City and Environment*, 15(45), 9039 10-11. Consulted online March 2021.

237 AA Secció D Box 7.

238 Alomar Esteve G (1986): *Memorias de un urbanista*, 1939-1979. Palma. Font, 32.

239 Costa Ferrer J (1963): Sa Vall: Arte y arqueología Part 1 *Santanyi*. 13 April.138,4. http://ibdigital.uib.es/greenstone/sites/localsite/collect/santanyiVolums/index/assoc/Santanyi/_1963_06/_n138.dir/Santanyi_1963_06_n138.pdf. Costa Ferrer designed the plans for and promoted the Cala d'Hort urbanization, in Mallorca, which would later become Cala d'Or which was noted for its 'garden village' style.

240 Román Quetglas J (2001): Jardines públicos y jardines privado. La aportacion de Gabriel Alomar durante el franquismo, in: *Dos décadas de cultura artistica en el franquismo 1936-1956*, Granada Proyecto Sur de Ediciones 682-686.

241 Alomar Esteve G (1986): *Memorias de un urbanista*, 1939-1979. Palma. Font, 23-25.

242 Román Quetglas J (2001): Jardines públicos y jardines privado. La aportacion de Gabriel Alomar durante el franquismo, in: *Dos décadas de cultura artistica en el franquismo 1936-1956*, Granada Proyecto Sur de Ediciones, 683.

243 Alomar Esteve G (1950): Reconstrucción de las fachadas y trazado de los nuevos jardines en el Palacio de Lloseta en Mallorca. *Cuadernos de arquitectura*, 6,32-35.

244 Informe técnico. Incoación del expediente 399/13 para dejar sin efecto la declaración como Bien de Interés Cultural del Palacio de Aiamans de Lloseta y su declaración como Bien Catalogado Fabian. *Alta Mar* 27/02/2015. Consulted on line 21/06/2018.

245 Artigues Bonet A and Blázquez Salom M (2012): ¿Reconversión o desregulation? Analisis de planes de reconversión turístico-inmobiliaria de la playa de Palma (Mallorca). *Cuadernos de Turismo*, 29,11-34.

246 Horrach Estarellas B (2014): Nuevas pautas de regeneracion de los destinos turisticos maduros. *Architecture, city and environment*. 25, 349-372. Electronic offprint.

247 The estate which was originally very productive agriculturally but was divided a number of times. The lower part (Son Verí de Baix) was eventually bought by the Roses family who made their fortune in Puerto Rico in sugar, coffee and tobacco accumulating capital which then was invested in banking and land, land that proved valuable for the new tourism industry that grew from the mid-1950s.

248 The garden suburb first evolved in the United States with Llewellyn Park, New Jersey. It soon spread under the influence of Frederick Law Olmsted, whose suburban designs are amongst the finest of their kind including Riverside, Illinois, Druid Hills in Atlanta, Georgia and Parkside, Buffalo, New York.

249 Diez Monge F (1988): Ciudad Jardín de Palma: un nombre impropio para una urbanizacíon en la costa de Mallorca a comienzo del siglo. *El Bollettí De La Societat Arqueològica Lul.luliana*. 44, 307-323.

250 Ramos Gorostiza J L (2008): El descontento frente a la ciudad industrial: reformismo social y "ciudad jardín" en España, 1900-1923. *Revista de Historia Industrial*, 37(2), XVII.1,19.

251 For an account of the influence of early British ideas on garden suburbs on Spanish town planning especially in Madrid see: Sambricio C (1982): La política urbana de Primo de Rivera; del plan regional a la política de casas baratas. *Ciudad y Territorio*,54, 38-42.

252 Calmés i Riera. A (1989) Un caire del arquitecte D. Gabriel Alomar Esteve *El Bollettí De La Societat Arqueològica Lul.lulian)*,407-410.

253   The building was designed by the Mallorcan architect Guillem Reynés Font (1877-1918) in the Modernist and Regionalist styles fashionable in the early part of the 20C. It is a massive looking house built on a square plan around a courtyard with a tower. It was modified in the 1930s by another local architect with whom Alomar had worked, Guillem Forteza Pinya.

254   Alomar Esteve G (1964): Housing groups in Cala Guya (Mallorca). *Cuadernos de Arquitectura*, 57,16-18, Consulted on line 10/06/2016.

255   Alomar Esteve G (1969): Mise en valeur d'un monument: 'La Almudaina', Palais des rois de majorque a Palma et reconstitution de 'S'hort del rei', le jardin royale, 1969-1970. *Monumentum*. (ICOSMOS), 3,4-49.

256   To help, neither Alomar nor Francisco Prieto-Moreno, with whom he shared the project, collected a fee. The cost of the work was 25,000,000 pesetas.

257   Report on the death of Maximó Alomar, 22nd June 2008. *Diario de Mallorca*. While mayor Maximó progressed the development of the early industrial *poligonos* and schools. He was one of the few mayors in the Franco era that Alomar admired.

258   Francisco Prieto-Moreno, originally an active member of the Falange in the late '30s and '40s, became one of the new 'technocrats' in architecture in the 1960s. He was responsible for the restoration of the Alhambra in Granada and making it accessible to tourists. Like Alomar, he was an advocate of the historical in architecture and garden design. In 1973 he published *Los jardines de Granada*.

259   Harvey D (1985): *The urbanization of capital*. Oxford, Basil Blackwell, 174-178.

260   At least two graphic artists helped draw Alomar's maps. The first was Juan Vila Moncau who worked for a well-known advertising company in Palma. He may well also have been an accomplished painter since he exhibited with Xam (Pedro Quetglas Ferrer) and José Vila Moncau (possibly his brother – an equally well- known artist) at Granja Palau in January 1953. *History of Publicitat Matas,* a well-known cinema advertising company in Palma, Chapter X. 2015. Consulted online, November 2019 at, http://www.pmatas.com/index.php/medio-siglo-de-nuestra-historia-en-12-entregas-x/ and Ysasi Alonso A: *La obra grafica (estampas y matrices) de Pedro Quetglas Ferrer 'Xam' (1915-2001). La riqueza de un patrimonio*. Tesis Doctoral UIB. Departamento de Ciencias Históricas y Teoría de las Artes. Consulted online at http://ibdigital.uib.es/greenstone/collect/tesisUIB/import/Ysasi_Alonso_Alejandro.pdf . Oct 2020. The second was Jaime Mora but there is no trace of him.

261   Serrano Suñer R (1940): La exposición de la Reconstrucción en España,' *Reconstrucción*, 3.

262   Almonacid Canseco R (2017): La continuidad de 'le moderno' en la arquitectura española de los años 40 in *Los años CIAM en Espagne: La otra modernidad*. C2C Proyectos, Editoriales de Arquitectur, 212.

263   Letter to Gaspar Blein, 14 December 1946. AA Box K.

264   Alomar Esteve G (1986): *Memorias de un urbanista*, 1939-1979. Palma. Font, 21.

265   Buswell R J (2011): *Mallorca and tourism; history, economy and environment*. Bristol. Channel View Publications, Chapter 4.

266   Gonzáles Pérez J M (2017): *Les ciutats de les Balears; processos d'urbanització i urbanisme*. Palma. Muntaner. Chapter 5.

267   Frank, A, Mironowicz I, Lourenco J et al. (2014): Educating planners in Europe: a review of 21st century study programmes. *Progress in Planning* 91, 30-94.

268   Letter to Gaspar Blein 14, December 1946. AA Box K.

269   Tumbler University Note Book, AA Box K. (nd),100-101.

270   Consellaria de medi ambient, ordenacio del territori i litoral, 1997,111-3.

271   Buswell R (2013): *Mallorca; the making of the landscape*. Edinburgh, Dunedin Academic Press,219.

272   Buswell R (2011): *Mallorca and tourism; History, economy and environment*. Bristol. Channel View Publications,58.

273   http://www.mcu.es/patrimonio/CE/Bien Culturales/Definición.htm. Consulted on line 13 Nov 2018.

274   Buswell R (2011): *Mallorca and tourism; history, economy and environment*. Bristol. Channel View Press. 97-101.

275   Alomar Esteve G (1950): *La Reforma de Palma*. Palma. Mossen Alcover,84-5.

276   Dyckoff T (2017): *The age of spectacle; adventures in architecture and the 21st century city*. London. Random House,131-139.

277   By 1961 the flyleaf of his *Sociologica Urbanistica*, Madrid, Aguila was describing him as '*doctor arquitecto*' and *Profesor de sociologica urbana* in ILEA. While he may have held the title professor there is no evidence he held a doctorate.

278   Alomar Esteve G (1980): *Teoria de la ciudad*. Madrid.IEAL.2nd Edition,37.

279   Alomar Esteve G (1955): *Comunidad planeada; principios de sociologia aplicada al urbanismo y al planeamento rural*. Madrid. IEAL,62.

280   Preston P. (2020): *A people betrayed; a history of corruption, political incompetence and social division in Spain,1874-2018*. London, Harper Collins,244.

281   March's stint in jail was hardly that of an ordinary prisoner. He had 'two large cells, one as a bedroom and the other as a sitting room. Two prison orderlies were in attendance on him throughout the day. His meals were hurried from the Palace Hotel in big steaming receptacles.' Buckley H (2nd Edn. 2014): *The life and death of the Spanish Republic*, London. I.B. Taurus,122. Was Alomar aware of this kind of detail?

282   Preston P. (2020): *A people betrayed; a history of corruption, political incompetence and social division in Spain,1874-2018*. London, Harper Collins ,246.

283   Fundació initiciatives del Mediterrani (2018): *Capacitat de càrrega turística; estudi al centre històric de Palma*. Consulted online at http://palmaxxi.com/informes/ October 2020.

284   Vives-Miró S, Rullan O and González-Pérez J M (2018): *Geografies de les desposses d'habitage a través de la crisi; els desnonaments Marca Palma*. Barcelona. Icaria. (English version), 305-310.

285   Coords: Garau i Salas J and Holles J (2018): *Capacitat de càrrega turística, Estudi al centre històric de Palma*. Palma. Fundació iniciatives del Mediterrani. Consulted online at palmaxxi.com/wp-content/uploads.

GABRIEL ALOMAR ESTEVE: MALLORCAN TOWN PLANNER

www.ingramcontent.com/pod-product-compliance
Lightning Source LLC
Chambersburg PA
CBHW060930180426
43192CB00045B/2888